# COMPUTER AND LANGUAGES

DPH ENGINEERING SERIES

# COMPUTER AND LANGUAGES

*By*

Poonam Yadav

DISCOVERY PUBLISHING HOUSE
NEW DELHI-110002

Reprinted - 2019

First Published - 2005

ISBN: 978-81-8356-041-2



**Computer and Languages**

*Published by:*

**DISCOVERY PUBLISHING HOUSE PVT. LTD.**

4383/4B, Ansari Road, Darya Ganj
New Delhi-110 002 (India)
*Phone*: +91-11-23279245, 23253475; 43596065
*E-mail*: discoverybooksindia@gmail.com
discoverypublishinghouse@gmail.com
*web*: www.discoverypublishinggroup.com

*Printed at:*
Infinity Imaging Systems
Delhi

# Preface

This fascinating title "Computer and Languages" has been carefully compiled and edited to meet the long felt needs of increasingly large number of those who have to deal with the different aspects of computers and languages in Colleges, Universities and research institutes. It provides a balanced and integrated treatment of the entire field of computer. The title is intelligible to the educator layman but it deals with some complex ideas. It is an adequate text for all requirements in this area for most university students. Special efforts have been made to explain ideas in non-mathematical terms. The primary aim throughout has been clarity, simplicity and the high standard. It will definitely prove to be a boon to teachers and research workers in the field of computer.

It has been the constant endeavour of the author to furnish maximum substance, keeping in view the limitations of size of the volume. Efforts have been made to condense the matter as far as practiceable. The book features both a text and a laboratory guide. It is hoped that this book will not only meet the requirement of undergraduate students but will also be useful as a guideline to the teachers in their teaching.

The author tried hard to be accurate and upto date in statement and realises the impossibility of completely avoiding errors therefore, the author will greatly appreciate having her attention called to any questionable statement.

Special thanks are given to Mr. Wasan and staff of M/s Discovery Publishing House for their whole hearted co-operation in the publication of this book.

**Author**

# CONTENTS

Real Time Systems, (i) Soft Real Time System, (ii) Hard Real Time System, Real Time Operating System, Concept of Channels, Network Operating System, Distributed Operating System, Different Modes of Operating System, (i) Interrupt model, (ii) Mail box model, (iii) The polling model, Comparison of the models, File Concept, File Types, Tape-Based System, Disk-Based System, Blocking, File Operations, Creating a File, Writing a File, Reading a File, Rewinding a File, Deleting a File, Device directory, File Organisation And Access Mechanism, Access Methods, Sequential Access, Direct Access, Indexed Access, Free Space Management, Allocation Methods, Contiguous Allocations, Dynamic Storage Allocations, First-fit:, Best-fit:, Worst-fit:, Linked Allocation, Indexed Allocation, Directory System, Search:, Create file:, Delete file:, List directory:, Backup up:, Single-Level Directory, Two-Level Directory, Tree Structured Directory, Acyclic Graph Directories, File Protection, Implementation Issues: Layered File System, Interleaving, Authentication Parameter in File System, File Sharing, Multiple Users, Remote File Systems, Consistency Semantics, Immutable-Shared-Files Semantics, Directory Implementation, Linear List, Hash Table, MSDOS memory Types, Conventional Memory, Expanded memory, Extended Memory, Upper Memory Blocks, The High Memory Area, MSDOS.SYS, Command.COM, The Boot Process, The Bootstrap, Loading the OS, Establishing The Environment, DOS Commands SYNTAX, Command Syntax Elements, 1. Command Name, 2. Space, 3. Drive Designation, 4. A Colon, 5. Pathname, 6. Filename, 7. Filename Extension, 8. Switches, 9. Brackets, 10. Ellipses, 11. Vertical Bar, DOS Commands, List of DOS Commands, Additional Commands & Operators in Batch Files, Command Editing, File Comparison command, DOS input and output keys, Commonly used extensions and the type of file they indicate, Brief Description of Some Newever DOS Commands, DriveSpace and Double Guard, Mem Maker, Backup, Anti-Virus, Undelete, ScanDisk, Multi Config, Interactive Start, Defrag, SmartDrive, Interlink,

# Chapter 1

# Computer Hardware

## THE COMPUTER

In all spheres of life computer is used today. It makes an important contribution in this modern age. Information technology collectively bounded all the uses of computers and the new revolutions in the area of communication. A computer system can fly an aeroplane, can control the machines of a factory, can check your balance in your account and many more endless things. All this talk would have naturally kindled an interest in you to learn more about the Computer and its internal details. In this chapter, we will study about this marvel gazzet of science.

A no. of different subcomponent systems made a computer system and allow the system to perform complicated tasks & calculations. You might think, so is my calculator. It is an electronic machine. A computer is a device to store and manipulate data and produce desired outcome. High speed calculations is its main capability.

Computer is different in the sense that it not only store the data but also the instructions for the data. The computer does nothing without explicit instructions that specify each step it must take which is what you call the program. A set of programs developed for the purpose of performing a particular task is called software. Every instruction has aspecific operation to be performed. Each instruction specifies an operation to be performed. After interpreting each instruction computer executes the specified operation. The computer interprets each instruction and executes the specified operation.

In digital computer binary system is used. In this the data is in the binary form i.e.-o's and 1's. The instructions are also represented in the form of binary code. Such a program is said to be in machine language. All computers work in machine language. As machine languages are very difficult to practice and learn, there are special programs called compilers that accept programs in High Level Languages (HLLs) and translate into machine language programs like English HLLs are simple and easy to learn.

The physical units of a computer called Hardware, such as CPU, Memory, Input and output. Hardware is your entire computer from the standpoint of running a program. Hardware is what puts your instructions into action. Every computer is built from an array of components, each of which performs a specific function in making the overall machine work. As with the world of physical reality, a computer is built from fundamental elements combined together. Each of these elements adds a necessary quality, or feature to the final computer. These building blocks are hardware components, built of electronic circuits and mechanical parts to carry out a defined function. All the components of computer perform their functions individually yet collectively. The Operating Systems, compilers as well as user programs (high level language or machine language) form the software.

**Today computers make our life easier and quicker. They become much powerful in last few years as they have been used in all spheres of life and are ready to insert in few other new fields of our life. But computers are just not wonderful because they are so powerful. A computer is a way of doing all work and also play.**

## Characteristics of a Computer

There are few major characteristics of computers. Which can be discussed as speed, accuracy versatility, diligence and memory.

### *Speed*

Computer work very fast so it takes only few seconds for the complicated calculations which may take hours. Suppose you are asked to calculate the average month income of one thousand persons in your neighborhood. For this you have to add income from all sources for all persons on a day-to-day basis and find out the average for each one of them. How long will it take for you to do this? One day, two days or one week? Your small computer can finish this work in few seconds! The weather forecasting that you see every day on TV is the result of compilation and analysis of a huge amount of data on temperature, humidity, pressure, etc. of various places on computers. Computers can perform several millions (1,000,000) of instructions per second or even more than that?

### *Accuracy*

Along with speed computer also has accuracy & correctness. The degree of accuracy of computer is very high and every calculation is performed with the same accuracy. The accuracy level is determined by the design of computer. The only error we find in the computing are due to programming error or the human error of inaccurate data.

### *Diligence*

Unlike human there is no tiredness, fatigue and lack of concentration is seen in computer. It can work for hours without committing any error. If millions of calculations are to be performed, a computer will perform every calculation with the same accuracy. Because of this capability it overcome the human beings in monotonous type of work.

### *Versatility*

It means the capacity to perform completely different type of work. You may use your computer to prepare payroll slips. Next moment you may use it for inventory management or to prepare electric bills.

### *Power of Remembering*

Computer can store the huge amount of data. Any information can be stored and recalled as long as you require it, for any numbers of years. Its up to you how much date you want to store & how much you want to erase from the memory.

*No IQ*

Computer cannot do any work without any instructions it is just like a dumb machine. It performs only the instructions that you give with tremendous speed and with accuracy. It is up to you to decide what you want to do and in what sequence.

*No Feelings*

It does not have feelings or emotion, taste, knowledge and experience. Thus, it does not get tired even after long hours of work. It does not distinguish between users.

*Storage*

You can store a large amount of data in its in-built memory. You can also store data in secondary storage devices such as floppies, CD's which can be kept outside your computer and can be carried to other computers.

## COMPUTER GENERATIONS

Computer evolved in 16th century and reached to the stage which we see today. The present day computer, however, has also undergone rapid change during the last fifty years. This period, during which the evolution of computer took place, can be divided into five distinct phases known as Generation of Computers. On the basis of the switching circuits used each phase is different from others.

### First Generation Computers

Thermion valves were used in first generation computers. These computers were large in size and programming them was difficult. Some of the computers of this generation were:

ENIAC: It was the first electronic computer built in 1946 a University of Pennsylvania, USA by John Eckert and John Mauchly. It was named Electronic Numerical Integrator and Calculator (ENIAC). The ENIAC was 30X50 feet long, weighed 30 tons, contained 18,000 vacuum tubes, 70,000 reistors, 10,000 capacitors and required 150,000 watts of electricity. Today your favourite computer is many times as powerful as ENIAC. Still its size is very small.

**EDVAC:** It stands for Electronic Discrete Variable Automatic Computer and was developed in 1950. The concept of storing data and instructions inside the computer was introduced here. This allowed much faster operation since the computer had rapid access to both data and instructions. The internal logical decision making was the major advantage for storing instructions in them.

### Other Important Computers of First Generation

**EDSAC:** It stand for Electronic Delay Storage Automatic Computer and was developed by M.V. Wilkes at Cambridge University in 1949.

**UNIVAC-1:** Eckert and Mauchly produced it in 1951 by Universal Accounting Computer setup.

### Limitations of First Generation Computers

Major drawbacks of the first generation computers.

- Slow operating speed.
- High power consumption.
- A lot of heat was generated in its operation. Elaborate arrangements were required for heat dissipation.
- Required large space for installation.
- Low programming capability.

### Second Generation Computers

In 1950's the bulky electric tubes were replaced by the device called transistor in Ist generation computer. Transistors are much smaller than electric tubes and have higher operating speed.

Their power consumption is much lesser and therefore, much less heat needs to be dissipated. Manufacturing cost was also very low. Because of that the computer size got reduced. Thus, the size of the computer got reduced considerably.

COBOL, FORTRAN were the programming languages which were developed during this period. Some of the computers of the Second Generation were:

**IBM 1620:** Its size was smaller as compared to First Generation computers and was mostly used for scientific purposes.

**IBM 1401:** Its size was small to medium and was used for business applications.

**CDC 3600:** Its was large and was used for scientific purposes.

### Third Generation Computers

In 1964 the IIIrd generation computers were introduced. They used Integrated Circuits (ICs). These ICs are popularly known as Chips. A single IC has many transistors, registers and capacitors built on a single thin slice of silicon. So the size of the computer got further reduced. Some of the computers developed during this period were IBM-360, ICL-1900, IBM-370, and VAX-750. During this period higher-level languages such as BASIC (Beginness all-purpose symbolic instruction code) were developed.

Computers of this generation were small in size, low cost, large memory and processing speed was high as compared to the earlier generation. But further developments in technology led to the next generation of computers.

### Fourth Generation Computers

Around 1975 todays computers which were called IVth generation computers come into the picture. They use Large Scale Integrated Circuits (LSICs) built on a single silicon chip called microprocessors. Due to the development of microprocessors it is possible to place computer's Central Processing Unit (CPU) on a single chip. These computers are called microcomputers. LSICs later on replaced by Very Large Scale Integrated Circuits (VLSIC).

Thus, the computer that was occupying a very large room in earlier days can now be placed on a table. The Personal Computer (PC) that you see everywhere is a Fourth Generation Computer.

### Fifth Generation Computer

The next generation computer are said to be Fifth Generation computers. In Vth generation computers the expected speed to be very high. Apart from this it can perform parallel processing. The concept of Artificial intelligence has been introduced. It is still in a developmental stage. In Japan, US & Europe verious researches in this field are going on.

Few important achievements have been successfully made towards the development of the Fifth Generation Computer. Some of these are Natural Language based interfaces for interacting with the computer, voice recognition based interfaces, options, Character recognition etc. In natural language based interface you can interact with the computer in plain English or any other normal language. A voice recognition based interface allows you speak out the commands in natural language into a microphone connected to the computer and the computer then responds your commands. All these are available to some extent but not with full generality. However, in a few years from now you may just be able to completely do away with the keyboard/ mouse interfaces that you take so many pains to learn now.

## DIFFERENT TYPES OF MODERN - DAY COMPUTERS

The development in computers shown by the various generations of computers. But all computers are not the same type even today. There are a whole variety of computers that you talk about and refer to them using a wide variety of names. The table below summarizes the chief characteristics of each type:

| *Type* | *Processor Speed* | *Common use* |
|---|---|---|
| Supercomputer | 60 billion to 3trillion MIPS | Scientific calculation, Complex system modeling and simulation. |
| Mainframe | 5000 MIPS+ | Enterprise wide Systems, Corporate database management. |
| Minicomputer | 1000 MIPS+ | Department level or a small company or for a particular purpose. |
| Workstation | 1000 MIPS+ | Engineering/CAD software development. |
| Microcomputer | 500 MIPS+ | Personal/workgroup productivity, communication. |
| Network Computer | 500 MIPS+ | Personal/workgroup productivity, communication. |

The different types of computers that you come across are:

### Microcomputer

The lowest end of the computer range in terms of speed & storage is called microcomputer. Its CPU is a microprocessor. The first microcomputers were built of 8-bit microprocessor chips. The most common application of Personal Computers (PC) is in this category. The PC supports a number of input and output devices. Nowadays these are built using Pentium 4 and Pentium III CPUs. These are most commonly used as office desktops.

### Minicomputer

They support more than one user at a time. It operates at a higher speed and possesses large storage capacity. The mini computer is used in multi-user system in which various users can work at the same time. Minicomputers are generally used for processing large volume of data in an organization. They are also used as servers in Local Area Networks (LAN).

### Mainframes

They have very large storage capacity and can handle the work load of many users at very high speed. They are generally used in centralized databases. They are also used as controlling nodes in Wide Area Networks (WAN). Example of mainframes are DEC, ICL and IBM 3000 series.

### Supercomputer

They are most expansive & fastest machine. Their speed is very high compared to other computers. They are the fastest and most expensive machines. They have high processing speed compared to other computers. Supercomputers are mainly being used for weather forecasting, biomedical research, remote sensing, aircraft design and other frontier areas of science and technology. Some of the example of supercomputers are CRAY YMP, CRAY2, NEC SX-3, CRAY XMP and PARAM from India).

### Laptop and Notebook computers

are small, easily transportable, lightweight microcomputers that fit easily into a briefcase. Laptops and notebooks are designed for maximum convenience and transportability, allowing users to have access to processing power and data without being bound to the office environment. The additional benefit of these computers is to provide internet access anytime, anywhere.

**Palmtop Computers**

are the microcomputers, small enough to carry in one hand. Although still capable of general purpose computing, palmtops are configured for specific applications and limited in the number of ways in which they can accept the user input and provide output.

**A Personal Digital Assistant (PDA)**

PDA is a hand-held palmtop computer that uses a pen rather than a keyboard input. PDAs provide electronic notepad, calendar, and wireless communication facilities. PDAs differ from the other PCs in that they are specialized for individual users. Users must train their PDAs to recognize their handwriting by writing each letter and digit several times. The PDA may be thought of as a computing appliance rather than an as general purpose computing device.

PDA is a hand-held palmtop computer in which pen is works as a keyboard input. It provide calender, notepad & wireless communication facilities.

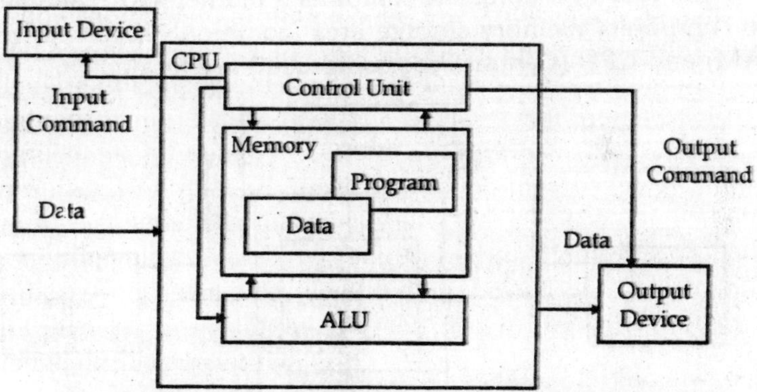


**Fig. 1.1 Basic functional units of a computer.**

## STRUCTURE OF A COMPUTER

The structure of a basic micro computer or the personal computer you shall learn in this section. Although the discussion is on the PC (because in all probability you are familiar with one having worked on it or at least seen one somewhere or the other) most of the concepts outlined have general applicability to other computers. There are main five functional blocks present in a computer. Arithmetic/Logic Unit (ALU), Control unit, Memory, Input unit and Output unit.

The Ist one is ALU (Arithmetic & logical unit) which contains electronic circuits for performing arithmetic & logical operations. The control unit analyses each instruction in the program and sends the relevant control signal to all the other units. The memory is for data and instruction storage e.g. floppy disks, hard disks, CD-ROMs etc. The input and output devices are for communication with the human world e.g. the monitor, keyboard, mouse, printer etc.

The CPU fetches the instructions and data from the memory and executes the instructions. It then places the results back in the memory. Therefore, the data paths in the figure below are bidirectional i.e. from the memory and to the memory. The CPU provide control signals for the coordination of all the devices. Thats why, the control paths are shown by unit-directional in the figure.

The base unit holds the computer's motherboard, on which the computers memory storage area (commonly referred to as RAM) and CPU (Central Processing Unit) are located.

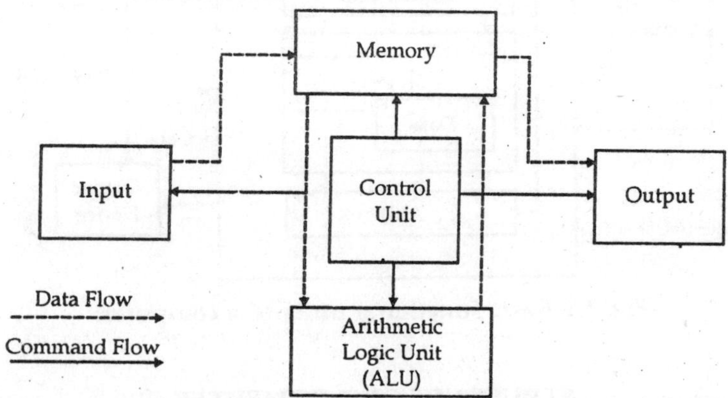


**Fig 1.2 Block diagram showing the command and data flow.**

RAM Random access memory holds both data & programs. The complicated programs can be seen & more data that can be processed depends upon the size of RAM. RAM is measured in Megabytes (one MB = 1 million characters). Typical size for today's personal computer systems is 128 MB.

The storage devices that are used to keep the copies of programs & data are the floppy drive and hard drive. The floppy drive support a removable media disk, which the user can taken away and use on another computer system. The hard drive is considered a non-removable media disk because it is permanently fixed inside the base unit. About 1.44 MB of data can be support by a Floppy drive 10 GB upwards (10000MB or 10000 Million characters).

All programs & processing of data actually run by the CPU. It is the main functional unit which does all the work. The PSU (Power Supply Unit) is also located in the base unit, and provides power to the memory, CPU and other devices. Keyboards allow users to enter commands and data into the computer system. Monitors are devices that allow the computer to display information back to the user. This might be in either a text or graphical display. Monitors come in various sizes, 14", 15", 17" and so on. The larger the monitor, the more expensive it is, and the large the image displayed on the screen is. Monitors have a number of important features. Screen resolution refers to the number of dots in the X and Y coordinates, and refresh rate specifies the number of times per second that the image is drawn on the screen (60Hz means 60 times per second). Higher screen resolutions like 1024 ´ 768 require a large monitor size like 21" (otherwise it looks very small when viewed on a 14" monitor), and also require a higher refresh rate in order to prevent the image on the screen flickering.

The modern day computer is working in the following manner. The program that you provide for execution is stored in the memory. The instructions in the program fetches by the CPU one by one, decodes them & executes them. This is called the fetch-decode-execute cycle and is the paradigm of computing in a majority of computers right from the smallest to the largest one. The origin of this concept of the "stored program" which is "fetched and executed" by the CPU is credited to John Von Neumann. It is to the credit of Von Neumann that his concept, although more than fifty years old, still forms the basis of our modern day computers.

This is the traditional way of describing the major components of the computers & their functions. However, an alternative way to understand the working of computer is to draw an analogy with the functions that the human beings perform as intelligent and articulate persons. In this respect, the major functions of modern PC in running its software are five: **thinking, remembering, listening, monitoring, and communicating.** Each of these functions requires one or more hardware components to carry out. These are:

- The thinking part (the system)
- The remembering part (mass storage)
- The listening part (the keyboard and mouse control system and various input devices)
- The monitoring part (the display system)
- The communicating part (various parts and external devices).

During the development of PC, many of there individual components have turned out not to be hard & fast. What once were separate component have merged together; others have been separated out. These, however, do not change the fact that all three functions are necessary and do need to be performed. Only for the pedagogical purposes, the division of the functions & the naming of the various devices should have been done.

## Common Input and Output Devices

### *Mouse*

To point and select an option on VDU and input device is used which is called mouse. A mouse can be classified on the basis of the number of buttons it has, the technology it uses and the kind of interface it has with the computer.

Maybe one, two or three buttons are found in a mouse. The program that uses the mouse determined the function of each button. A software package may use one, two or all three of them. In its simplest form, a mouse has one button. Moving the mouse on a flat surface produces a corresponding movement of a pointer on the screen. Placing the pointer on an option and clicking the button results in selecting that option.

On the basis of the technology & uses a mouse may be classified as an optical mouse or a mechanical mouse. In a *mechanical mouse,* the ball that projects through the bottom surface rotates as the mouses moved along a flat surface. The direction of rotation is detected and relayed to the computer by the switches inside the mouse. Microsoft, IBM and Logitech are some well-known makers of the mechanical mouse.

In optical mouse a light beam is used instead of rotating ball to detect movement across a specially patterned mouse pad. MSC Corporation makes the optical mouse that uses *LEDs* and photodetectors trap movement.

***Scanners***

Scanner is the another input device that is being increasingly used. Often, there are situations when some information (picture or text) is available on paper and is needed on the computer disk for further editing. The simplest way would be to take a photograph of the image directly from the source, and convert it into a form that can be saved on the disk and then printed.

An image is scanned and transferred to ASCII code by scanner. ASCII codes are used by the computer to represent the characters of the keyboard letters of the alphabet, numbers, punctuation marks and graphics. These can be edited, manipulated and printed.

There are 2 types of scanners :

1. The flat-bed type.

2. Roller-feed type.

While in a *roller-feed* scanner, the image is passed over a roller where it is captured, the *flat-bed* scanner works like a photocopier. Flat-bed scanners can scan and store images from books without having to remove the page, which is difficult in the case of the roller-feed scanner.

Many of the scanners available now-a-days are capable of not only scanning text and graphics, but also integrating text and graphics files.

Photographs can be reproduce on the computer screen by the scanner. They can be employed in training programs using the computer and in desktop publishing. Businesses use scanners for storing documents on the computer.

### *Touch Screens*

Imagine a cardiac surgeon performing an intricate bypass surgery. In between, the surgeon needs to check on the laboratory test results of the patient. Assuming that the information is stored on a computer, the surgeon can access the information through a keyboard, or better still, through a mouse. But how much more convenient it would be if the surgeon could only touch the screen on the option that is required to display the information. This is exactly done by the touch screen. When information has to be accurred with minimum effect touch screens are normally used there.

Two popular technologies exist for touch screens. In one, the screen is made sensitive to touch and the exact position is detected. In the other, the screen is lined with light emitting devices and photodetectors. When the user's finger approaches the screen, the light beam is broken and is detected by the photodetectors.

Touch screens are used in information-providing systems like the one explained above. It is also used in airline and railway reservation counters. The users indicate their current location and the destination by touching the screen (maybe on a map), and all the possible routes with timings and rates are displayed. These interfaces are also used in travel agencies to display the names and addresses of all hotels, restaurants, and other places of interest, at a desired destination. Touch screens are also used in stock.

### *Light Pens*

To select an option by simply pointing at it a pointing device is used called light pen.

A light pen has a photodetector at its tip. This detector used to detect changes on the bright screen. When the pen is pointed at a particular spot on the screen, it records change in brightness instantly and informs the computer about this. The computer can find out the exact spot with this information. Thus, the computer can identify where you are pointing on the screen.

For menu-based applications light pens are used. Instead of moving the mouse around or using a keyboard, the user can select an option by pointing at it.

For drawing graphics in CAD light pen is useful. An engineer, architect or a fashion designer can draw directly on the screen with the pen. Using a keyboard and a light pen, the designer can select color and line thickness, reduce or enlarge drawings, and edit drawings.

### *Printers*

Output devices that print the result of an operation on paper are called printers. Printer produce the output in form of printed words. It is also capable of printing straight lines and simple figures like squares, rectangles and circles. Printers are classified based on a number of parameters, like the mechanism used for printing, the speed of printing, the quality of output, the direction of printing, and the kind of interface they have with the computer. The following sections will elaborate on these parameters.

### Mechanism

Printers can be classified into 2 broad categories depending upon the technique used for printing—impact & non-impact printers.

In *impact printers,* characters are printed by pressing a typeface against an inked ribbon, which makes a mark on the paper. The most commonly-used impact printer is the Dot Matrix Printer (DMP).

An arrangement of tiny hammers or pins strike the ribbon to produce the desired characters in a DMP. These tiny pins typically print in a matrix of 7 dots across and 9 dots down. The impact of the appropriate pins on paper through the inked ribbon forms letters made up of dots. There are printers which use up to 24 vertical pins to print characters with a higher resolution.

DMPs are inexpensive & they can print both graphics aswellas text. With out additional hardware they can print in any language. They can also be made to print in color by changing ribbons. These printers are used to produce internal reports and memos needed by organizations. The other types of impact printer are *drum printers, daisy wheel printers* and *golf ball printers.* However, these printers are not as popular as DMPs.

Examples of DMPs are: CENTRONICS-702 HP-2635A, OLIVETTI TC480 Epson LX-80.

There is no contact between the typeface & the paper in non-impact printers. An example of a non-impact printer is the *laser printer.*

A light beam is used to form images on the paper using toner ink as medium in laser printers. The light beam strikes parts of a drum surface to form an image. Those parts of the drum surface, which are exposed to the light beam, become electrically charged. Only these electrically charged areas attract the tone ink particles. These toner particles are then deposited on, and permanently fixed to the paper using heat or pressure.

The thermal printers are the other types of non-impact printers that use heat to print character on paper and *ink-jet* printers that use jets of ink to print characters on paper.

A very high quality output is generated by laser printers, both graphics & text are typically used for publishing. Most organizations use them for business correspondence, newsletters, brochures and presentations. Laser printers are expensive.

Examples of laser printers are: Xerox 4010 from Rank Xerox UK, LASER Jet IIISI from Hewlett Packard USA and Lexmark Optra from Lexmark USA.

**Speed**

Printer's speed measured in character per seconds (CPS), lines per second (IPS) or pages per minute (PPM). The speed of a dot matrix printer is measured in *cps.* The speed can vary from 200 cps to 540 cps. A line printer prints a line at a time. Its speed can vary from 5 to 50 Ips. A laser printer prints within the range of 4 to 40 ppm.

**Quality of Output**

Draft near letter Quality (NLQ) letter quality are the 3 different mode in which printers can operate.

In the *draft-quality*-mode, a DMP forms a character by arranging dots to assemble it. Although the characters can be distinguished, the output is not as good as that of *near letter quality* printouts. A laser printer prints sin the draft mode by using less toner ink to form the characters.

The DMP prints a character twice, thereby making its appearance darker for printing in letter quality. A laser printer prints in the letter quality by using more toner ink than it uses while printing in the draft mode.

## Direction

Dot *matrix* printers and ink-jet printers can be *unidirectional, bidirectional,* or reverse. In a *unidirectional* printer, printing takes place in one direction only. After printing a line from left to right, the printer head ( the component that carries the pins or characters) returns to the left without printing.

A *bidirectional* printer prints both ways, with *logic-seeking* capability, i.e. it selects the characters in the reverse direction while printing in reverse. A reverse printer supply the characters in reverse order.

## Interface

Printer can be serial or parallel depending upon the number of characters received at a time. A serial printer receives one character at a time for printing. A parallel printer receives more number of characters and is faster.

## Plotters

To create high-quality visuals on paper which cannot be obtained using a printer, a plotter is used. A *plotter* is an output device that is used to create presentation visuals, charts, graphs, tables and diagrams.

A plotter consists of an *arm* that moves across the paper on which the diagram or graph needs to be drawn (refer Figure 1.5). A *pen* move along the arm, and the arm itself moves relative to the paper. A combination of the two thus provides movement along the *horizontal* and *vertical axis.*

The paper is held stationary in some plotters while the arm and the pens move over it. This is called a *flat-bed plotter*. In the other type of plotter, the paper is wrapped around a drum and anchored at both ends. While the pen move laterally along a fixed rail the drum rotates. This is called a drum plotter.

To draw clear, high-quality diagrams, a plotter need high-quality pens with special inks of different colors.

Through the parallel port a plotter can be connected to a PC. A plotter is more software-dependent than any other peripheral, and needs much more intructions than the printer for producing output.

In applications like computer aided Design (CAD) which require high quality graphics on paper plotter are used. Many of the plotters now available in the market are desktop models that can be used with PCs. Businesses typically use plotters to present an analysis in visual terms (bar chart, graph, diagrams, etc.) as well as for engineering drawings.

### Storage Media

For later use data need to be stored on storage media. Floppy disks are enough to store if the volume of data is small. However, when the amount of data to be stored is huge, storage media with larger storage capacities are required. In this section, you will learn about three such storage media—*cartridge tape*, CD-ROM and *Magneto-optical disks.*

### Cartridge Tape

Assume that an organization has bought a powerful computer to meet it growing need. Now the problem is arises to shift the marine databases from the old machine to the new one. Diskettes are not good enough as they cannot store large amounts of data. In such cases, a cartridge tape is a very convenient backup media as it can store many megabytes of data. Cartridge tapes are available in capacities of 60 MB, 150 MB and 500 MB.

Cartridge tape is similar to a video cassette tape made up of plastic & coated with a magnetic material. The tape is divided into tracks, which run along the entire length of the tape. Data is recorded along these tracks. Just as you need a disk drive to read or write data onto a disk, you need a cartridge tape drive which is an input-output device for a cartridge tape.

Data on a cartridge tape is stored sequentially. Therefore, if you want to access data stored at the end of the tape, you will have to run through the entire tape till you come to the end. This is in direct contrast to accessing data on disks wherein data can be accessed randomly. We can easily understand the concept by the example of audio tape & the gramophone record. If you want to listen to a song recorded in the middle of the tape, you have to forward the tape till you come to the point where the song starts whereas in the gramophone record you can directly place the gramophone head on the required sound track. Cartridge tapes are used wherever the volume of data or software to be backed up is very large, for example, backup copies of DBMS. Cartridge tape drives are present only in large machines.

## CD-ROM

Imagine that you are viewing a video film about an Antarctic expedition on your computer. It would be ideal if you can see the recording of the expedition, hear a commentary on the expedition at the same time and listen to the conversation of members of the expedition on your computer. This is possible by using a storage medium A CD-ROM. The CDs used in a CD-ROM are similar to audio CD and can store vast quantities of data-600 MB or more.

An input device called the CD-ROM drive is used to read a CD-ROM. A CD-ROM can not be erased or written onto without the help of a special device called the *CD-Recorder*.

Whenever large volumes of data need to be stored and distributed, CD-ROM are used. Many types of databases such as on, medicine, tourism literature etc. are available on CD-ROMs. Encyclopedia and dictionaries are also available on CD-ROMs.

## Megneto-optical Disk

The data storage requirements of organizations have increased manifold. At the same time software has also become powerful and voluminous. With usually more than several hundred megabyte or even gigabytes, the storage capacity of 1.44 MB diskette is insufficient.,

At 3½ inch Magneto-optied (M-O) disk has developed by maxell corporation USA having storage capacities in excess of 640 MB. M-O disks with capacities of 2 GB are also available. Data can be read as well a written onto these disks. The new disks are compatible with all 3½ inch magneto-optical drive, such as those manufactured by Fujitsu, Olympus, and others. Some of the significant improvements of the M-O disk over the conventional 1.44-MB diskette are:

- 100% faster speed than that of conventional media. This is achieved by passing the erase data phase during a rewrite operation. Thus data can be directly overwritten on existing data during an overwrite operation.
- It can store up to 4 GB of data if the M-O disk is double-sided which is more than what many hard disks can store.
- The disks are rewriteable one 1 million time, an archival life of times.
- To safeguard surface form heat or moisture a protective layer of exceptionally durable hard coaling.

Some applications of the new M-O media include: mass archival storage, document/image storage, and multimedia storage using data compression technology.

Now that you have become familiar with the PC environment, you will see where the PC fits in the computer spectrum. You will be given a bird's eye view of the computer range, from microcomputer (of which the PC is a well-known example) to supercomputers, the emphasis being on their capabilities and application areas. In this session, you will also take a closer look at the PC range itself.

## CLASSIFICATION OF COMPUTERS

Depending upon performance, size and cost the computer industry classifies than ink the following categories.

- Microcomputer (also referred to a micros)
- Minicomputers (also referred to as minis)
- Mainframes
- Supercomputers

The performance of computer is measured in terms of data storage capacity, ability to handle a large number of input & output device, speed of processing & types of operation it can perform. Generally, computers with better performance are larger in size and cost more than computer with less processing power.

### Microcomputers

At the lowest end of the computer range microcomputers are situated. The highly visible personal computers you see on desktops fall into this category.

Onlyone user can use at any time that means single-user systems. The microcomputer. Microcomputer have small to medium data storage capacities (500 MB-2 GB). Their processing power is also limited in terms of the number of instructions that they can process per second. Therefore, Microcomputer are not suitable for complex mathematical calculation & for the application that require large storage capacities such as weather forecasting or aircraft design.

The most common applications of the PC are word processing, spreadsheet calculation and database management. The other applications are desktop publishing (using computers for publishing), accounting, statistical analysis, graphics designing, investment analysis and project management. Microcomputers are also used in the field of teaching (the computer act as a teacher) and entertainment (computer games).

Examples of desktop PCs are: IBM PC, PS/2 and Apple's Macintosh.

### Minicomputers

Minicomputers are larger in size and more costly, & perform better. More than one user use them at a time. They possess larger storage capacities and operate at higher speed. They support faster peripheral devices like high-speed printers, which print hundreds of lines per minute. They can also communicate with mainframes.

When the volume of processing is large these computers are used, for example, data processing for a medium-sized organization. They are used to control and monitor production processes, to analyze result of experiments in laboratories, to meet instructional needs of colleges, etc. They are also used as servers in Local Area Networks (LANs).

Examples of minis are: Digital Equipment's PDP11/45 and VAX 11.

**Mainframes**

Mainframes have very large storage capacities & operate at very high speed and can support hundreds of user.

They are used for data processing in large organizations where the records of thousand of employees have to be processed. They are also used to manage large centralized databases. Such databases are normally queried by hundreds of users who need to access information from different locations. They are used as controlling nodes in Wide Area Networks (WANs).

Examples of mainframes are: IBM 3000 series, Boroughs B 7900 and Univac 1180.

**Supercomputers**

On the apex of the computer range are the Supercomputers. They are most expensive machine and the fastest and are considered a national resource. Although initially used for weapons design, they are also used for commercial purposes, like designing automobiles that will offer better protection to passengers in case of accidents. They are required (and can be afforded) only by a few organizations. There are less than 500 conventional supercomputers in the world.

# Chapter 2

# Operating System

A program that manages the computer hardware is an operating system. It acts as an intermediate between a user and the computer hardware and also provide the basis for application programs. An amazing aspect of operating systems is how varied they are in accomplishing these tasks Mainframe operating system are designed primarily to optimize utilization of hardware. Personal computer (PC) operating systems support complex game, business applications, and everything in between. Handheld computer operating systems are designed to provide an environment in which a user can easily interface with the computer to execute programs. Because of that some operating system are designed for their efficiency, some for their convince & some with both qualities.

We must understand the development operating system before understanding what are the operating systems. In this chapter, we trace the development of operating system from the first hands-on system through multi-programmed and time-shared system to PC, and handheld computer. We also discuss operating system variations, such a parallel, real-time, and embedded systems. We see how the components of operating systems evolved as natural solutions to problems as we move through the various stages.

### What is an Operating System?

Operating system is found almost in every computer system as an important part. A computer system can be divided roughly into four components; the *hardware, the operating system,* the *application programs,* and the *users.*

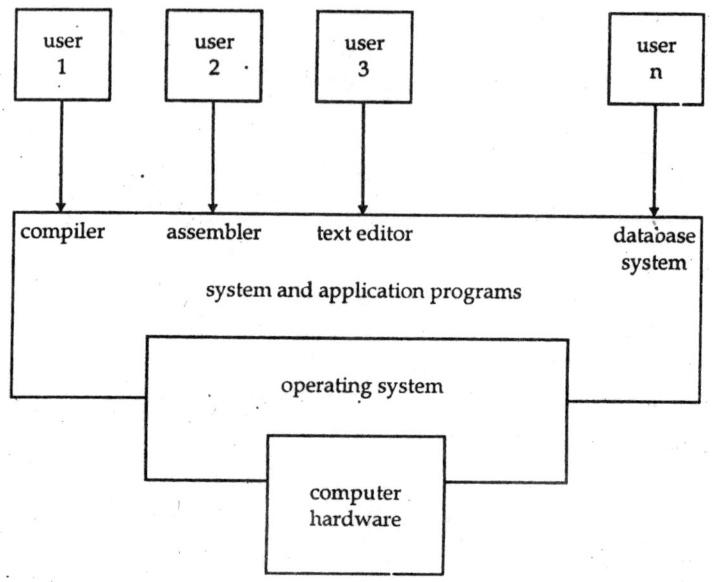


**Fig.2.1 Abstract view of the components of a computer system.**

The central processing unit (CPU), the memory and the input/output (I/O) device form the—Hardware which provide the basic computering resources. The **application programs—such as word processor, spreadsheets, compilers, and web browsers—define the ways in which these resources are used to solve the computing problem of the users. The use of hardware among the various application programs control & coordinated by the operating system.**

Hardware, software and data are the components of a computer system. The operating system provide the means for the proper use of these resources in the operation of the computer system. An operating system is similar to a *government.* Like a government, it performs no useful function by itself. It simply provides an *environment* within which other programs can do useful work. Operating system can be explored from two viewpoints: the user and the system.

**Functions of Operating System**

An operating system play an intermediate role between the computer and computer hardware. The purpose of an operating system is to provide an environment in which a user can execute programs in a convenient and efficient manner. For this, operating system performs following four operations:

(a) Memory management (b) Processor management

(c) Device management and (d) File management.

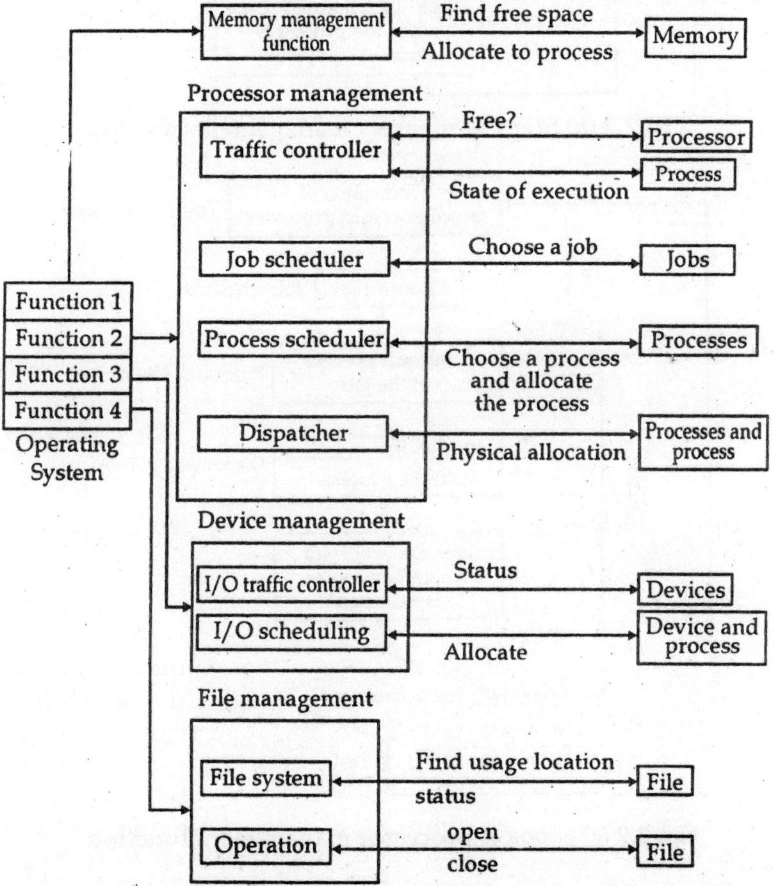


**Fig. 2.2 *(a)* Functions of operating system.**

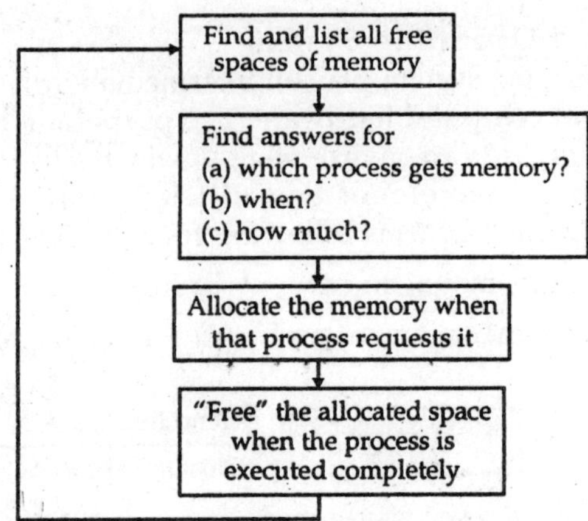


**Fig. 2.2 *(b)* Steps of memory management function.**

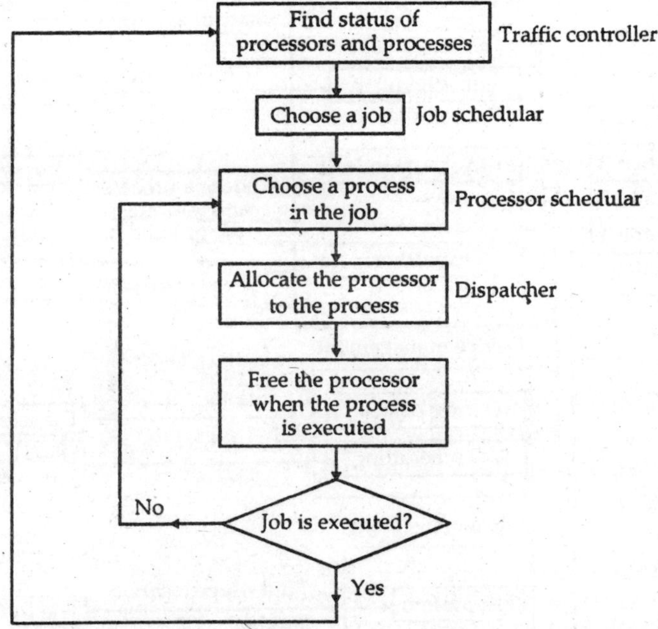


**Fig. 2.2 *(c)* Steps of processor management function.**

To find free space in memory and to allocate it for processor memory management works. To allocates the processor the execute the process processor management functions; To allocates a device to a process device management functions and to keep track of all information about file and opens/closes the file, management functions. The Figs. 2.2*(a)*, *(b)*, *(c)*, *(d)* and *(e)* clear more concept about the functionality of operating system.

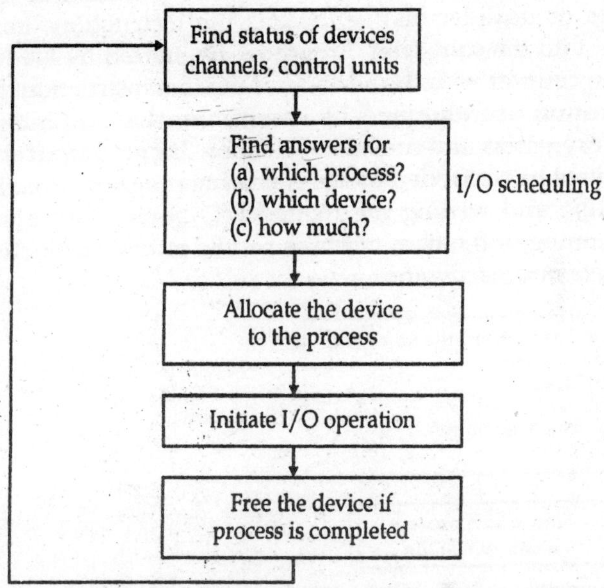


**Fig. 2.2 *(d)* Steps of device management function.**

## EVOLUTION OF OPERATING SYSTEMS

An operating system processes its work serially or concurrently. That is, resources of the computer system may be dedicated to a single program until its completion, or they may be dynamically reassigned among a collection of active programs in different of execution. Operating systems which execute multiple programs in interleaved fashion often referred as multiprogramming systems. Several variations of both serial and multi-programmed operating systems exist. In order to motivate the need for certain types of services that each of these varieties provides, we briefly and informally sketch the evolutionary path of operating-system development. In particular, we describe serial processing, multi-programming and batch processing.

**(i) Serial Processing**

Every computer system programmed in its machine language with out any support of system-software. Programs for bare machine can be developed by manually translating sequences of instructions into binary or some other code whose base is usually an integer power of 2. By means of console switches or hexadecimal keyboards the instructions and data interred into the computer. Programs are started by loading the program counter with the address of the first instruction. Results of execution are obtained by examining the contents of the relevant registers and memory locations. Input/output devices, if any, must be controlled by the executing program directly, say, by reading and writing the related I/O ports. With evidence, programming of the bare machine results in low productivity of both users and hardware.

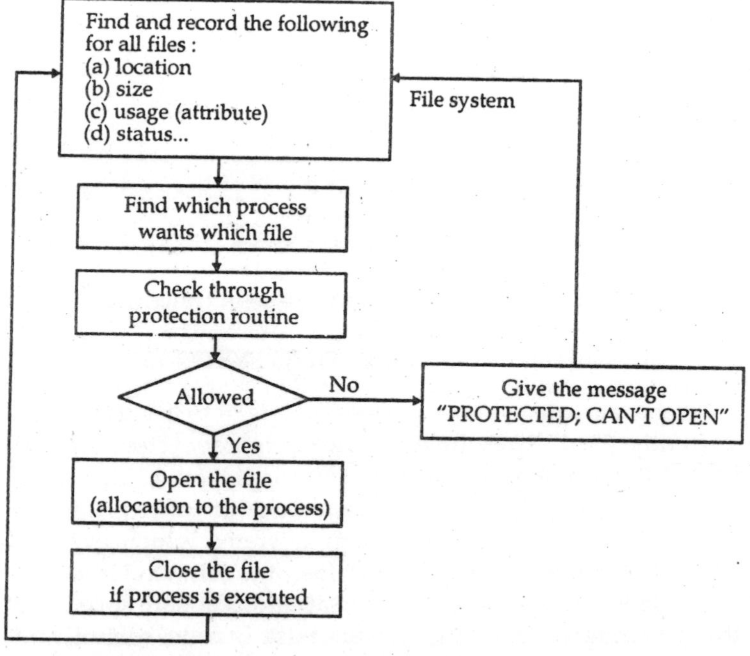


**Fig. 2.2 *(e)* Steps of file management function.**

The next significant evolutionary step in computer-system usage came about with the advent of input/output devices, such as punch cards and paper tape and language translators. Programs, now coded in programming language, are translated into executable form by a computer program called the loader, automate the process of loading executable programs into memory.

**(ii) Multi-programming**

The another method to increase the CPU utilization is multi-programming. Executing more than one program at one instant is called as multiprogramming. In this method, there is more than one job present in the memory at one instant. By doing so the CPU utilization will be increased as it will always have something to execute.

***Requirement***

Memory management methods and Scheduling methods are required.

As shown in Fig. there are five jobs present in the memory.

| O | | | | | 512K |
|---|---|---|---|---|---|
| OS | J1 | J2 | J3 | J4 | J5 |

**Fig. 2.5**

In general, either the CPU or the input/output device keep busy all the time by a single user. Multi-programming is an attempt to increase CPU utilization by always having something for the CPU to execute.

The operating system selects one of the jobs from the job pool and start executing it. Eventually the job may have to wait for something such as tape to mount, or command to be typed on a keyboard or an input/output operation to complete. In a non-multiprogrammed system the CPU would sit idle.

The editor program is loaded to prepare the source code of the user programm in a typical require. The next step is to load and execute the language translator and to provide it with the source code of the user program. When serial input devices, such as card readers are used, multiple-pass language translators may require the source code to be repositioned for reading during each pass. If syntax errors are detected, the whole process must be repeated from the beginning. Eventually, the object code produce from the syntactically correct source code is loaded and executed. If run-time errors are detected, the state of machine can be examined and modified by means of console switches or with the assistance of a program and called a debugger.

### (iii) Batch Processing

A group of job defined as batch. The jobs of each batch sequentially executes the computer.

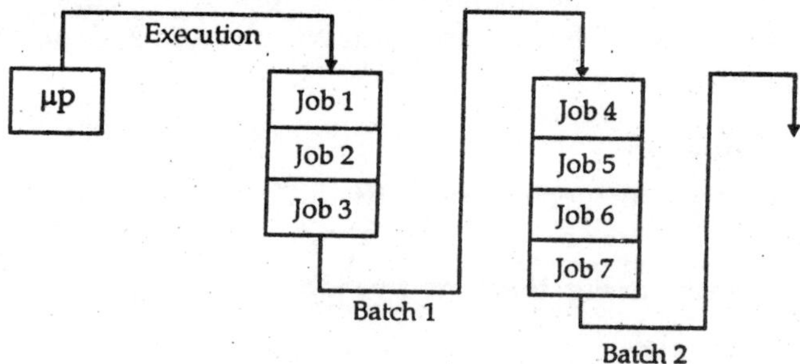


**Fig. 2.6 Batch and batch processing.**

Processing all the job of a batch considering them as a single process is called batch processing.

### Batch Operating System

The program, data and appropriate system commands to be submitted together in the turn of a job requires generally for batch processing. Batch operating system usually allow little or no interaction between users and executing program.

- In batch systems scheduling is very simple. Jobs are typically processed in the order of submission, that is in first-come-first serve fashion. Some other ordering of jobs such as shortest job next is sometimes employed to provide a fair distribution of turnaround times.
- Memory management in batch system is also very simple. Memory is usually divided into two areas, one of them is permanently occupied by the resident portion of the operating system and the other is used to load transient programs for execution. When a transient

program terminates, a new program is loaded into the same area of memory.

- Batch system does not require any time–critical device management since at most one program is in execution at any time. For this reason many serial and ordinary batch operating systems use the simple program control method of input-output. The lack of contention for input-output devices makes their allocation and deallocation trivial.
- Simple terms of the file management often provide by batch systems. Since access to files is also serial, little protection and no concurrence control of the file access is required.

**Memory Management for Batch Processing**

Normally single contiguous allocation memory is preferred for batch processing. Their are two main parts of the whole memory, one which is permanently allocated to the operating system and other remaining portion for the batch.

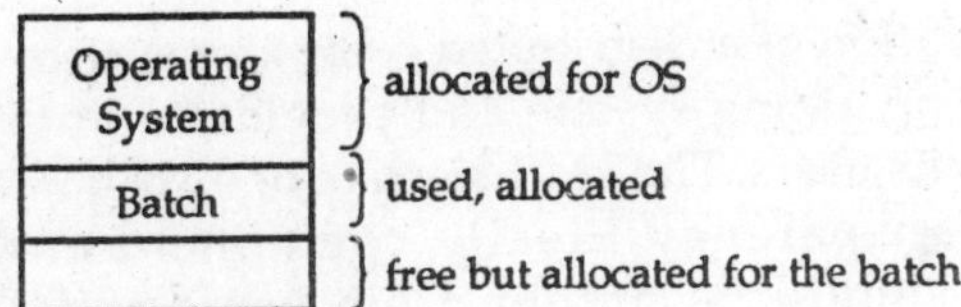


**Fig. 2.6 *(a)* Memory Management in batch processing system.**

The main disadvantage of the above allocation is that, no portions of memory are actively being used by the CPU, hence allocating free spaces to a batch becomes much complicated.

**Interactive System or Single User System**

There is direct communication between the user and system in such system and there is only one user using the system at one instance.

**Time Sharing or Multitasking**

There are number of users using the system in such systems. The CPU time is divided into different time slots depending upon the number of users. Each user is allowed to use the system for cne time slot. The switching of CPU between two users is so rapid that it gives the impression to the user that he is working on his own computer (but actually it is shared between different users).

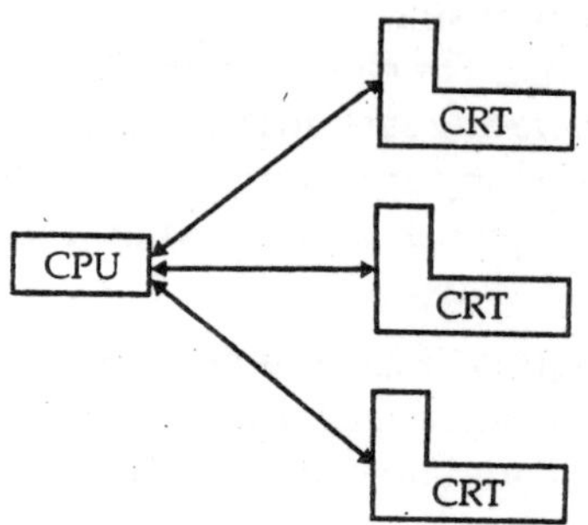


**Fig. 2.7 Time sharing system.**

### Distributed Operating System

A distributed computer system is a collection of autonomous computer systems capable of communication and cooperation via their hardware and software interconnections.

The operation of a distributed computer system governs by a distributed operating system and provides a virtual machine abstracting to its users. The key objective of distributed operating system is transparency Ideally component and resource distribution should be hidden from users and application programs unless they explicitly demand otherwise.

### Real Time Systems

A number of events present in Real Time operating system that must be accepted and processed in a short time or with in certain deadlines. Rocket launching, Flight control, Telephone switching equipment & real time simulation etc. are the some applications of this Real time systems can be classified into two categories:

#### *(i) Soft Real Time System*

Nothing catastrophic will occur but performance will be degraded in this if certain deadlines are missed. These types of the system are called as soft real time systems, *e.g.*, video conferencing.

***(ii) Hard Real Time System***

Something catastrophic will occur or the system will fail, if any deadline is missed in these types of systems. In hard real time system, all the processing must be completed with in the certain period of time.

These systems are often used as control device in a dedicated system. It has well-defined fixed time constraint and processing should be done within this time period, otherwise the system will fail.

**Real Time Operating System**

To provide quick event response time is a primary objective of real time system and thus meet the scheduling deadlines. User convenience and resource utilization are secondary concern to real-time system designers.

Each process assigned a certain level of priority that corresponds to the relative importance of the event that it services. The processor is normally allocated to the highest priority process among those that are ready to execute. Higher priority processes usually preempt execution of the lower-priority processes. This term of scheduling called priority-based preemptive scheduling which is used by majority of real time systems.

Memory management in real-time systems is comparatively less demanding than in other types of multiprogramming systems. The primary reason for this is that many processes permanently reside in memory in order to provide quick response time. Process in real time systems tends to cooperate closely thus necessitating support for both separation and sharing of memory.

Time-critical device management is one of the main characteristics of real-time systems. In additional to providing sophisticated forms of interrupt management and input output buffering, real-time operating systems often provide system calls to allow user processes to connect themselves to interrupt vectors and to service events directly.

In large installation of real-time systems usually found the file management. In fact some embedded real-time systems such as an onboard automotive controller, may not even have any secondary storage. However, where provided file management of real-time system, it must satisfy the requirement of protection and access control. The primary objective of the file management in real time system is usually speed of access rather than efficient utilization at secondary storage.

**Concept of Channels**

For handling I/O independently of the main processor of the computer system channel is a special purpose computer system. In computer system a processor executes a "start I/O" instruction to initiate I/O transfer over a channel to inform the processor. The main advantage of channel is that they allow simultaneous execution of I/O operations and CPU programs.

*Network Operating System*

This system is multiple independent computer system which communicates or file information between them. Each computer system has it our operating system in this system 4 operates independently.

*Distributed Operating System*

The collection of autonomous computer system is called distributed computer system & is capable of communication & cooperation through their hardware and software interconnections.

It provides sharing of resources such as computational capacity, file and I/O devices. For typical operating system, services provided at each mode for the benefit of local clients. A distributed local operating system may facilitate access to remote resources, communication with remote processes and distribution of computations.

## DIFFERENT MODES OF OPERATING SYSTEM

To divide the work between two or more user there are many possible ways. The users can agree on method of dividing the work with cooperation and sharing tool in a manner so that they could complete the whole work in the minimum span of time for organising the work in three ways. The interface between two users is necessary to achieve the task. The best example is the library management system where the demand of a book is fulfilled by the librarian if the book is available. If the book is not available, the librarian tells the user to wait for a time until the book available in the library.

The following are the important method:

(i) Interrupt model.

(ii) Mail box model.

(iii) The polling model.

**(i) Interrupt model**

The regular flow of work is interrupted by the user in this method. Taking the example of library system the request prompts an action while the librarian processes the request, the user (or borrower) continues working independently. When the librarian receives the book again it becomes necessary to interrupt the user by giving him the message that the book is available. Now the user suspends his routing work and goes to the library to get the book.

**(ii) Mail box model**

On the request sent by the user this method is basically based. The user fills a request form and put it into a proper place for example, in a librarian's tray for the librarian. The librarian checks the tray and processes further if any request is there. When the book arrives it is placed at the proper position for the user. The user come to library to check the book. Now if the book is there, the user can take it. In this method there is no need to communicate directly with each other.

**(iii) The polling model**

Another possible model for the communication between the two user is polling model. The user enquires about the book on regular basis to the librarian. In comparison to the interrupt model this model requires more of the user's time. For example, the librarian can ignore the telephone ring until the book has been received.

**Comparison of the models**

If we compare the models, each one has some advantages. The interrupt model is most efficient in terms of minimum communication between two persons. This is the fastest model while polling model is neither faster nor more efficient. The mail box model approach is quite easy. Both users can process independently but do not provide least time and efficiency.

**File Concept**

A collection of related information is called a file defined by its creater. Commonly program and data are represented by the files. Data files may be numeric, alphabetic or alphanumeric. Files may be free-form such as text files or may be rigidly formatted. In general a file is a sequence of bits, bytes, lines or records whose meaning is defined by its creator and user.

A file is named and is referred to by its name its type, the time of its creation, name of its creater, its length are certain other.

**File Types**

Creator of the file defined the information in a file. Source program, object programs, numeric data, text, payroll records, and so on. A file has a certain defined structure according to its use. A text file is a sequence of characters organized into lines, a source file is a sequence of subroutines and functions, each of which is further organized as declarations followed by executable statements, an object file is a sea-of words organized into loader record blocks.

How much of this structure should be known and supported by the operating system is of major consideration. If an operating system knows the structure of a file, it can then operate on the file in reasonable ways.

For example, a common mistake occurs when a user tries to print the binary object form of a program. This attempt normally produces garbage, but can be prevented if the operating system has been told that the file is a binary object program.

There are disadvantages to having the operating system know the structure of a file. One problem is the resulting size of the operating system. If the operating system defines fourteen different file structures, it must then contain the code to support these file structures correctly. In addition every file must be definable as one of the file types supported by the operating system. Seven problems may result from new applications that require information structured in ways not supported by the operating system.

To include the type as part of the file name is a common technique for implementing file types. The name is split into two parts a name and an extension. Various file types are shown in following table. In this way, the user and the operating system can tell from the name alone what the type of file is,

| *File type* | *usual extension* | *function* |
|---|---|---|
| executable | exe, com, bin or none | read to run machine-language program |
| object | obj, o | compiled, machine language, not linked |
| source code | c,cc, java, pas, asm, a | source code in various languages |
| batch | bat, sh | commands to the command interpreter |
| text | txt, doc | textual data, documents |
| word processor | wp, tx, rrf, doc | various word-processor formats |
| library | lib,a,so,dll, mpeg, mov, rm | libraries of routines for programmers |
| print or view | arc, zip, tar | ASCII or binary file in a format for printing or viewing |
| archive | arc, zip, tar | related files grouped into one file, sometimes compressed, for archiving or storage |
| multimedia | mpeg, mov, rm | binary file containing audio or A/V information. |

**Fig. 2.8 Common file types.**

## Tape-Based System

Earlier only time based systems were found-by mapping one file onto its own reel of tape each file was implemented. The advantage of this approach is its simplicity, but is suffers from a certain inefficiency. Since physical tape reels are quite large. Studies have shown that most files are small.

Only small amount of tape would take by the file because many files are quite, small. Some files are very large, which may require several tapes for storage. Such files are known as multi-reel or multi-volume tape files. To solve the problem of small files. system were created which store multiple files on one tape. This improves tape utilization. Now, there is the problem of determining which files are on which tape. To solve this problem; a directory is added to the tape. This directory is also called a volume table of contents (VTOC).

The name and location of each file listed by the directory on the tape. Additional information about a file such as the size of file, time of creation also kept in directory. Each tape or device will have its own device directory. The device directory is a convenient place to keep summary information about the files on that device.

There are some problems in file system. For this, consider a program which reads lines alternately from two files on the same tape. Either one file must first be copied to another tape, or the tape drive would spend significant amounts of time moving from one file on the tape to the other and back. Also, remember that the physical nature of tapes generally precludes rewriting in place. If a file is to be modified then it requires copying the entire tape over. All files, even those which are not being modified, must be copied and rewritten. Typically it is necessary even if a new file is being added to the end of the tape, since almost any change requires rewriting the directory. The directory is normally kept at the front of the tape to speed access. Thus if the directory is modified, the entire tape may need to be rewritten.

### Disk-Based System

When a disk based system is used many of the problems associated with storing multiple files on a tape are resolved. A disk is divided into tracks. Each disk drive varied from another diskdrive in number tracks and each track is too subdivided into sectors. A sector is the smallest unit of information which can be read from or written to the disk. Large disk systems may have several platters. Each platter has two switches. To access a sector we must specify the surface, track and sector. The read/write heads are moved to the correct track, (seek-time) electronically switched to the correct surface and then we wait (latency time) for the requested sector to rotate below the heads. A cylinder is a set of tracks which are at the same track position of the disk, but on different platter surfaces. No seek is necessary for accessing tracks in the same cylinder.

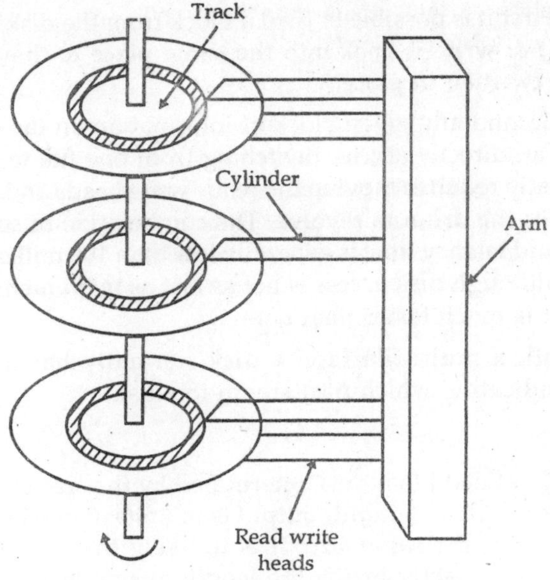


**Fig. 2.9 Disk-Based System.**

In units of one or more sectors the input/output transfers between memory and disks are performed. Addressing a particular sector requires a track (cylinder) number, a surface number and a sector number. Thus the disk can be viewed as a three-dimensional array of sectors. Commonly, this is treated by the operating system as a one-dimensional array of disk blocks and each block is a sector. Typically block addresses increase through all sectors on a track, then through all the tracks in a cylinder and finally from cylinder 0 (zero) to the last cylinder on the disk.

- If *s* is the number of sectors per track and *t* is number of track per cylinder, then we can convert from a disk address of cylinder *i*, surface *j*, sector *k* to a one-dimensional block number *b* by

$$b = k + s \times (j + i \times t)$$

Disk and drum differ from tapes in two ways which are important now.

1. First it is possible to read a block from the disk, modify it & write it back into the same place & they can be rewritten in place.
2. Second any given block of information on the disk we can directly access. Switching from one file to another only requires moving the read/write heads and waiting for the drum to revolve. The combination of seek time and latency time is generally less than 100 milliseconds; although disk access is not as fast as main memory but it is much faster than tape.

As with a multi-file tape a disk normally has a device directory indicating which files are on the disk.

**Blocking**

A well defined block size determined by the size of a sector in disk system. All disk input/output is in units of one block and all blocks are of the same size. It is unlikely that the physical record size will exactly match the length of the desired logical records. Packing a number of logical records into physical blocks is a common solution to this problem.

For example, the unix operating system defines all files to be simply a stream of bytes. Each byte is individually addressable by its offset from the beginning of the file. In this case, the logical record is one byte. The file system automatically packs and unpacks bytes into physical disk blocks as necessary.

Notice that always allocating disk space in blocks means that, in general, some portion of the last block of each file may be wasted. If each block is 512 bytes, then a file of 1949 bytes would be allocated 4 blocks, the last 99 bytes would be wasted. The wasted bytes allocated to keep everything in units of blocks internal fragmentation. All file systems suffer from internal fragmentation. Larger block size cause more internal fragmentation.

**File Operations**

To define a file properly, we need to consider the operations that can be performed on files.

Following are the five operations on a file:

(i) Creating a file

(ii) Writing a file

(iii) Reading a file

(iv) Rewinding a file

(v) Deleting a file.

**Creating a File**

To create a file two steps are necessary. First is space in the file system must be found for the file and second, an entry for the new file must be made in the directory. The directory entry records the name of the file and its location in the file system.

**Writing a File**

The name of the file and the information to be written to the file a system call is made specifying to write a file. Given the name of the file, the system reaches the directory to find the location of the file. The directory entry will need to store a pointer to the current end of the file. By using this pointer the address of the next block can be computed and the information can be written. The write pointer must be updated. In this way successive write operation can be uses to write a sequence of blocks to the file.

**Reading a File**

The name of the file and where the next block of the file should put, a system call specifies to read from a file. Again, the directory is search for the associated directory entry. And again, the directory will need a pointer to the next block to be read. Once that block is read the pointer is updated.

**Rewinding a File**

Any actual input-output not involved to rewinding a file. Rather the directory is searched for the appropriate entry & the current file position is simply reset to the beginning of the file.

'le

ch the directory for the named file to delete the file. d the associated directory entry, we release all file invalidate the directory entry.

ctory

perating system to operating system the particular tion kept for each file in the directory various. The following is a list of some of the informations which may be kept in a directory entry. Of course not all system keep all this information.

- **File Name:** The symbolic file name.
- **File Type:** For those systems which support different types.
- **Location:** A pointer to the device and location on that device of the life.
- **Size:** The current size of the file and the maximum allowed size.
- **Current Position:** A pointer to the current read or write position in the file.
- **Protection:** Access control information to control reading, writing, executing and so on.
- **Usage Count:** Indicating the number of processes which are currently using this file.
- **Time, Date and Process Identification:** This information may be kept for creation of last modification and last use.

These can be useful for protection and usage monitoring.

**File Organisation And Access Mechanism**

To use a file, it is very important to organize the file in a proper manner so that the access can be done easily. Some common file organization schemes are as follows. (i) Sequential Access (ii) Direct Access (iii) Index Access.

## Access Methods

File store information must be accussed and read into computer memory. There are several ways that the information in the file can be accessed:

(i) Sequential Access

(ii) Direct Access

(iii) Index Access

## Sequential Access

The most of the operations on a file are reads and writes. The next portion of the file reads by a read operation and automatically advances the file pointer. Similarly, a write appends to the end of the file and advances to the end of the newly written material. Such a file can be rewound and on some systems a program may be able to skip forward or backward *n* records for some integer *n*. This scheme is known as sequential access to a file sequential access.

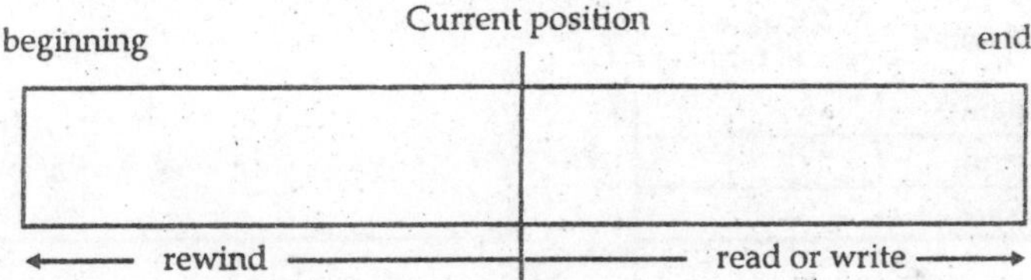


**Fig. 2.10. Sequential access file.**

## Direct Access

Direct access is an alternative method. This method is based upon a disk model of a file. For direct access, the file is viewed as a numbered sequence of blocks or records. A block is generally a fixed-length quantity, defined by the operating system as the minimal positioning unit.

Arbitrary block to be read or written allowed by a direct assess file. Thus we may read block 14, then read block 53 and then write block 7. There are no restrictions on the order of reading or writing for a direct access file.

For immediate access to large amounts of information direct access files are of great use. They are often used in accessing large data bases. When a query concerning a particular subject arrives, we compute which block contains the answer and then reads that block directly to provide the desired information. The file operations in this method uses block.number as a parameter. The block number provided by the user to the operating system is normally a relative block number. This block number is relative to the beginning of file.

### Indexed Access

In this method an index is created which contains a key field and pointers to the various blocks. To find an entry in the file for a key value, we first search the index and then use the pointer to directly access the file and find the desired entry.

With large files, the index file itself may become too large to be kept in memory. One solution is to create an index for the index file. The primary index file would contain pointers to secondary index files, which would point to the actual data items. Fig. Shows a situation as implemented by VMS index and relative files.

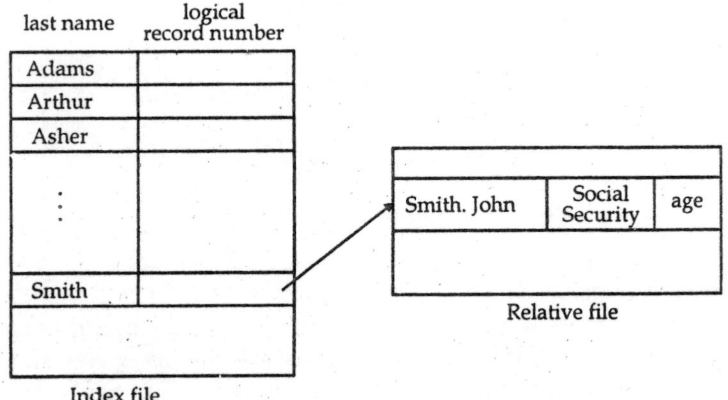


**Fig. 2.11 Example of Index and Relative Files.**

### Free Space Management

To manage space on the secondary storage is an important function of the file system. This includes keeping track of both disk blocks allocated to files and the free blocks available for allocation.

File System maintains a free space list to keep track of free disk space. To create a file, we search the free space lst for the required amount of space and allocate it to the new file. This space is then removed from the free space list. When a file is deleted, its disk space is added to the free space list.

As a bit map or bit vector it is implemented frequently. Each block is represented by one bit. If the block is free, the bit is 0, if the block is allocated the bit is 1. For example consider a disk where block 2,3,4,5,8,9, are free, space bit map would be: 11000011001......

Keeping a pointer to the first free block is the another approach to link all the free blocks together. This block contains pointer to the next free disk block, and so on. In previous example, we would keep a pointer to block 2, as the first free block. Block 2 would contain a pointer to block 3, which would point to block 4 and so on.

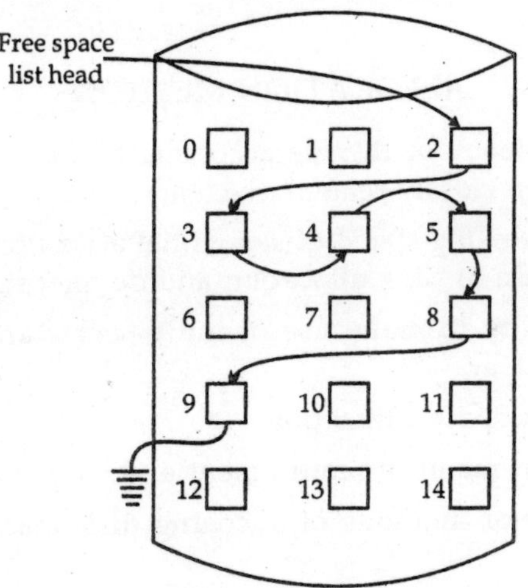


**Fig. 2.12 Free space management.**

This scheme is not very efficient since to traverse the list, we must read each block, requiring substantial input/output time.

File system maintains a free space list to keep track of free disk space. All the disk blocks which as free are recorded by the free space list.

A modification of this approach would store the addresses of a $n$ free blocks in the first free block. The first $n - 1$ of these are actually free. The last one is the disk address of another block containing the addresses of another $n$ free blocks. The importance of this implementation is that the addresses of a large number of free blocks can be found quickly.

To take advantage of the fact that, generally several contiguous blocks may be allocated or freed simultaneously is the another approach. Particularly when contiguous allocation is used. Thus rather than keeping a list of $n$ free disk addresses, we can keep the address of the first free block and the number $n$ of free contiguous block which follow it. Each entry in the free space list then this consists of a disk address and a count. While each entry requires more space than a simple disk address the overall list will be shorter, as long as the count is generally greater than one.

## ALLOCATION METHODS

The efficiency of the file accessing & the space allocation storage is often closely related. Such as:

(i) Processing speed of sequential access to files, random access to files, allocation and de-allocation of blocks.

(ii) Ability to make use of multi-sector and multi-track transfer.

(iii) Disk space utilization.

(iv) Main memory requirement also.

Three major methods of allcoatng disk space are in wide use:

(1) Contiguous Allocation

(2) Linked Allocations

(3) Indexed Allcoation

Several related and interactive factors must take into consideration by a good space allocation strategy.

### Contiguous Allocations

The contiguous allocation method requires each file to occupy a set of contiguous addresses on the disk. Disk addresses define a linear ordering of the disk. Notice that with this ordering, accessing block ($b$+1) after block normally requires no head movement. When head movement is needed, it is only one track.

The disk address of the first block and its length defined the contiguous allocation of a file. If the file is $n$ blocks long and starts at location $b$, then it occupies blocks $b,b,+1,b+2,....b+n-1$. The directory entry for each block indicates the address of the starting block and the length of the area allocated for this file.

It is easy to access a file which has been contiguously allocated. For sequential access, the file system remembers the disk address of the last block and, when necessary reads the next block. For direct access to block $i$ of a file which starts at block $b$, Thus both sequential and direct access can be supported by contiguous allocation.

The difficulty with contiguous allocation is finding space for a new file. If the file to be created is $n$ blocks long we must search the free space list for $n$ free contiguous blocks.

Directory

| File | Start | Length |
|---|---|---|
| Current | 0 | 2 |
| Tr | 14 | 3 |
| F | 6 | 2 |

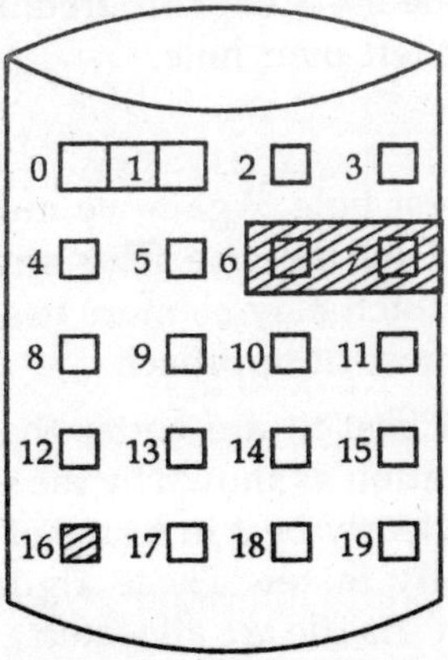

**Fig. 2.13 Contiguous Allocation**

The disadvantages of contiguous allocation are:

(a) External fragmentation

(b) May not know the file size in advance.

**Dynamic Storage Allocations**

As a large arrary of disk blocks the disc can be viewed. At any given time, some of these blocks are allocated to files and others are free. Disk space can be seen as a collection of free and used segments, each segment is a contiguous set of disk blocks. An unallocated segment is called a hole. The dynamic storage allocation problem is how to satisfy a request of size *n* from a list of free holes. There are many solutions to this problem. The set of holes is searched to determine which hole is best to allocate.

First-fit, Best-fit and Worst-fit are the most common strategies used to select a free hole from the set of available holes.

***First-fit:***

Allocate the first hole that is big enough. Here searching can start either at the beginning of the set of holes or where the previous first-fit search ended. We can stop searching as we find large enough free hole.

***Best-fit:***

Allocate smallest hole that is big enough. We must search the entire list, unless the list is kept ordered by size. This strategy produces the smallest left-over hole.

***Worst-fit:***

Allocate the largest hole. Again we must search the entire list, unless it is sorted by the size. This strategy produces the largest leftover hole, which may be more useful than the smaller leftovers hole from a best-fit approach.

Both first fit and best-fit are better than worst-fit in both time and storage utilization as shown by the simulations. Neither first-fit nor best-fit is clearly best in terms of storage utilization, but first-fit is generally faster. These algorithms suffer from external fragmentation. As file are allocated and deleted, the free disk space is broken into little pieces. External fragmentation exists when enough total disk space exists to satisfy a request, but it is not contiguous, storage is fragmented into a large number of small holes. To prevent losing significant amounts of disk space to external fragmentation, the user must compact all free space into one hole.

Some other problems are also there with contiguous allocation. The major problem is determining how much space is needed for a file. When the file is created the total amount of space it will need must be found and allocated. But user does not know the size of file to be created.

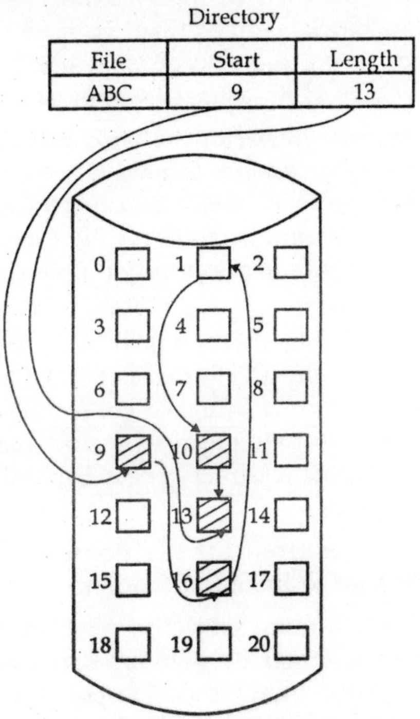


**Fig. 2.14. Showing Linked Allocation**

### Linked Allocation

Each file is a linked test of disk blocks in linked allocation and the disk blocks may be scattered any where on the disk. The directory contains a pointer to the first block of the file. For example, a file of 5 block which starts at block 9, might continue at block 16 then block 1, block 10 and finally block 13.. Each block contains pointer to the next block. These pointers are not made available to the user.

Thus if each sector is 512 words and a disk address requires two words, then the user see block of 510 words.

It is easy to create a file, we imply create a new entry in the device directory with linked allocation each directory entry has a pointer to the first disk block of the file. This pointer is initialized to nil to signify an empty file. A write to a file removes the first free block from the free space list and write to it. To the end of file this new block is linked then. To read a file we simply read blocks by following the printer from block to block. With linked allocation there is no asternal fragmentation.

*There is no external fragmentation with linked allocation. Any free block on the free space list can be used to satisfy a request since all blocks are linked together. Notice also that there is no need to declare the size of a file when it is created. A file can continue to grow a long as there are free blocks. Consequently it is necessary to compact disk space.*

- The major problem with linked allocation is that it can only be used effectively for sequential of that file and follow the printers until we get to the $i^{th}$ block. Each access to a pointer requires a disk read. Hence we cannot support a direct access capability for linked allocation files.
- The space required for the pointers is the another disadvantage to linked allocation.
- Reliability is a more subjective problem. Since the files are linked together by pointers scattered all over the disk. Consider what would happen if a pointer is lost or damaged. A bug in the operating system s/w or a disk hardware failure may result in picking up the wrong pointer. This error could result in linking into the free space list or into another file.

## Indexed Allocation

In indexed allocation, all pointers are brought together into one location: *The index block.*

Each file has its own index block which is an array of disk block address. The $i^{th}$ entry in the index block points to the $i^{th}$ block of the file. The directory contains the address of the index block. To read the $i^{th}$ block, we use the pointer in the $i^{th}$ index block entry to find and read the desired block. When the file is created all pointer in the index block are set to nil. When the $i^{th}$ block is first written a block is removed from the free space list and is address is put in the $i^{th}$ index block entry.

With out suffering from external fragmentation indexed allocation supports direct access. A request for more space may satisfied by any free block any where on the disk. Indexed allocation dose suffer from wasted space. The pointer overhead of the index block is generally worse than the pointer overhead of linked allocation. Most files are small. Assume that we have a file of only one or two block with linked allocation we only lose the pace of one pointer per block. With indexed allocation an entire index block must be allocated even if only one of two pointers will be non-nil.

The index block should be as small as possible because every file must have an index block. If the index block is too small however it will not be able to hold enough pointers for a large file. An index block is normally one disk block. Thus it can be read and written directly by itself. For large files several index files may be linked together. For example an index block might contain a small header giving the name of the file and a set of the first 100 disk block addresses. The next address is nil or a pointer to another index file. For a very large file this second index file could point to a third and so on.

Inspite of using this linked allocation for the index blocks; another representation may use a separate index block to point to the index blocks which point to the file blocks themselves. The first level index be used by the operating system to access a block to find the second level index to a third or fourth level but two level are generally sufficient.

## DIRECTORY SYSTEM

The entries in a device directory or volume table of contents are represented by files. A device directory may be sufficient for a single user system with limited storage space. As the amount of storage and the number of users increases it becomes very difficult for the users to organize and keep track of all files. The solution to this problem is imposition of a directory structure on the file system.

Many system actually have to separate directory structures: the devices directory is stored on each physical device and describe all files on that device. The device directory entry mainly concentrates on describing the physical properties of each files: where it is, how long it is, how it is allocated and so on. A logical organization of the files on all devices are the file directories. The file directory entry concentrates on logical properties of each file: name, file type, owing user, accounting information, protection access codes and so on.

The operations which are to be performed on a directory are:

*Search:*

We need to search a directory structure to find the entry for a particular file. Since files have symbolic names and similar names may indicate a relationship between the files, we may want to be able to find all files which match a particular pattern.

*Create file:*

New files need to be created and added to the directory.

***Delete file:***

When a file is no longer needed, we want to remove it from the directory.

***List directory:***

We need to be able to list the files in a direction and the contents of the directory entry for each file in the list.

*Backup up:*

In case of system failure this provides a backup copy. Or if the file is simply no longer in use.

Different Directory Structure are:

**Single-Level Directory**

The single level directory is the simplest directory structure for example. The device directory is a single level directory. All files are contained in the same directory, which is very easy to support and understand.

A single-level directory has significant limitations, however, when the number of files increases or when there is more than one user. Since all files are in the same directory, they must have unique names. With multiple users as the number of files increases it becomes difficult to remember the names of all the files in order to create only files with unique names.

**Two-Level Directory**

The major disadvantage to a single-level directory is the confusion of file a names between different users. To create a separate directory for each user is the standard solution.

Each user has his own user file directory in two-level directory structure. Each user has a similar structure but lists only the files of a single user. When a user job starts or a user logs-in, the system's master file directory is searched. The master file directory is indexed by the user name or account no. and each entry points to the user directory for that user.

When users refers to a particular file, only their own user file directory is searched. Thus different users may have files with the same name as long as all the names within each user file directory are unique.

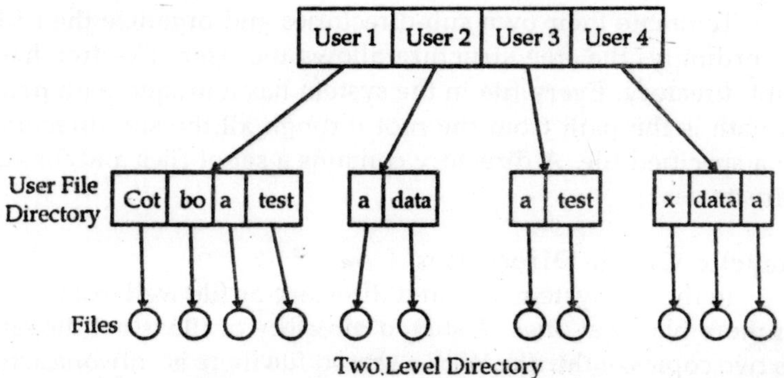


**Fig. 2.15 Two Level Directory**

It isolates one user from another is the problem with too-level directory. This is disadvantage when the users want to cooperate on some task and access files of other users. If this type of access is to be permitted we must name particular file uniquely by giving both the user name and the file name. A user name and a file name define a path name. Every file in the system has a unique path name.

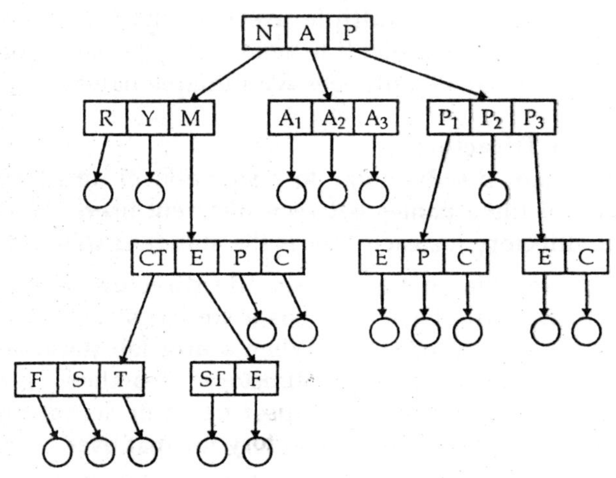


**Fig. 2.16 Tree structured directory.**

## Tree Structured Directory

To create their own sub-directories and organize their files accordingly, the tree structure allows the user. The tree has a root directory. Every file in the system has a unique path name. A path is the path from the root through all the sub directories to a specified file. A directory contains a set of files and/or sub-directories.

## Acyclic Graph Directories

In the file system a shared directory or file well exist in two or more places at ones.. A shared directory or file is not the same as two copies of the file. With a shared file there is only one actual file and any changes made by one person would be immediately visible to the other.

An acyclic graph allow directories to have shared sub-directories and files. The same file or sub-directory may be in two different directories.

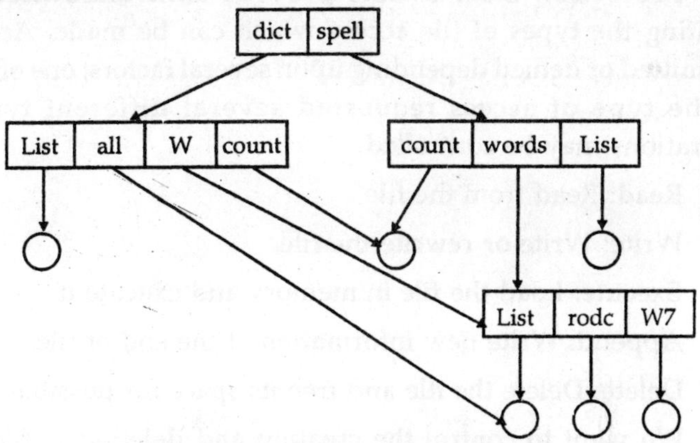


**Fig. 2.17 Acyclic graph directory.**

An acyclic graph directory structure is more flexible and also more complex than a simple tree structure. We have multiple complex path names, like a file. Consequently distinct file name may refer to the same file. If we are trying to traverse the entire file system (to find a file or copy all files to backup storage) this problem becomes significant, since we do not want to traverse shared structure more than once.

## File Protection

A major concern is a protection from both physical damage and improper access when information is kept in a computer system.

By making duplicate copies of files reliability is generally provided. Many operating systems will automatically copy disks files to tape at regular intervals to maintain a copy. File system can be damage by hardware problems such as error in re-adding or writing, power surges or failures, head crashes, din, temperature and vandalism. Bugs in the file system can also cause file content to be lost.

In many ways protection can be provided. For a small single-user system, protection might be provided by physically removing the dikettes and locking them in a desk drawer or file cabinet.

Protection mechanisms provide controlled access by limiting the types of file access which can be made. Access is permitted or denied depending upon several factors, one of which is the type of access requested several different types of operations may be controlled.

Read: Read from the file

Write: Write or rewrite the file.

Execute: Load the file in memory and execute it.

Append: Write new information at the end of file.

Delete: Delete the file and free its space for possible refuse.

We want to control the creation and deletion of files in a directory. In addition we probably want to control whether a user can determine the existence of file in directory. It itself significant the knowledge of resistance and name of file. Thus listing the content of directory must be a protected operation.

The inability of users to access a file which they cannot name determines the protection schemes of several systems. If a user cannot name a file they cannot operate on it. Another approach is to associated password with each file. Just as access to computer system itself is controlled by a password, access to each file can be controlled by a password.

**Implementation Issues: Layered File System**

As show in chart the file system itself generally composed of many different levels as shown in chart. Each level in the design uses the features of lower level to create new features for use by higher levels.

To actually transfer information between memory and the disk system the lowest level, input output control consists device drivers and interrupt handless. The basic file system uses this to read and write particular blocks to and from the disk. Each disk block is identified its numeric disk address.

Application Program

↓

Logical file system

↓

File Organization module

↓

Basic file system

↓

Input output control

↓

Device

**Chart for layered file system**

About both files and disk blocks the file organization modules knows. By knowing the type of file allocation used and the location of the file; the file organization module can generate the addresses of the blocks for the basic file system to read. Finally the logical file system uses the directory structure to provide the file organization module with the values it needs from a symbolic file name.

To create a new file an application program calls the logical file system. The logical file system knows the format of the directory structures. To create a new file, we read the appropriate directory into memory update it with the new entry and write it back to the disk. The directories can be treated exactly files with the type field indicating that they are directories. Thus the logical file system can call the file organization module to map the directory input/output into disk block number which are passed on to the basic files system and input/output control system.

### Interleaving

A sector numbering scheme is called interleaving. It is made up of placing consecutive logical blocks into non contiguous physical sectors on a disk.

As a result some processing time is allowed between passage of two consecutive logical sectors under a read/write head.

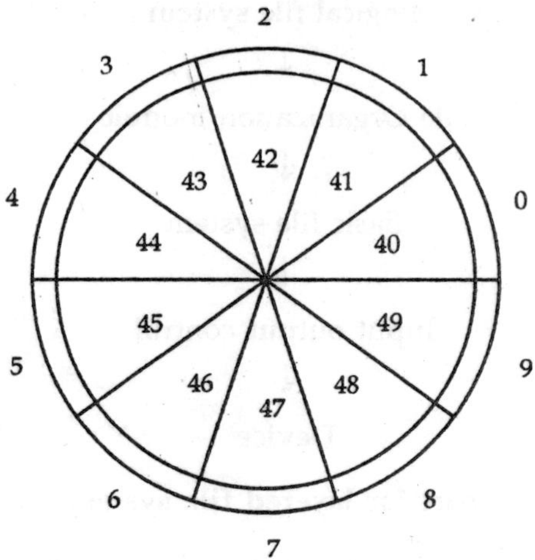


**Fig. 2.18 Without Interleaving.**

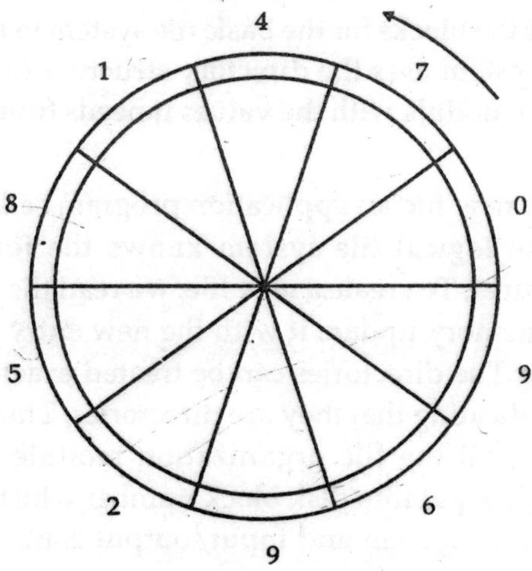


**Fig. 2.19 With Interleaving.**

On the rotational speed of the disk and on the size and number of interring physical disk sectors between consecutive logical block the duration of such gaps depends. The last component called the interleave factor is usually programmable to suit the intended use of a given system. The interleave factor is 3. As a result for logical blocks can be read and processed within a single disk revolution with interleaving.

**Authentication Parameter in File System**

On of the important parameter for file system is Authentication. Basically in this, we have considers the following two terms:

(i) **False acceptance ratio:** This is percentage (%) of illegitimate user enormously admitted.

(ii) **False rejection ratio:** This is the percentage % of legitimate users who are denied access to failure of authentication.

To minimize the both false acceptance and the false rejection ratios is the main objective here, which is always our need when we handle the file system.

Authentication is based on the following techniques:

1. Possession of a secret *i.e.* password.
2. Possession of an artifact.
3. Unique physiological or behavioural characteristics of user.

One of the important bases of authentication *i.e.* password which is described as: It is most common authentication mechanism based ones sharing of a secret. In this system, each file has a password and this may be assigned by the system or administrator. Many systems allow users to subsequently change their password.

To authenticate to the users the system stores all users passwords. At the time of logging-in, system requests to user to put secret password. Passwords are not required of special hardware and it is very easy to implement. But passwords offer limited protection since one can easy to obtain or guess. Encrypted password files are stored in a system.

For the protection of password various techniques are available. One technique is that password schemes are multilevel and users are required to supply additional passwords at the system's request at random intervals during computer use.

To have the system a dynamic challenge to user after login is the second technique. This challenge can take the form of random number generated by computer. The user has to apply a secret transformation like squaring or incrementally. Failure may be used to detect unauthorized users.

The number of consecutive login attempt may also be controlled by disabling the users' account after certain number of unsuccessful attempts.

### File Sharing

For the users who want to collaborate and to reduce the effort required to achieve a computing goal file sharing is very desirable. Therefore, user-oriented operating systems must accommodate the need to share files inspite of the inherent difficulties.

### Multiple Users

When an operating system accommodates multiple users, the issues of file sharing, file naming, and file protection become pre-eminent.

The system must maintain more file and directory attributes than and single-user system to implement sharing and protection. Although there have been many approaches to this topic historically, most systems have evolved to the concepts of file/ directory *owner* (or *user* and *group*. The owner is the user who may change, attributes, grant access, and has the most control over the file or directory. The group attribute of a file is used to define a subset of users who may share access to the file.

With the other file attributes the owner and group IDs of a given file or directory are stored. When a user requests an operation on a file, the user ID can be compared to the owner attribute to determine if the requesting user is the owner of the file. Likewise, the group IDs can be compared. The result indicates which permissions are applicable. The system then applies those permissions to the requested operation, and allows or denies it.

**Remote File Systems**

Between remote computers communication allowed by the advent of networks. Networking allows the sharing of resources spread within a campus or even around the world. One obvious resource to share is data, in the form of files. Through the evolution of network and file technology, file-sharing methods have changed. In the first implemented method, users manually transfer files between machines via programs like ftp. The second major method is a distributed file system (DFS) in which remote directories are visible from the local machine. In some ways, the third method, the **World Wide Web**, is a reversion to the first. A browser is needed to gain access to the remote files, and separate operations (essentially a wrapper for ftp) are used to transfer file.

**Consistency Semantics**

For evaluating any file system that supports file sharing consistency semantics is an important criteria. It is a characterization of the system that specifies the semantics of multiple users accessing a shared file simultaneously. In particular, these semantics should specify when modifications of data by one user are observable by other users. The semantics are typically implemented as code with the file system.

The UNIX file system uses the following consistency semantics:

- Writes to an open file by a user are visible immediately to other users that have this file open at the same time.
- One mode of sharing allows users to share the pointer of current location into the file. Thus, the advancing of the pointer by one user affects all sharing users. Here, a file has a single image that interleaves all accesses, regardless of their origin.

**Immutable-Shared-Files Semantics**

Immutable shared files is a unique approach. The file cannot be modified if it is once declared as shared by its creator. An immutable file has two key properties: Its name, may not be reused and its contents, may not be altered. Thus, the name of an immutable file signifies that the contents of the file are fixed, rather than the file being a container for variable information. The implementation of these semantics in a distributed system is simple, because the sharing is disciplined (read-only).

### Directory Implementation

One of the important concepts for implementing the directory is directory implementation. The selection of directory-allocation and directory management has a large effect on the efficiency, performance and reliability of the file system. In the directory implementation, we have used the following two approaches:

(i) Linear list

(ii) Hash table.

### Linear List

To use a linear list of file names with pointers to the data blocks is the simplest method of implementing a directory. A linear list of directory entries requires a linear search to find a particular entry. This method is simple to program but time-consuming to execute. A linked list is used for managing the time in the linear list.

The real disadvantage of a linear list of directory entries is the linear search to find a file. Directory information is used frequently, and users would notice a slow implementation of access to it. In fact, many operating systems implement a software cache to store the most recently used directory information. A cache hit avoids constantly rereading the information from disk.

### Hash Table

Hash table is a another data structure that has been used for a file directory. A linear list stores the directory entries, and a hash data structure is also used in this method. The has table takes a value computed from the file name and returns a pointer to the file name in the linear list. Therefore, it can greatly decrease the directory search time. Insertion and deletion are also fairly straightforward, although some provision must be made for **collisions**–situations where two file names has to the same location. The major difficulties with a hash table are its generally fixed size and the dependence of the hash function on that size.

**MSDOS memory Types**

MSDOS had come under threat with advances in hardware design and the increased memory available in different machines (PC=640KB, AT286=16MB,-386/486=4GB). MSDOS was still restricted by the old limitations of the 8086 processor of using 640KB of memory, for running MSDOS programs. MSDOS has not been rewritten to keep space with developing hardware, and as each new version of MSDOS has appeared, it has remained backward compatible with old machines (ie, still runs on a PC with 640 KB of memory).

Certain add-on features have appeared to patch MSDOS into recognizing the extra RAM available in 286/386 (and beyond) machines. They are called **memory manager,** and make available the extra memory in a number of different ways, primarily a disk cache and RAM drives.

There are a number of differnt memory areas in MSDOS:

**Conventional Memory**

A memory light of 1 MB, found in the original 8086 processor is being for use by MSDOS (0-640K), the second half for use by peripheral cards like video cards, network cards, the ROM BIOS program and the XT hard disk controller card.

**Expanded memory**

Earlier its maximum address range was 16 MB of RAM, when the 80286 processor was developed. As MSDOS still imposed the 640KB limits for running programs, several companies developed a memory manager for using the area between 640K and 1MB for storing programs and data.

A free block (normally about 64K) of memory space not being used by a peripheral card is found between 640KB and 1MB. Access and control of this block is under a memory manager device driver program.

Many 16K blocks of RAM were provided on an expansion card that plugs into a free expansion sect on the mother board within this memory block. Under software control, up to 4 of these 16KB banks were visible at any one time. By switching in and out these 16KB blocks of RAM, it could appear as though there was a large amount of memory available, all accessed through this expanded memory window.

This is called the LIM EMS standard, and this standard is supported by many modern program like lotus 123, Quattro pro, Borland c++ and many other. With 386/486 computers, it has the ability to simulate expanded memory using a device driver, and does not need a special card to do this.

**Extended Memory**

The 8086 processor was limited to 1MB of memory. A new way of accurring this extra memory introduced by designers of the 286/386/486 processors. In effect, they designed two processors inside a single chip.

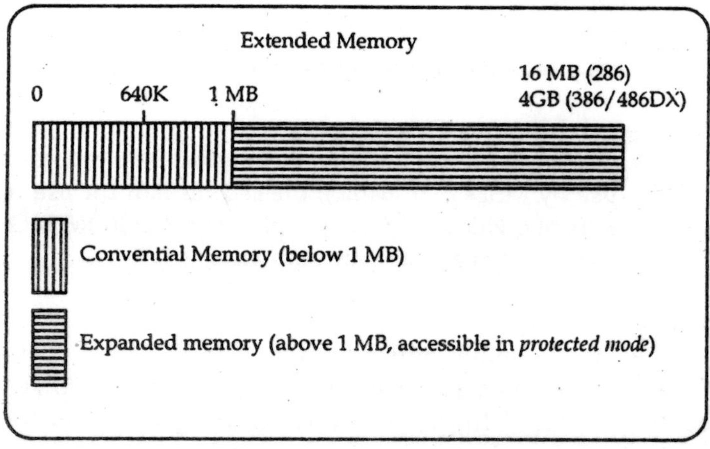


Fig. 2.20 Extended Memory

The first processor looked and behaved like a standard 8086, whilst the other acted as a super improved chip with extra functions and larger memory capability. The default mode of operation is a standard 8086, but a special software instruction can switch the chip into the new advanced mode. MSDOS, you must remember, is written in the old 8086 instructions, so it cannot take advantage of the improved chip and its extra functionality.

With the 286-486 chip acting as a PC (default), accessing memory is called real mode (<1MB), whilst the new way is called protected mode.

**Extended memory is ONLY accessible in protected mode.** In protective mode the exfinded memory is only occussible. When the chip is switched to act in its native form then this special mode of operation occur. Several operating systems have been written to take advantage of this mode, and thus access to the larger amounts of memory available. Examples are Windows and beyond and OS/2.

Extended memory can only be accessed on machines based on 286-486 and higher processors running in protected mode of operation with more than 1MB of RAM.

**Upper Memory Blocks**

For application programs MSDOS user the lower 640K of memory. The remaining memory below 1MB is reserved for system use, examples being the ROM BIOS and peripherals like networking and hard disk cards.

Peripheral cards often have memory on board, like video cards that have memory which holds the screen image, and a small ROM which hooks itself into the ROM BIOS to provide support for special displays (VGA) display cards are a good example.

Intelligent support chips were added to provide sophisticated memory manipulation and management when the 286-486 computers were designed. These are called the AT Chip Set, now common on virtually all PC based computers.

As memory chips expanded in size, it became common for 2MB or 4MB of memory to be fitted to motherboards, This complicated remapping the unused memory from the first 1MB (640KB used by MSDOS), so software was developed to remap the unused memory into the address space between 640KB and 1MB reserved for peripheral devices.

The types and numbers of peripheral cards installed in the computer system determines how much unused space is available. It can range from as little as 8KB to 128KB of unused space. This is called the **Upper Memory Area.**

The upper memory blocks become an integral part with the release of MSDOS 5.0 and are used for transferring device drivers into the upper memory, freeing up more conventional memory for MSDOS based applications. MSDOS provides an Upper Memory device driver (EMM386.EXE), which manages the memory area as a series of blocks, allocated under the control of MSDOS. This is available only for 386 or better computers.

### The High Memory Area

When Microsoft Windows v3.0 was released it was found that the first 64K of extended memory above 1MB was actually accessible in real mode, and therefore could be accessed by MSDOS. This is known as the **high memory area**, and is a maximum of 64K in size.

It is possible to load the DOS shell into the high memory area with MSDOS 5.0 and above, freeing up more conventional memory for DOS based applications.

### MSDOS.SYS

This is the core of MS-DOS versions up through 6.22. In the boot disk's directory the MSDOS.SYS file is listed second and is the second file to be loaded during the boot process. It contains the routines that handle OS disk and file access. The MSDOS.SYS File is loaded into low memory like IO. SYS where it resides throughout the system's operation. You will see some kind of book failure massage if the file is missing or the system might lock up.

### Command.COM

As the MSDOS shell and command processor the COMMAND. COM file serves. At the command line prompt you interact with this program. COMMAND.COM is the third file loaded when a PC boots, and it is stored in low memory, along with IO.SYS and MSDOS.SYS. On the version of MSDOS in use determines the number of commands that you have available. In normal operation MSDOS user two types of commands: resident and transient. Resident commands (also called internal commands) are procedures that are coded directly into COMMAND.COM. Resident commands execute almost immediately when called from the command line. CLS and DIR are two typical resident commands. Transient commands (also called external commands) represent a broader and more powerful group of commands. However, transient commands are not loaded with COMMAND. COM Instead, the commands are available as small. COM or EXE utility files in the DOS dirctory (such as sDEBUG and EMM386). Transient commands must be loaded from the disk and executed each time they are needed. By pulling out complex commands as separate utilities, the size of COMMAND.COM has been kept relatively small.

## THE BOOT PROCESS

Computer initialization is not an event it is a process power is applied until this system sits idle at the command-line prompt from the moment, the PC boot process is a sequence of predictable steps that verify the system and prepare it for operation. You can develop a real appreciation for the way that hardware and software relate to one another by understanding each step in system initialization—you also stand a much better chance of identifying and resolving problems when a system fails to boot properly. You will now look at a step-by-step review of a typical PC boot process.

### The Bootstrap

To fetch an instruction from address FFFF:0000h is the very first operation performed by a CPU. The instruction is almost always a jump command (JMP) followed by the actual BIOS ROM starting address. The BIOS ROM can then send program control anywhere in the particular ROM by making all CPUs start at the same point. This initial search of address FFFF: 0000h and the subsequent redirection of the CPUs traditionally referred to as the bootstrap in which the PC "pulls itself up by its bootstraps"—or gets itself going. Today, you have shortened the term to boot, and have broadened its meaning to include the entire initialization process.

A small program stored in ROM on the motherboard gains control of the microprocessor, when the computer is turned on. The program performs the following sequence of steps:

- Tests available memory and determines the amount of RAM in the system.
- Initializes the various support chip on the motherboard.
- Initializes the video display system.
- Initializes the keyboard.
- Resets the floppy disk controller.
- Attempts to load MSDOS from floppy disk.
- Attempts to load MSDOS from hard disk if one is present.

The MSDOS files (MSDOS.SYS, IO.SYS) must be the first files stored on the disk. Because of this Otherwise, this special boot program would not be able to locate them as it assumes they are always located at the start of the disk.

The ROM program loads the file ink RAM, and then, the processor executes the instructions contained in them (they are actual programs). These program in turn help bring up the rest of MSDOS, reading configuration files from disk which allocate RAM space for storage and load command com.

### Loading the OS

IO.SYS Cor 1BM-BIO COM) is loaded and executed if no problems are detected in the disk's DOS volume boot sector. For such things as the keyboard printer, and block devices, IO.SYS contains extensions to BIOS that start low-level device drivers. IO.SYS also contains initialization code that is only needed during system startup. At the top of comentional memory a copy of this initialization code is placed that takes over initialization. The next step is to load MSDOS.SYS (or IBM-DOS.COM), such that it overlaps the part of IO.SYS containing the initialization code. MSDOS.SYS (MSDOS kernel) is then executed to initialize base device drivers, detect system status, reset the disk system, initialize devices (such as the printer and serial port), and set up system-default parameters. The MSDOS essentials are now loaded and control returns to the IO.SYS/WINBOOT.SYS initialization code in memory.

## ESTABLISHING THE ENVIRONMENT

To suit the particular application that you intend to run, you can customize MSDOS. By reading special configuration files when it first loads MSDOS supports this customigation. The two configuration files must be in the root directory of the drive from which MSDOS is being loaded, and have the following filenames,

Config.SYS

autoexec.bat

If a CONFIG.SYS file is present, it is opened and read by IO.SYS. In the order they appear the device statement are processed first. Then INSTALL statements are processed in the order they appear. A SHELL statement is handled next. The COMMAND.COM processor is loaded, if no shall statement is present. When COMMAND.COM is loaded, it overwrites the initialization code left over from IO.SYS (which is now no longer needed).

COMMAND.COM will loaded and execute the patch file when an AUTOEXEC.-BAT file is present. The familiar DOS prompt will appear after the batch file processing is complete. If there is no AUTOEXEC.BAT in the root directory, COMMAND.COM will request the current date and time, then show the DOS.

## DOS COMMANDS SYNTAX

Each DOS command must be entired in a particular way, to be functional this command entry structure is known as the command's "syntax". To reproduce the command syntax in print the notation is a way.

For example, you can determine the items that are optional, by looking for information that is printed inside square brackets. The notation [d:], for example, indicates an optional drive designation. The command syntax, on the other hand, is how YOU enter the command to make it work.

## Command Syntax Elements

### 1. *Command Name*

To start the DOS program you enter the DOS command name. The DOS command name is always entered first. You can enter command names as either lowercase or uppercase or a mix of both i.e. DOS command interpreter is not case-sensitive.

### 2. *Space*

Always leave a space after the command name.

### 3. *Drive Designation*

For many DOS commands the drive designation is an option. However, some commands are not related to disk drives, and therefore, do not require a drive designation. You are already working in the drive in question, you don't have to enter the drive designator whenever you enter a DOS command that deals with disk drives. If you do not enter a drive designation, DOS always assumes you are referring to the drive you are currently working in (sometimes called the "default" drive).

### 4. *A Colon*

You must always follow the drive designator with a colon (:) when referring to a drive in a DOS command.

### 5. *Pathname*

A pathname (path) refers to the path you want DOS to follow in order to. Act on the DOS command. It indicates the path from the current directory or sub directory to the files that are to be acted upon. The path starting from the root directory a pathy may specify alternatively.

### *6. Filename*

The name of a file stored on disk is a filename. A filename can be of eight or fewer x letter or other legal character.

### *7. Filename Extension*

To further identify it a filename extension can follow the filename. The extension follows a period and can be of three or fewer characters. A filename extension is optional.

### *8. Switches*

Characters shown in a command syntax that are represented by a letter or number and preceded by a forward slash (for example, "/P") are command options (sometimes known a "switches"). Use of these options activates special operations as part of a DOS command's functions.

### *9. Brackets*

Items enclosed in square brackets are optional; in other words. Without entering the information contained inside the brackets the command will work in its basic form.

### *10. Ellipses*

An item in command syntax can be repeated as many times as needed indicated by ellipses (.....).

### *11. Vertical Bar*

When vertical bar (|) seperated two or more items than it means that you enter one of the seperated items. For example : ON | OFF means that you can enter either ON or OFF, but not both.

## DOS COMMANDS

### *List of DOS Commands*

A table of the internal commands and the external commands is given as follows—

| COMMAND | Command syntax | Command description |
|---|---|---|
| APPEND (External) | ANNEND;<br>APPEND [d:]path[d:]path[...]<br>APPEND [/X:on/off][/path:on/off] [/E] | Displays or sets the search path for data files. DOS will search the specified path(s) if the file is not found in the current path. |
| ASSIGN (External) | ASSIGN x=y [...] /sta | Redirects disk drive requests to a different drive. |
| ATTRIB (External) | ATTRIB [d:][path]filename [/S]<br>ATTRIB [+R/-R] [+AI-A] [+SI-S] [+HI-H] [d:][path]filename [/S] | Sets or displays the the read-only, archive. system, and hidden attributes of a file or directory. |
| BACKUP (External | BACKUP d:[path][filename] D:[/S][/M]/A][/ F:(size)] [/P][/D:date] [/T:time] [/L:[path filename] | Makes a backup copy of one or more Files. |
| BREAK (Internal) | BREAK =on/off | Used from the Dos prompt or in a batch file or in the CONFIG.SYS file to set (or display) whether or not DOS Should check for a Ctrl + Break key combination. |
| BUFFERs (Internal) | BUFFERS=(number),(read-ahead number) | Used in the CONFIG.SYS file to set the number of disk buffers (number) that will be available for use during data input. Also used to set a value for the number of sectors to be read in advance (read-ahead) during data input operations. |
| CALL (Internal | CALL [d:][path]batchfilename [options] | Calls another batch file and then returns to current batch file to continue. |
| CHDIR (Internal) | CHDIR (CD) [d:]path<br>CHDIR (CD) [..] | Displays working (current) directory and/or changes to a different directory |

| | | |
|---|---|---|
| CHKDSK (External) | CHKDSK [d:][path][filename] [/F][/V] | Checks a disk and provides a file and memory status report. |
| CLS (Clear Screen) (Internal) | CLS | Clears the screen. |
| COMMAND (External) | COMMAND [d:][path] [device] [/P][/E:(size)] [/MSG][/Y [/C (command)[/K (command)] | Starts a new version of the DOS command processor (the program that loads the DOS Internal programs). |
| COPY (Internal | COPY [/Y]-Y] [/A][/B] [d:][filename [/A][/B] [d:][path][filenmane [/V]<br>or<br>COPY [/Y]-Y][/A][/B] [d:][path]filename+[d:][path]filename[...][d:][path [filename] [/V] | Copies and appends files. |
| COUNTRY (Internal) | COUNTRY=country code, [code page][,][d:] [filename] | Used in the CONFIG.SYS file to tell DOS to use country-specific text conventions during processing. |
| DATE (Internal) | DATE mm-dd-yy | Displays and/or sets the system date. |
| DBLSPACE (External) | DBLSPACE / automount=drives<br>DBLSPACE / chkdsk [/F] [d:]<br>DBLSPACE /compress d: [/newdrive=host:] [/reserve=size] [/size=size]<br>DBLSPACE /defragment [d:] [/F]<br>DBLSPACE /delete d:<br>DBLSPACE /doubleguard=0I1<br>DBLSPACE /format d:<br>DBLSPACE /[info] [d:]<br>DBLSPACE /list]<br>DBLSPACE /mount[=nnn] [/newdrive=d:]<br>DBLSPACE /ratio[=ratio] [d:] [/all] | A program available with DOS 6.0 that allows you to compress information on a disk. |

| | | |
|---|---|---|
| | DBLSPACE /size[=size] [/reserve=size] d:<br>DBLSPACE /uncompress d:<br>DBLSPACE /unmount [d:] | |
| DEBUG (External) | DEBUG [pathname] [parameters] | Used to test and edit programs. |
| DEFRAG | DEFRAG [d:] [/F][/S[:][order] [/B][/skiphigh<br>DEFRAG [d:] [/V][/B][/skiphigh] [/LCD]I/BWI/GO] [/H] | Optimises disk performance by reorganizing the files on the disk. |
| DEL (ERASE)- (Internal) | DEL (ERASE [d:][path]filename [/P] | Delete (erases) files from disk. |
| DELTREE (External) | DELTREE [/Y] [d:]path [d:]path[...] | Deletes (erases) a directory including all files and subdirectories that are in it. |
| DEVICE (Internal) | DEVICE=(driver name) | Used in the CONFIG.SYS file to tell DOS which device driver to load. |
| DEVICEHIGH (Internal) | DEVICEHIGH=(driver name) | Like DEVICE, DEVICEHIGH is used in the CONFIG.SYS file to tell DOS which device driver software to use for devices; however, this option is used to install the device driver into upper memory area. |
| DIR (Internal) | DIR [d.][path][filename] [/A:(attributes)] [/O:(order)] [/B][/C][/CH][/L][/S][/P][/W] | Displays directory of files and directory stored on disk. |
| DISKCOMP (External) | DISKCOMP [d:] [d:][/1][/8] | Compares the contents of two diskettes. |
| DISKCOPY (External) | DISKCOPY [d:] [d:][/1][/V][/M] | Makes an exact copy of a diskette. |
| DOS (Internal) | DOS=[highllow],[umblnoumb-] | Used in the CONFIG.SYS file to specify the memory location for DOS. It is used to load DOS into the upper |

| | | |
|---|---|---|
| | | memory area and to specify whether or not the upper memory blocks will be used. |
| DOSKEY (External) | DOSKEY [reinstall] [/bufsize=size][/macros] [/history][/insert/overstrike] [macroname=[text] | Loads the Doskey program into memory that can be used to recall DOS commands so that you can edit them. |
| DOSSHELL (External | DOSSHELL [/B] [/G:[resolution][n]I[/T:[resolution][n] | Initiates the graphic shell program using the specified screen resolution. |
| ECHO (Internal) | ECHO on/off<br>ECHO (message) | Displays message or turns on or off the display of commands in a batch file. |
| EDIT (Internal) | EDIT [d:][path]filename [/B][/G][/H][/NOHI] | Starts the MSDOS editor, a text editor used to create and edit ASCII text files. |
| EMM386 (External) | EMM386 [on/offlauto] w=on/off] | Enables or disables EMM386 expanded-memory support on a computer with an 80386 or higher processor. |
| EXE2BIN (External | EXE2BIN [d:][path]filename [d:][path]filename | Converts.EXE (executable) files to binary format. |
| EXIT (Internal) | EXIT | Exits a secondary command processor |
| EXPAND (External) | EXPAND [d:][path]filename [d:][path]filename[...] | Expands a compressed file. |
| FASTHELP (External) | FASTHELP [command][command]/? | Displays a list of DOS commands with a brief explanation of each. |
| FASTOPEN (External) | FASTOPEN d:[=n][/X] | Keep track of the locations of files for fast access. |
| FDISK (External) | FDISK [/status] | Prepares a fixed disk to accept DOS files for storage. |
| FILES (Internal) | FILES=(number) | Used in the CONFIG.SYS file to specify the maximum number of files that can |

| | | |
|---|---|---|
| | | be open at the same time. |
| FIND (External) | FIND [/V][/C][/I][/N] ÒstringÓ [d:][path]filename[...] | Finds and reports the location of a specific string of text characters in one or more files. |
| FOR (Internal) | FOR% (variable) IN (set) DO (command) or (for interactive processing) FOR% (variable) IN (set) DO (command) | Performs repeated execution of commands (for both batch processing and interactive processing). |
| FORMAT (External) | FORMAT d:[/1][/4][/8][/F:(size)] [/N:(sectors) [/T:(tracks)[/BI/S][/C][/V: (label)] [/Q']/U][/V] | Formats a disk to accept DOS files. |
| GOTO (Internal) | GOTO (label) | Causes unconditional branch to the specified label. |
| HELP (External) | HELP [command] [/B][/G][/H][/NOHI] | Displays information about a DOS command. |
| IF (Internal) | IF [NOT] EXIST filename (command) [parameters] IF [NOT] (string1)==(string2) (command) [parameters] IF [NOT] ERRORLEVEL (number (command) [parameters] | Allows for conditional operations in batch processing. |
| INCLUDE (Internal) | INCLUDE=blockname | Used in the CONFIG.SYS file to allow you to use the commands from one CONFIG.SYS block within another. |
| INSTALL (Internal) | INSTALL=[d:][/path]filename[parameters] | Used in the CONFIG.SYS file to load memory-resident programs into conventional memory. |
| KEYB (External) | KEYB [xx][,][yyy][,][d:][path]filename [/E] [/ID: (number)] | Loads a program that replaces the support program for U.S. keyboards. |
| LABEL (External) | LABEL [d:][volume label] | Create or change or deletes a volume label for a disk. |
| LASTDRIVE (Internal) | LASTDRIVE= (drive letter) | Used in the CONFIG.SYS file to set the maximum number of drives that can |

| | | be accessed. |
|---|---|---|
| LOSADFIX (Internal) | LOADFIX [d:][path][filename [parameiers] | Ensures that a program is loaded above the first 64K of conventional memory, and runs the program. |
| LOADHIGH (Internal) | LOADHIGH (LH) [d:][path]filename [parameters] | Loads memory resident application into reserved area of memory (between 640K-1M). |
| MEN (External) | MEN [/program[/debug/classify/freel/module(name)] [/Page] | Displays amount of installed and available memory, including extended. expanded, and upper memory. |
| MEMMAKER (External | MEMMAKER [/B][/batch][/session][/swap:d] [/T][/undo][/W:size].size2] | Starts the MemMaker program a program that lets you optimise your computer's memory. |
| MENUCOLOR (Internal) | MENUCOLOR=textcolor,[background] | Used in the CONFIG.SYS file to set the colours that will be used by DOS to display text on the screen. |
| MENUDEFAULT (Internal) | MENUDEFAULT=blockname, [timeout] | Used in the CONFIG.SYS file to set the startup configuration that will be used by DOS if no key is pressed within the specified timeout period. |
| MENUITEM (Internal) | MENUITEM=blockname, [menutext] | Used in the CONFIG.SYS file to create a start-up menu from which you can select a group of CONFIG.SYS commands to be processed upon reboot. |
| MKDIR (MD) (Internal) | MKDIR (MD) [d:]path | Creates a new subdirectory. |
| MODE (External) | MODE n<br>MODE LPT#[:][n][,][m][,][P][retry],<br>MODE [n],m[,T]<br>MODE (displaytype,linetotal) | Sets mode of operation for devices or communications. |

| Command | Syntax | Description |
|---|---|---|
| | MODE COMn[:]baud[,][parity][,][databits][,][stopbits][,][retry] | |
| MORE (External) | MORE < (filename or command)<br>(name) MORE | Sends output to console, one screen at a time. |
| MOVE (Internal) | MOVE [/YI/-Y<br>[d:][path]filename[,][d:][pathfilename[...]destination | Moves one or more files to the location you specify. Can also be used to rename directories. |
| MSAV (External) | MSAV [d:] [/SI/C]/R][/A][/L][/N][/P][/F][/video]<br>[/mouse] MSAV /video | Scans your computer for known viruses. |
| MSBACKUP (External) | MSBACKUP [setupfile] [/BWI/LCDI/MDA] | Used to backup or restore one or more files from one disk to another. |
| MSCDEX (External) | MSCDEX /D:driver [/D:driver2...]<br>[/E][/K][/S][/V][/L:letter] [/M:number] | Used to gain access CD-ROM drives (new with DOS Version 6). |
| MSD (External) | MSD [/B][/I]<br>MSD [/I] [/F[d:][path]filename [/P[d:][path]filename<br>[/S[d:][path]filename | Provides detailed technical information about your computer. |
| NUMLOCK (Internal) | NUMLOCK=on/off | Used in the CONFIG.SYS file to specify the state of the NumLock key. |
| PATH (Internal) | PATH;<br>PATH [d:]path[;][d:]path[...] | Sets or displays directories that will be searched for programs not in the current directory. |
| PAUSE (Internal) | PAUSE [comment] | Suspends execution of a batch file until a key is pressed. |
| POWER (External) | POWER [adv:max/reg/min]std/off] | Used to turn power management on and off, report the status of power management. and set levels of power conservation. |
| PRINT (External) | PRINT [/B:(buffersize)] [/D:(device)] [/M:(maxtick)]<br>[/Q:(value] [/S:(timeslice)][:(busytick)] [/C][/P][/T] | Queues and prints data files.<br><br>[d:][path]filename] [...] |

| Command | Syntax | Description |
|---|---|---|
| PROMPT | PROMPT [prompt text] [options] | Changes the DOS command prompt. |
| RECOVER (External) | RECOVER [d:][path]filename<br>RECOVER d: | Resolves sector problems on a file or a disk. (Bigning with DOS Version 6, RECOVER is no longer available). |
| REM (Internal) | REM [comment] | Used in batch files and in the CONFIG.SYS file to insert remarks (that will not be acted on). |
| RENAME (REN) (Internal) | RENAME (REN) [d:][path]filename [d:][path]filename | Changes the filename under which a file is stored. |
| REPLACE (External) | REPLACE [d:][path filename [d:][path] [/A][/P][/R][/S][/U][/W] | Replaces stored files with files of the same name from a different storage location. |
| RESTORE (External) | RESTORE d: [d:][path]filename [/P][/S][/B:mm-dd-yy] [/A:mm-dd-yy][/E:hh:mm:ss] [/L:hh:mm:ss] [/M][/N][/D] | Restores to standard disk storage format files previously stored using the BACKUP command. |
| RMDIR (RD) (Internal) | RMDIR (RD) [d:]path | Removes a subdirectory. |
| SCANDISK (External) | SCANDISK [d: [d:...]I/all][/checkonlyI/autofix [/nosave]I/custom][/surface][/mono][/nosummay]<br>SCANDISK volume-name[/checkonlyI/autofix[/nosave]I/custom][/mono][/nosummary]<br>SCANDISK /fragment [d:][path]filename<br>SCANDISK /undo [undo-d:][/mono] | Starts the Microsoft ScanDisk program which is a disk analysis and repair tool used to check a drive for errors and correct any problems that it finds. |
| SELECT (External) | SELECT [d:] [d:] [path][country code][keyboard code] | Formats a disk and installs country-specific information and keyboard codes (starting with DOS Version 6, this command is no longer available). |
| SET (Internal) | SET (string1)=(string2) | Inserts strings into the command environment. The set values can be used later by programs. |

| Command | Syntax | Description |
|---|---|---|
| SETVER (External) | SETVER [d:] ]:path][filename (number)] [/delete][/quiet] | Displays the version table and sets the version of DOS that is reported to programs. |
| SHARE (External) | SHARE [/F:space] [/L:locks] | Installs support for file sharing and file locking. |
| SHELL (Internal) | SHELL =[d:][path][filename [parameters] | Used in the CONFIG.SYS file to specify the command interpreter that DOS should use. |
| SHIFT (Internal | SHIFT | Increases number of replaceable parameters to more than the standard ten for use in batch files. |
| SORT (External) | SORT [/R][/+n] < (filename) SORT [/R][/+n] > (filename2) | Sorts input and sends it to the screen or to a file. |
| SYS (External) | SYS [sourced] d: | Transfer the operating system files to another disk. |
| TIME (Internal) | TIME hh:mm[:ss][.cc][AIP] | Displays current time setting of system clock and provides a way for you to reset the time. |
| TREE (Internal) | TREE [d:][path]filename | Displays the contents of a file. |
| UNDELETE (External | UNDELETE [d:][path][filename] [/DT/DSI/DOS] UNDELETE [/listI/all/purge[d:]I/statusI/loadI/UI/S[d:]I/Td:[-entries] | Restores files deleted with the DELETE command. |
| UNFORMAT (External) | UNFORMAT d: [/J][/L][/test][/partn][/P][/U] | Used to undo the effects of formatting a disk. |
| VER (Internal) | VER | Displays the DOS version number. |
| VERIFY (Internal) | VERIFY on/off | Turns on the verify mode; the program checks all copying operations to assure that files are copied correctly. |

| | | |
|---|---|---|
| **VOL (Internal)** | **VOL [d:]** | **Displays a disk's volume label.** |
| **VSAFE (External)** | **VSAFE [/option[+I-j[...] [/NE][/NX][AxI/Cx] [/N][/D][/U]** | **VSAFE is a memory-resident program that continuously monitors your computer for viruses and displays a warning when it finds one.** |
| **XCOPY (External)** | **XCOPY [d:][path][filename] [/A][/D:(date)] [/E][/M][/P][/S][/V][/W][Y\-Y]** | **Copies directories, subdirectories, and files.** |

***Several special characters may be used when referring to directories and files***

\ root directory or a directory separator

. current directory

.. parent directory

***Wildcard characters may be used in filenames or extensions***

? any character

* any tail or extension

X switches to current working directory (cwd) on drive X.

DOS provides facilities for extending the capability of DOS by creating lists of commands that can be executed together when you execute the program in addition to the internal and external commands. Batch files are a very powerful facility. In fact you have almost all the features of a full-blown High Level Language supported in a batch file.

*Additional Commands & Operators in Batch Files*

| | |
|---|---|
| IF | Conditional operator |
| EXIST | Test existence of a file |
| == | Equality test |
| %1, %2, etc. | Command line arguments |
| :<name> | Reference point for GOTO statement. |

*Command Editing*

DOS commands are stored in a template and previous commands can be recalled, character by character enabling editing as required. The following keys can access the template:

F1 get next character from template

F2 C get characters up to but excluding character C

F3 get remaining characters from template

del skip one character in template

F4 C skip characters up to but excluding character C

ESC clear command line

INS toggle overwriting of template

F5 copy command to template for reediting

F6 puts in Ctrl Z new template

The arrow keys may also be used to recall the previous command.

*File Comparison command*

The comparison of two files enables by FC (File comparison) command.

FC *pathname 1 pathname 2*

compare two files, or two wildcarded sets of files

/a Abbreviate output of ASCII comparison

/b Force binary comparison (byte-by-byte)

/c Ignore case

/L Force ASCII comparison (line-by-line)

/Lb# Use line buffer of # lines

/n Display line numbers in ASCII mode

/t Do not expand tabs-default expands to spacing of 8

/w Compress white space (tabs and spaces) to single space (leading or trailing white space always ignored).

*DOS input and output keys*

By the help of following control key sequences the DOS input and output may be controlled. (=the CTRL key).

^C Abort current command

^H Destructive backspace

^J Linefeed-physical newline to input long lines

^N Toggle copying of terminal output to printer

^P Toggle redirection of terminal output to printer

^S Suspend/restart terminal output

^X Cancel current line, and output \-CR-LF

^Z End of file

*Commonly used extensions and the type of file they indicate*

| | |
|---|---|
| BAK | Backup file |
| BAS | Basic program |

| | |
|---|---|
| BAT | Batch file; it contains a group of DOS commands the user wants to run |
| COM | Command line |
| DOC | Document |
| EXE | Executable file, Similar to COM file |
| PRN | Print file |
| SYS | System file |
| $$$ | Temporary file |

## BRIEF DESCRIPTION OF SOME NEWEVER DOS COMMANDS

In a little more detail some of the newer commands are described because of their movelly and relative importance.

**DriveSpace and Double Guard**

Both hard disk and floppy disks supported by DriveSpace integrates disk compression into the operating system. DriveSpace includes Double Guard safety checking, which protects data by verifying data integrity before writing to the disk.

**Mem Maker**

To free conventional memory by moving device drivers Mem Maker is a memory-optimisation program and memory-resident program from conventional memory into the Upper Memory Area (UMA).

**Backup**

For backing up your hard drive backup is a utility. MSDOS 6.22 includes a version of Backup for both DOS and Windows 3.1x.

**Anti-Virus**

The Anti-Virus utility can identify and remove more than 1000 different computer viruses. A version of anti-virus includes MSDOS 6.22 for both DOS and Windows 3.1x.

**Undelete**

The Undelete feature allows you to recover deleted files. MSDOS 6.22 includes a version of Undelete for both DOS and Windows 3.1x.

**ScanDisk**

MSDOS 6.22 includes the latest version of ScanDisk, which detects, diagnoses, and repairs disk errors on uncompressed drives and DriveSpace-compressed drives. ScanDisk can repair file-system errors (such as cross-linked files and lost clusters) and physical disk errors.

**Multi Config**

Multi Config allows you to define more than one configuration in you CONFIG.SYS file. If your CONFIG.SYS file defines multiple configuration, MSDOS displays a menu that enables you to choose the configuration you want to use each time you boot the computer.

**Interactive Start**

When you turn on your computer by pressing the <F8> key the interactive start feature gives you the ability to bypass startup commands. This allows you to choose which CONFIG.SYS and AUTOEXEC.BAT commands MSDOS should carry out.

**Defrag**

MSDOS 6.22 includes the latest version of Defrag, which reorganizes files on your hard disk to minimize the time it takes your computer to access them.

**SmartDrive**

The SmartDrive program included with MSDOS 6.22 speeds up your computer by using a disk cache, which stores information being read from your hard disk or CD-ROM drive. SmartDrive can also be set to cache information being written to your hard disk.

**Interlink**

The Interlink feature enables you to easily transfer files between computers. With Interlink and a cable, you can access information on another computer without using floppy disks to copy data from one computer to another.

# Chapter 3

# Windows Environment

## THE "FIRST" WINDOWS

You would certainly have encountered windows OS as a PC users and for performing a wide variety of tasks easily and quickly used its facilities. As its operating system the original CP had DOS. However, the need for a user-friendlier interface led to the development of the Windows OS and with Microsoft's excellent market strategies it has become the dominant OS on the PC platforms. You will learn more about the windows environment in this chapter.

Windows 95, Windows NT workstation and windows 2000 professional operating systems are essentially single user systems. To perform tasks on the computer system they provide you the capability such as printing & accessing files and writing programs and documents. Consider a typical home computer. There is a single keyboard and mouse that accept input commands, and a single monitor to display information output. There may also be a printer for the printing of documents and images. In essence, a single-user operating system provides access to the computer system by a single user at a time. If another user needs access to the computer system, he/she must wait till the current user finishes what he/she is doing and leaves. Students in computer labs at colleges or University often experience this. You might also have experienced this at home, when you want to use the computer but someone else is currently using it. To finish before you can use the computer system you have to wait for them.

More than one user access the computer system at one time in a multiuser operating system. Access to the computer system is normally provided via a network, so that users access the computer remotely using a terminal or other computer. Large multiuser computers, multiple terminals (keyboards and associated monitors) were provided in the early days. These terminals sent their commands to the main multi-user computer for processing, and the results were then displayed on the associated terminal monitor screen. Terminals were hard-wired directly to the multi-user computer system. Today, these terminals are generally personal computers and use a network to send and receive information to the multi-user computer system. Examples of multi-user operating systems are UNIX, Linux (a UNIX clone) and mainframes such as the IBM AS400.

It lets a number of user share the expensive hardware resources the advantage of having a multiuser OS. The cost is divided amongst the users and it also makes better use of the resources. Since the resources are shared, they are more likely to be in use than sitting idle being unproductive.

As more user access it the performance becomes slower and slower is one of the problem with multiuser system. The cost of hardware is the another disadvantage as a multi-user operating system requires a lot of disk space and memory. In addition, the actual software for multi-user operating systems tends to cost more than single-user operating systems. That is why a single-user OS like the Windows is firmly ensconced in the PC segment as the dominant OS. In this chapter, you will look at the various versions of Windows from the historical perspective (briefly), internal working and the user point of view. You will look at the UNIX multi-user system in the next chapter.

**Enter Windows**

DOS was being used in an environment that was far beyond its capabilities by the introduction of 80486 and pentium. The power of these processors simply could not be exploited by the DOS. This led to the development of concepts like multitasking and multi-programming.

It just sat there waiting for the user to tell it what to do was one of the major criticisms of DOS. It did not help him/her in any way in deciding on this. This made it difficult for new users to become productive till they could learn to use and also "memorise" at least a few of the basic commands. Thus, learning to use a PC in DOS environment could be a slow and arduous process.

Microsoft began the development of a Graphical user interface (GUI) that would be interposed between the user and the OS, to combat this in the early eighties. The intent was to compete with Macintosh whose OS was unsurpassed for the ease of use it offered. Windows is a GUI that transforms your screen into a colourful array of graphics and allows you to quickly access multiple programs at the same time. The programs are represented by the Icons or menu items on the screen that can be selected using your mouse.

Windows 3.0 was released by microsoft, by 1990. The early WINDOWS 3.0 had problems of unreliability. One faulty application could cause a data killing system crash. The biggest complaint was its inherent instability. Another problem was Unrecoverable Application Error (UAE).

The first commercially successful Windows to have a long stint in the market was the Windows 3.1. Some of the important features of Windows 3.1 are as under:

- The UAE disappeared because microsoft added methods for validating system requests in WINDOWS 3.1. Every time an application wants to perform disk access or some other task, WINDOWS 3.1 makes sure that is can succeed before it executes it.
- WINDOWS 3.1 can use virtual memory, method of using a part of the hard disk to simulate a RAM. To provide driver support this additional memory is used.
- Using protected mode access also enables WINDOWS 3.1 to be a little more stable.
- WINDOWS 3.1 has 32-bit memory access. This feature reduces the opportunity for system crashes and enhances the overall speed.
- You can associated every task with a single application, in WINDOWS 3.1, Under cooperative multitasking, an hourglass means that the system is tied up. More about this later.

- For enhanced mode WINDOWS 3.1 microsoft used segmented memory. This model is harder for a programmer to use than a flat memory model. After many complaints, Microsoft set aside two heaps-the first one contains graphic resources and the other one contains non-graphic resources like dialogue boxes, even with two 64 KB heaps; WINDOWS 3.1 ran out of memory.
- This version of Windows still needed DOS and ran on top of it.

**Windows 95**

It is discussed at the end because of its different purpose, although WINDOWS NT came earlier than WINDOWS 95. Microsoft released Windows 95 in August of 1995 as a major upgrade to Windows 3.1x Windows 95 was designed:

- To offer superior performance.
- Take advantage of emerging PC hardware, such as Plug-and-Play, power conservation, PCI bus architecture, etc.

WINDOWS 95 not only runs most Windows 3.1x and DOS programs, but also supports improved features, such as a built-in uninstaller, dial-up networking, multitasking, and long filenames. WINDOWS 95 represents a halfway point between Windows for Workgroups and WINDOWS NT. It performs better, faster and is more reliable and also supports new interface as well To include plug and play as an integral part of the OS, it is the first version.

A few words about the concept of processes and multi-tasking of processes are in order here.

In some stage of execution a process or task is a portion of a program. Several process can be in memory at the same time as per the concept of multiprogramming described earlier.

To hold information about the process each process is assigned a process control block (PCB).

Only a portion of a program is loaded at anyone time in modern OSS. Till it is needed the rest of the program sits waiting on a disk unit. The rest of the program sits waiting on a disk unit till it is needed. This saves RAM space. Some systems run only a single process at a time, other system run multiple processes at once. Most computer systems are single processor based, and a processor can only execute one instruction' at a time, so how is it possible for such a single processor system to run multiple processes? The simple answer is that it doesn't. The processor of the computer runs on process for a short period of time, then is switched to the next process and so on. As the processor executes millions of instructions per second, this gives the appearance of many processes running at once.

The processes allocated the processor in round robin fashion which are ready to run in memory. To determine arrow often the process receives processor time the processor priority is used. The OS may run all processes with the same priority, or it may run some processes more often than others. Processes that have been waiting a long time for execution by the processor may have their priority increased so that they will be more likely to be executed in the future.

### What are process states?

A process in a computer system may be in one of a number of different possible states such as

Read-if it can run when the processor becomes free.

Running-it currently has the processor.

Blocked-it cannot run when the processor becomes free.

After completing its alloted time when a running process is interrupted the processor, its state is saved in its PCB, its process state changed to ready and its priority adjusted.

When a running process accesses an input or output device, or for some reason cannot continue, it is interrupted by the processor, the process state and associated data is saved in the associated PCB. The priority adjusted and the process state is changed to blocked and the priority adjusted.

When the scheduler decides the next task to run, it changes the process state of the selected process to running and loads the saved data associated with that process back into the processor.

**What is cooperative and preemptive switching?**

In a computer system that supports more than one process at once, some mechanism must be used to switch from one task to another. To perform this switching there are two main methods used.

- Co-operative switching means that a task that is currently running will voluntarily give up the processor at some time, allowing other processes to run.
- Pre-emptive switching means that a running task will be interrupted (forced to give up) and the processor given to another waiting process.

The major problem with this cooperative switching is that it deny execution of other processes when one process could hang due to this no work have been done. An example of a cooperative multi-tasking system to Windows 3.1.

Pre-emptive scheduling is better then the previous one. It helps prevent the dreaded machine lockup and gives more response to all processes. Windows NT workstation is an example of such an operating system. In Windows 95, there is a caveat. Only 32-bit programs in Windows 95 are preemptive switched. 16-bit programs are still cooperatively switched, which means it is still easy for a 16-bit program to lock up a Windows 95 computer.

**Internal working of the Windows 95**

Some of the important features of the internal working of the Windows 95 are as follows:

- A totally different system is used by WINDOWS 95 to access the disk than its predecessors. For reducing the chance of a system crash this new system runs in protected mode. As mentioned above WINDOWS 95 supports two kinds of multitasking-co-operative and preemptive. All 16-bit applications have to run in a cooperative multitasking mode. WINDOWS 95 also minimizes the impact of these applications by running them in shared space. Pre-emptive multitasking supports 32-bit applications. It monitors each application and interrupts it when the time is up.

- It also uses two hidden files USER.DAT and SYSTEM. DAT to store register information.
- Base system is the core and all the OS specifications stored by it. File management sub-system, Network sub-system, Operating System services, Virtual Machine manager, Device Drivers.
- From the release 2 of this OS Internet Explorer was bundled along with the OS for PCs that gave Windows 95 along with the PC.
- By taking better advantage of Intel 80386, 80486 and pentium processors it has major portions of the OS written in 32-bit code. The memory manager scheduler, and process manager are still written in 16-bit code to ensure compatibility with existing 16-bit applications.
- Stores the bulk of important hardware settings, system settings, applications settings in a central location called the registry. These settings were previously stored in a number of different files such as autoexec.bat, config.sys, win.ini and system.ini files. This arrangement allows for a more easily managed PC.
- For DOS applications it provides much more conventional memory space. This is because it implements device drivers such as smart drive, mouse drivers, share.exe, CD-ROM, and SCSI device drivers as 32-bit VxD's. This means that with WINDOWS 95 there is less chance of running out of memory for your DOS applications.
- Includes built-in-peer networking only with more efficient 32-bit network drivers as well support for the TCP/IP protocol.
- Incorporates Object Linking and Embedding (OLE) version 2.0 This allows you to easily create fancy compound documents using Windows packages like Microsoft Office combining information from several

different application programs, especially when using applications that support OLE 2.0.

## WINDOWS 98

Rather than being a new considerably different version of windows the windows 98 is a more maintenance release. It includes more than 150 updates, bug fixes, and usability tweaks to the original Windows 95 code. Some of the major points about Windows 98 are as given below:

- Windows 98 contains drivers for more than 1200 new devices and for simplified setup all of them support plug & play. Some categories of hardware supported in Windows 98 didn't even exist when Windows 95 first released. Most significant of all are peripherals that use the Universal Serial Bus (USB). You can plug just about any type of device into a USB port, including mice, keyboards, modems, scanners, digital cameras, speakers, telephones, and more. The technology makes your PC incredibly more flexible and does away with the need for serial and parallel ports, IRQs, and other configuration hassles.
- Windows 98 is generally faster overall.
- Its dependence on the old 16-bit FAT format was one of the most significant weaknesses in the original retail release of windows 95. That restriction becomes particularly painful when you add a hard drive greater than 2GB because FAT16 forces you to create multiple partitions that waste huge amounts of space. Microsoft fixed those problems with the introduction of the FAT32 disk format in OEM Service Release 2 of Windows 95. Windows 98 adds a major new tool that you need when upgrading: a utility that quickly coverts your existing data to the new format.
- Notebook users see improved power features, enhancements in the way Windows works with CP Cards, and support for the latest infrared devices.
- You'll find substantial improvements in the Dial-up features, if you have a dial-up Internet connection, including a simplified wizard for creating connections

and support for multilink connections, use of two phone lines for faster data transfers. When you use Windows 98, you'll have ready access to the web. There's a new Favorites option on the Start menu, which lets you jump quickly to your favorite web sites.

- Windows 98 includes software that automates some of the more unpleasant tasks. Most notable is the Tune-Up Wizard, which regularly scans local hard disks for errors, defragments disks, and cleans up unnecessary files—all without requiring any work from you.
- About system resources hardware, components and running tasks a new system information tool consolidates a wealth data in a single location. This well organized window is also a launching pad for other troubleshooting tools, such as the System File Checker (which undoes the damage when a crucial file becomes corrupted) and the Registry Checker (which automatically backs up your database of system settings for quick recovery in the event of trouble). And whenever Microsoft issues a Windows patch, you can install it automatically by clicking the Windows Update icon.
- For game players, there's DirectX5 technology and MMX support, two technologies that make multimedia more appealing.
- You'll find support for many more network cards windows 98 is smoother in operation for example, and you'll find it easier to connect with Windows NT or NetWare networks. And Windows 98 also makes it easier than it used to be to configure a TCP/IP connection (the default protocol in Windows 98).
- The windows 98 system files than not been modified or corrupted is easily verified by a system file checker utility. The utility also provides an easy mechanism for restoring the original versions of system files that have changed.
- The System Troubleshooter utility automates the routine troubleshooting steps used by support personnel

and users when diagnosing issues with the Windows configuration.

- The routine troubleshooting steps used by support personnel & users automated by the system troubleshooter utility.
- An enhanced version of the Dr. Watson utility included by Windows 98. When a software fault occurs (general-protection fault, hang, etc.), Dr. Watson will intercept it and indicate what software failed (and why). Dr. Watson also collects detailed information about the state of your system at the time the fault occurred.
- A new backup applet supports SCSI tape devices and makes backing up your data easier and more versatile.
- Windows 98 allows a CP to receive and display, television with a TV tuner board installed and other data distributed over the broadcast networks, including enhanced television programs (which combine standard television with HTML information related to the programs).
- A new media streaming architecture supported by windows 98 called Active-Movie that delivers high-quality video playback of popular media types, including MPEG audio, WAV audio, MPEG video, AVI video, and Apple Quick Time video.
- It provides support for software that uses the Pentium Multimedia Extensions (MMX) for fast audio and video support on Pentium processor.
- The FAT file system's improved version is FAT32, that allows disk over two gigabytes to be formatted as a single drive. FAT32 also uses smaller clusters than FAT drives, resulting in a more efficient use of space on large disks.
- Windows 98 includes support for the Advanced Configuration and Power Interface (ACPI), and support for the Advanced Power Management (APM) 1.2 extensions including: Disk spin down, PCMCIA modem power down, and resume on ring.

- To use multiple monitors & multiple graphics adapters on a single PC multiple display support allows you.
- Windows 98 includes all of the components necessary to enable your desktop to act as a dial-up server.
- All of the component necessary to enable your desktop to act as dialup server included by windows 98.
- There have been several enhancement to Windows 98 for PCMCIA support, including support for PC Card32 (Cardbus) for implementing high-bandwidth applications, such as video capture and 100Mbps networking. There is support for PC Cards that operate at 3.3 V and there is support for multifunction PC Cards (such as LAN and Modem, or SCSI and sound) to operate on a single physical PC Card.
- User can easily connect to peripheral devices or other PCs without using connecting cables–windows 98 supports IrDA for wireless connectivity. Infrared-equipped laptop or desktop computers have the capability of networking, transferring files, and printing wirelessly with other IrDA-compatible infrared devices.
- Distributed Component Object Model (DCOM) in Windows 98 (and Windows NT 4.0) provides the infrastructure that allows DCOM applications provided by distributed component object Model (DOM) (the technology communicate across networks without needing to redevelop applications.
- Windows 98 includes Client Services for Net Ware that support Novell NetWare Directory Services (NDS). This enables Windows 98 users to log on to Novell NetWare 4.x servers running NDS to access files and print resource.

## WINDOW NT

DOS was the predominant PC operating system during the NT's development period. Servers and engineering work stations were exclusively used by unix. Microsoft built support in NT for DOS, Windows 3.x, OS/2 and POSIX.

Customer were highly interested the POSIX and OS/2, during early 90's. To capture the corporate-level customers, Microsoft realizes that it would have to develop their own 32-bit API.

PCA used Intel's X86 processor, during the NT's development period. Microsoft designated NT to run out of the box on any of the RISC processor chips to make NT as portable as possible. Although Windows 3.1 had a good graphical user interface, it has no real networking support. In 1980s, Microsoft intended to avoid repeating these networking mistake with the support for most of the APIs and networking protocols. Net BIOS, remote procedure call (RPC) file server nail slots and Beskeley sockets included by APIS. The protocols included TCP/IP, IPX/SPX, Apple Talk and DLC. Microsoft opened the door to the sites that were dominated by Maintosh or Netware by including protocols in NT.

Neither DOS or not Windows 3.x is capable of true multitasking with preemptive scheduling but NT has a multitasking preemptive scheduling system. Only one program or task can executed by DOS at a time. Windows 3.x can execute several programs concurrently, but each program must be aware that other programs may need to run, and it must therefore, yield the machine at regular intervals. This design means that a malicious program can halt the computer simply by entering an infinite loop. In NT, a centralized scheduling authority divides CPU time to programs that need it. Once a program's turn has ended, the scheduler has the power to preempt it and give another program a run. Microsoft wanted NT to incorporate one major feature: it had to be truly 32-bit and provide protected address space.

**Architecture of NT**

Kernel mode and user mode are the two modes which provide the protection by most of the operating system. Windows NT also supports these two modes.

Modified micro-ro kernel is the unique approach taken by NT that falls between pure micro-rokernel and monolithic design. The basic operating system, subsystems, including the Process Manager and the Virtual Memory Manager, execute in kernel mode and they are complied into one file image. These kernel-model subsystems are not separate processes and they can communicate with each other by using function calls for maximum performance.

As a microkernel based operating system NT is sometimes refused. The main idea behind the pure microkernel concept is that all operating system components except a small core execute as user-mode processes, just as spreadsheets. So they can access hardware directly the core components in the microkernel executein privileged mode.

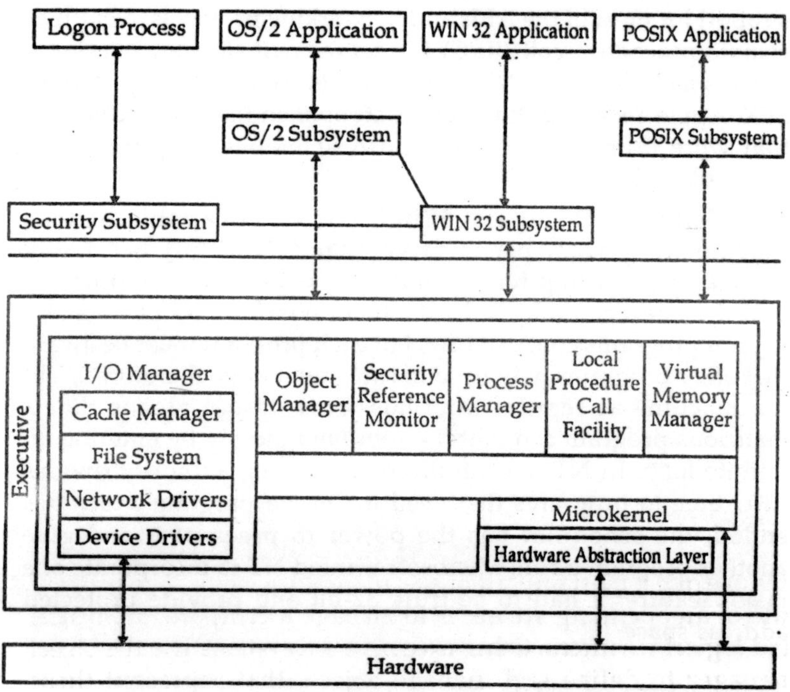


**Fig. 3.1 Windows NT Architecture.**

Microkernel architecture gives a system configurability and fault tolerance, because an operating system subsystem like the Virtual Memory Manager in NT, runs as a distinct program in microkernel design. The bug is likely to bring down the whole machine if the virtual memory manager has a bug in a monolithic system.

In microkernel design every interaction between operating system components requires an inter-process message. NT's operating system environment relies on the kernel mode services. The services invoked in kernel mode are known as NT's native API. A software-exception system call is a hardware-assisted way to change execution modes from user mode to kernel mode.

Basic hardware functionality used by NT's Executive components implemented in microkernel. The microkernel which is known in NT as the kernel, contains the scheduler. The kernel also manages the executive's use of NT's hardware and software interrupt handlers.

Device drivers and the kernel use the HAL (Hardware Abstraction Layer) to interact with the computer's hardware. The HAL exports its own API, which translates abstract data into processor-specific commands.

### The Executive

Most of the functions traditionally associated with operating systems perform by NT's executive. The executive subsystems have separate responsibilities and names, so sometimes it seems that they are different processes. To a different system process there is no context switch. The purpose of the system process in perform is to own executive threads that carry out work, usually of a background nature for executive subsystems.

### Object Manager

The last known NT's executive subsystems is object manager. It is one of the most important executive subsystems. The primary rate of an operating system is to manage a computer's physical and logical resources. Other executive subsystems use the object manager to define and manage objects that represent these resources.

Object management duties which are the identification and reference counting performed by the object manager. When the reference count goes to zero, the object representing the resource is no longer in use and the object manager deletes the objects.

To provide object identification object manager implements NT's name space. The object manager pass the file's name to locate the file-system driver for the disk that store the file, when a program opens a file. When a program opens a file, the object manager parse the file's name to locate the file-system driver for the disk that stores the file. Similarly when an application opens a Registry key, the object manager determines from the Registry key's name that the configuration manager must be called.

Object Manager creates an associated process object for an open process and invokes the process manager's function for opening processes.

### Virtual Memory Manager

Two major duties performed by the virtual memory manager: to create and manage address maps for processes and to control physical memory allocation.

The demand-page virtual memory implemented by the virtual memory manager which means of manager memory in individual pages. The total memory application requirement can exceed the computer's physical memory on the hard disk in page files. When an application requests the data the virtual memory manager transfers data to physical memory from a passing file.

NT uses memory sharing to enhance physical memory use and to communicate between processes.

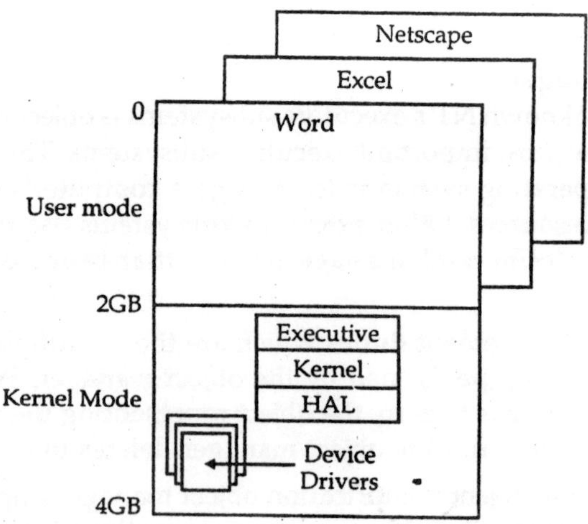


**Fig. 3.2 Virtual Memory in Windows NT.**

## Security Reference Monitor

The object manager and the security reference monitor are closely associated. The object manager calls the security reference monitor for an access check before letting an application, open an object. The Security Reference Monitor (SRM) implements a security model based on identifies and Access Control Lists (ACLs).

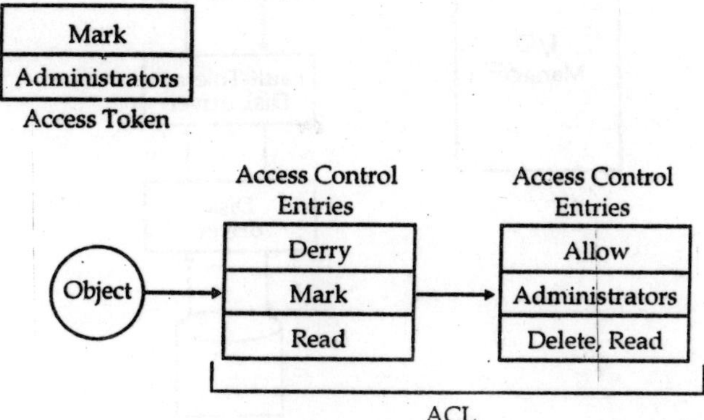


**Fig. 3.3 Function of Security Reference Monitor.**

The action that particular IDs can perform on an object specified ACLS. An ACL can contain any number of access control entries (ACEs), including no entries, which contain the information, about the actions that IDs can perform.

When a user attempts to open the object NT references the ACE.

## Cache Manager

Closely with the virtually memory manager and file system drivers the cache manager works. The cache manager maintains NT's global file system, cache. When the working set tuner takes memory containing modified file data, away from the cache manager, the I/O manager invokes file systems that manage the moved files to write their data back to the disk.

## I/O Manager

For integrating add on device drivers with NT the I/O manager is responsible. The I/O manager supports 64-bits file offsets and layered device drivers. Using 64-bit offsets lets NT's file system address extremely large files and lets disk device drivers address extremely large disks.

The NTFS driver is layered above the fault-tolerant disk driver.

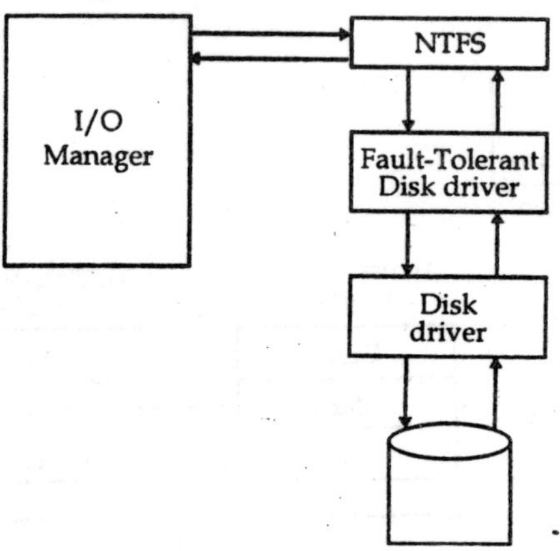


**Fig. 3.4 Layered device drivers.**

### Process Manager

To define process and thread objects the process manager works with the kernel. The process manager wraps the kernel's process object and add to it a process identifier (PID), the access taken, an address map and a handle table.

An interface that lets other executive subsystems and user mode applications manipulate process and threads operated by the process manager.

### NT's Kernel

NT's kernel operates more closely with hardware than the executive does, and it contains CPU-specific code. NT's thread schedular, called the dispatched by NT's developers, resides in the kernel.

Preemptive schedular is a type of NT dispatcher. The CPU time is divided into slices called quantum.

In kernel NT implements most synchronization primitives.

NT has a rich set of synchronization types including semaphores, events and spin locks.

In most cases, NT wraps kernel objects with executive objects so that application can access them from user mode through the native API. NT stores all the priority-related information and statistical information related to scheduling in the kernel's object. The interuppts are also managed by the kernel.

**The Hardware Abstraction Layer (HAL)**

To the raw CPU the HAL is NT's interface. To make the portability feasible, NT's developers isolated as much CPU specific code as possible into a separate, dynamically replacable module, the HAL. The HAL exports a common processor model that masks the difference in various processor clips from NT.

A common difference between motherboards in the same processor family is that some are for multiprocessor systems and other are for uniprocessor systems.

The debug version of NT for device driver developers provided by microsoft.

**Porcess Management and CPU Scheduling in NT**

A preemptive multi-threading operating system is windows NT. lets several programs run simultaneously and switches among them often enough to create the illusion that each program is the only program running on the machine.

The NT scheduler must honour the relative priorities that the application programmers designate for each thread and attempt to provide responsiveness to user-interactive method.

**Paging**

Virtual memory divided by window NT into equal size blocks called pages. Similarly, it divides physical memory into blocks called frames which are used to hold pages in memory.

Pages, which are in physical memory, are called valid pages and those on disk are called invalid pages. Paging is the process of moving pages from physical memory to disk.

A demand paged, virtual memory system is the architecture of NT. To multiple page files the virtual memory manager can transfer pages. If the page files are located on separate physical disks then multiple page can be transferred to separate files simultaneously.

Store pagetable entries a cache is used to facilitate fast page table look-ups. The most recently used entries stored by this cache. If the entry does not exist in the cache then software is used to access to page table in memory.

**Memory Protection**

Windows NT protected the memory using following techniques:

(1) The type of access allowed in user and kernel mode indicates the set of flage present in each virtual page.

(2) A thread is not allowed to access the virtual memory addresses of another process. This is done by the hardware.

(3) User mode can be used to restrict access to system data and code.

(4) When a process accesses an object, Windows NT security reference monitor checks whether the process has to the object.

When a thread uses a virtual address, the virtual memory manager and hardware translate the address into a physical address. This automatic translation prevents threads from one process accessing a frame of another process.

## WINDOWS 2000

A 32-bit preemptive multitasking operating system is the microsoft windows 2000 for intel pentium and later micro-processor. The successor to the Windows NT operating system, it was previously named Windows NT Version 5.0. Key goals for the system are portability, security, Portable Operating System Interface (POSIX or IEEE Std. 1003.1) compliance, multiprocessor support, extensibility, international support, and compatibility with MS-DOS and Microsoft Windows applications. In this chapter, we discuss the key goals for this system, the layered architecture of the system that makes it so easy to use, the file system, networks, and the programming interface.

**History**

To develop the OS/2 operating system, which was written in assembly language for single processor Intel 80286 systems Microsoft and IBM cooperated in the mid-1980s. In 1988, Microsoft decided to make a fresh start and to develop a "new technology' (or NT) portable operating system that supported both the OS/2 and POSIX application-programming interfaces (APIs). Dave cutler, the architect of the DEC VAX/VMS operating system in October, 1988, was hired and given the charter of building this new operating system.

Originally, the team planned for NT to use the OS/2 API as its native environment, bit during development, Windows NT was changed to use the 32-bit Windows API (or Win32 API), reflecting the popularity of Windows 3.0. The first versions of NT were Windows NT 3.1 and Windows NT 3.1 Advanced Server. (At that time, 16-bit Windows was at Version 3.1) Windows NT version 4.0 adopted the Windows 95 user interface and incorporated Internet web-server and web-browser software. To improve performance code were moved into the kernel in addition to user interface routines and graphics, with the side effect of decreased system reliability. Although previous versions of NT had been ported to other microprocessor architectures, Windows 2000 discontinues that practice due to marketplace factors. Portability among Intel architecture systems refers to portability. Windows 2000 uses a microkernel architecture (like Mach), so enhancements can be made to one part of the operating system without greatly affecting other parts. With the addition of Terminal Services, Windows 2000 is a multiuser operating system.

With significant changes the windows 2000 was released in 2000. It adds an X.500-based directory service, better networking support, support for Plug-and-Play devices, a new file system with support for hierarchical storage, and a distributed file system, as well as support for more processors and more memory.

Windows 2000 have four versions. For desktop use the professional version is intended. The other three are server versions. Server, Advanced Server, and Datacenter Server. These differ primarily in the amount of memory and number of processors that they support. They use the same kernel and operating-system code, but Windows 2000 Server and Advanced Server versions are configured for client-server applications and can act as application servers on NetWare and Microsoft LANs. Windows 2000 Datacenter Server now support up to 32 processors and up to 64 GB of RAM.

All versions of UNIX licenses were sold than in 1996 to more windows NT server licenses. Interestingly, the code base for Windows 2000 is on the order of 30 million of code. Compare this size with the code base of Windows NT version 4.0: about 18 million lines of code.

**Design Principles**

Microsoft has stated the design goals for windows 2000 include extensibility, portability, reliability, compatibility, performance, and international support.

The capacity of an operating system to keep up with advances in computing technology refers to the esctensibility. So that changes are facilitated over time, the developers implemented Windows 2000 using a layered architecture. The Windows 2000 executive, which runs in kernel or protected mode, provides the basic system services. On top of the executive, several server subsystems operate in user mode. Among them are **environmental subsystems** that emulate different operating systems. Thus, programs written for MS-DOS, Microsoft Windows, and POSIX can all run on Windows 2000 in the appropriate environment. (See Section 21.4 for more information on environmental subsystems.) Additional environmental subsystems can be added because of the modular structure without affecting the executive. In addition, Windows 2000 uses loadable drivers in the I/O system, so new file systems, new kinds of I/O devices, and new kinds of networking can be added while the system is running. Windows 2000 uses a client-server model like the Mach operating system, and support distributed processing by remote procedure calls (RPCs) as defined by the Open Software Foundation.

Operating system can be moved from one hardware architecture to another with relatively few changes hence it is portable. Windows 2000 is designed to be portable. The majority of the system is written in C and $C^{++}$ as true UNIX operating system. All processor-dependent code is isolated in a dynamic link library (DLL) called the **hardware-abstraction layer (HAL).** A DLL is a file that gets mapped into a process' address space such that any function in the DLL appear to be part of the process. The upper layers of Windows 2000 depend on HAL, rather than on the underlying hardware, and that helps Windows 2000 to be portable. HAL manipulates hardware directly, isolating the rest of Windows 2000 from hardware differences among the platforms on which it runs.

To handle error conditions including the ability of the operating system to protect its users and itself from defective or malicious software Reliability is the ability. Windows 2000 resists defects and atacks by using hardware protection for virtual memory, and software protection mechanisms for operating-systems resources. Also Windows 2000 comes with a native file system—the NTFS file system—that recovers automatically from many kinds of file-systems errors after a system crash. Windows NT Version 4.0 has a C-2 security classification from the U.S. government, which signifies a moderate level of protection from defective software and malicious attacks. Windows 2000 is currently under evaluation by the government for that classification as well. For more information about security classifications, see Sections 19.8.

To applications that follow the IEEE 1003.1 (POSIX) standard the source level compatibility is provided by Windows 2000. Thus, they can be compiled to run on Windows 2000 without changes to the source code. In addition, Windows 200 can run the executable binaries for many programs compiled for Intel X86 architectures running MS-DOS, 16-bit Windows, OS/2, LAN Manager, and 32-bit Windows, by using the environmental subsystems mentioned earlier. These environmental subsystems support a variety of file systems, including the MS-DOS FAT file system, the OS/2 HPFS file system, the ISO9660 CD file system, and NTFS. Windows 2000' binary compatibility however, is not perfect. In MS-DOS, for example, applications can access hardware ports directly. Windows 2000 prohibits such access for reliability and security.

To afford good performance Windows 2000 is designed. The subsystems that constitute Windows 2000 can communicate with one another efficiently by a local-procedure-call (LPC) facility that provides high-performance message passing. Except for the kernel, threads in the subsystems of Windows 2000 can be preempted by higher-priority threads. Thus to external events the systems can respond quickly. In addition, Windows 2000 is designed for symmetrical multiprocessing. Several threads can run at the same time, on a multiprocessor computer. The current scalability of Windows 2000 is limited, compared to that of UNIX. As of late 2000, Windows 2000 supported systems with up to 32 CPUs, whereas Solaris ran on systems with up to 64 processors. Previous versions of NT supported only up to 8 processors.

For international use Windows 2000 is designed. For different locales via the national language support (NLS) API it provides support. NLS API provides specialized routines to format dates, time, and money in accordance with various national customs. String comparisons are specialized to account for varying character sets. UNICODE is Windows 2000's native character code; Windows 2000 supports ANSI characters by converting them to UNICODE characters before manipulating them (8-bit to 16-bit conversion).

### System Components

The architecture of Windows 2000 is a layered system of modules. The main layers are the HAL, the kernel, and the executive, all of which run in protected mode, and a large collection of subsystems that run in user mode. Two categories are present in user-mode subsystems. The environmental subsystems emulate different operating systems; the protection subsystems provide security functions. One of the chief advantages of this type of architecture is that interactions between modules can be kept simple. The remainder of this section describes these layers and subsystems.

### Hardware-Abstraction Layer

To make Windows 2000 portable HAL is the layer of Software that hides hardware differences from upper levels of the operating system. HAL exports a virtual-machine interface that is used by the kernel, the executive, and the device drivers.

One advantage of this approach is that only a single version of each device driver is needed—it can run on all hardware platforms without porting the driver code. HAL also provides the support for symmetric multiprocessing. For performance reasons, I/O drivers (and graphics drivers in Windows 2000) can access the hardware directly.

**Kernel**

The foundation for the executive and the subsystems provided by the kernel of Windows 2000. The kernel is never paged out of memory, and its execution is never preempted. It has four main responsibilities: thread scheduling, interrupt, and exception handling, low-level processor synchronization, and recovery after a power failure.

A system defined data type is an object type in Windows 2000 that has a set of methods (that is, functions or operations). An **object** is just an instance of a particular object type. The kernel performs its job by using a set of kernel objects whose attributes store the kernel data and whose methods perform the kernel activities.

Two sets of objects are used in kernel. The dispatches objects comprised by the first set. **Dispatcher objects** control dispatching and synchronization in the system. Examples of these objects are events, mutants, mutexes, semaphores, threads, and timers. To record an event occurrence and to synchronize the after with some action the event object is used. The **mutant** provides kernel mode or user-mode mutual exclusion with the notion of ownership. The **mutex**, which is available only in kernel mode, provides deadlock-free mutual exclusion. A **semaphore object** acts as a counter or gate to control the number of threads that access some resource. The **thread object** is the entity that is run by the kernel and is associated with a **process object**. **Time objects** are used to keep track of the time and to signal timeouts, when operations take too long and need to be interrupted. The control objects are comprises in the second set of kernel objects. These objects include asynchronous procedure calls, interrupts, power notify, power status, process, and profile objects. To break into an executing thread and to call a procedure. The interrupt object binds an interrupt service routine to an interrupt source.

The system uses the power-notify object to call a specified routine automatically after a power failure, and all power status object to check whether the power has failed. A process object represents the virtual address space and control information necessary to execute the set of threads associated with a process. Finally, the system uses the profile object to measure the amount of time used by a block of code.

**Threads and Scheduling**

Windows 2000 uses the notions of processes and threads for executable code or do many modern operating systems. The process has a virtual memory address space, and information such as a base priority and an affinity for one or more processors. Each process has one or more threads, which are the units of execution dispatched by the kernel. Including a priority, processor affinity and accounting information, each thread has its own state.

Ready, standby, running, waiting, transition and terminated are the six possible thread states. Ready means waiting to run. The highest-priority ready thread is moved to the standby state, which means that it will be the next thread to run. In a multiprocessor system, one thread is kept in the standby state for each processor. A thread is running when it is executing on a processor. It will run until it is preempted by a higher-priority thread, until it terminates, until its time quantum ends, or until it calls a blocking system call, such as for I/O. A thread is in the waiting state when it is waiting for a signal such as an I/O completion. A new thread is in the transition state while it is waiting for the resources necessary for executions. When it finishes the execution, a thread enters the terminated state.

To determine the order of thread excution, the dispatcher uses a 32 level priority schemes. Priorities are divided into two classes. The variable class contains threads having priorities from 0 to 15, and the real-time class contains threads with priorities ranging from 16 to 31. The dispatcher uses a queue for each scheduling priority, and traverses the set of queues from highest to lowest until it finds a thread that is ready to run. If a thread has a particular processor affinity but that processor is not available, the dispatcher will skip past it, and will continue looking for a thread that is ready to run. If no ready thread is found, the dispatcher will execute a special thread called the idle thread.

If the thread is in the variable-priority class, its priority is lowered, and when a thread's time quantum runs out, the thread is interrupted. The priority is never lowered below the base priority, however. Lowering the thread's priority tends to limit the CPU consumption of compute-bound threads. The dispatcher boosts the priority, when a variable-priority thread is released from a wait operation. the amount of the boost depends on for what the thread was waiting; for example, a thread that was depends on for what the thread was waiting; for example, a thread that was waiting for keyboard I/O would get a large priority increase, whereas a thread waiting for a disk operation would get a moderate one. This strategy tends to give good response times to interactive threads that are using the mouse and windows, and enables I/O-bound threads to keep the I/O devises busy, while permitting compute-bound threads to use spare CPU cycles in the background. Several time sharing operating systems, including UNIX uses this strategy. In addition, the current window with which the user is interacting also receives a priority boost to enhance its response time.

When a thread terminates, when a thread entire the ready or wait state or when an application changes a thread's priority or processor affinity then scheduling can occur.

If a higher-priority real-time thread becomes ready while a lower-priority thread is running, the lower-priority thread will be preempted. This preemption gives a real-time thread preferrential access to the CPU when the thread needs such access. Windows 2000 does not guarantee that a real time thread will start to execute with in any particular time limit, thats why it is not a hard real-time operating system.

### Exceptions and interrupts

For exceptions and interrupts that kernel also provides trap handling that are generated by hardware software. Windows 2000 defines several architecture-independent exceptions, including memory-access violation, integer overflow, floating-point overflow or underflow, integer divide by zero, floating-point divide by zero, illegal instruction, data misalignment, privileged instruction, page read error, guard-page violation, paging file quota exceeded, debugger breakpoint, and debugger single step.

Simple exceptions can handle the trap handler, others are by the kernel's exception dispatcher. The exception dispatcher creates an exception record that contains the reason for the exception and finds are exception handler that can deal with it.

The exception dispatcher simply calls a routine to locate the exception handles, when an exception occurs in kernel mode. If no handler is found, a fatal system error occurs and the user is left with the infamous "blue screen of death" that signifies system failure.

Exception handling is more complex for user-mode processes, because an environmental subsystem (such as the POSIX system) can set up a debugger port and an exception port for every process that it creates. If a debugger port is registered, the exception handler sends the exception to that port. If the debugger port is not found or does not handle that exception, the dispatcher then attempts to find an appropriate exception handler. If a handler is not found, the debugger is called again so that it can catch the error for debugging. If a debugger is not running a message is then sent to the process' exception port to give the environmental subsystem a chance to translate the exception. For example, the POSIX environment translate Windows 2000 exception messages into POSIX signals before sending them to the thread that caused the exception. The kernel simply terminates the process, finally, if nothing works that contains the thread that caused the exception.

By calling either an interrupt service routine or an internal kernel routine, the interrupt dispatcher in the kernel handle interrupts. The interrupt is represented by an interrupt object that contains all the information needed to handle the interrupt. Using an interrupt object makes it easy to associate interrupt service routines with an interrupt without having to access the interrupt hardware directly.

Different types numbers of interrupts are found in various processor architechures, such as Intel or DEC Alpha. For portability, the interrupt dispatcher maps the hardware interrupts into a standard set. The interrupts are prioritized and are serviced in priority order. There are 32 interrupts levels (IRQLs) in Windows 2000. Eight are reserved for the used of the kernel; the other 24 represent hardware interrupts via the HAL (although most x86 use only 16 lines). the Windows 2000 interrupts.

To bind each interrupt level be a service routine the kernel uses an interrupt dispatch table. Windows 2000 keeps a seperate interrupt dispatch table for each processor in a muiltiprocessor computer, and each processor's IRQL can be set independently to mark out interrupts. All interrupts that occur at a level equal to or less than the IRQL, of a processor get blocked util the IRQL, is lowered by a kernel-level thread. Windows 2000 takes advantage of this property to use software interrupts to perform system functions. For instance, the kernel uses software interrupts to start a thread dispatch, to handle timers, and to support asynchronous operations.

| *Interrupt levels* | *Types of interrupts* |
|---|---|
| 31 | machine check or bus error |
| 30 | power fail |
| 29 | interprocessor notification (request another processor to act, e.g. dispatch a process or update the TLB) |
| 28 | clock (used to keep track of times) |
| 27 | profile |
| 3-26 | traditional PC IRQ hardware interrupts |
| 2 | dispatch and deferred procedure call (DPC) (kernel) |
| 1 | asynchronous procedure call (APC) |
| 0 | passive |

Windows 2000 interrupt request levels

To register a routine the power notify object provides a way for a device driver, that will be called on power restoration, and ensures that devices get set to the proper state on recover. For battery-backed-up systems, the power-status object is useful. Before it begins a critical operations, a driver examines the power-status object to determine whether or not the power has failed. If the driver determines that power has not failed, it raises the IRQL, of its processor to powerful, performs the operation, and resets the IRQL. The powerfail interrupt blocked by this sequence of actions until after the critical operation completes.

**Executive**

All environmental systems can use provided by the Windows 2000 executive. The services are grouped as follows: object manager, virtual-memory manager, process manager, local-procedure-call facility. I/O manager, and security reference monitor.

*Object Manager*

Window 2000 uses, objects for all its services and entities as an object oriented system. Examples of objects are directory objects, symbolic link objects, semaphore objects, event objects, process and thread objects, port objects, and file objects. the job of the object manager is to supervise the use of all objects. When a thread wants to use an object, it calls the object manager's open method to get a handle to the object. Handles are a standardized interface to all kinds of objects. An object handls is an identifier unique to a process just like a file handle that confers the ability to occurs and manipulate a system resource.

It is the natural place to check security since the object manager is the only entity that can generate an object handle. For instance, the object manager checks whether a process has the right to access an object when the process tries to open that object. The object manager can also enforce quotas, such as the maximum amount of memory that a process may allocate.

The object manager can keep track of which processes are using by each object. A count of the number of processes contained by each object header to handle that object. When the counter goes to zero, the object is deleted from the name space if it is temporary object name. Since Windows 2000 itself often uses pointers (instead of handles) to access objects, the object manager also maintains a reference count, which it increments when Windows 2000 gains access to an object and decrements when the object is no longer needed. When the reference count of a temporary object goes to zero, the object is deleted from memory. Permanent objects represent physical entities, such as disk drives, and are not deleted when the reference count and the open-handle counter to to zero.

A standard set of methods are used to manipulate the objects :-create, open, close, delete, query name, parse, and security. the latter three objects need explanation:

- query name is called when a thread has a handle to an object, but wants to know the object's name.
- parse is used by the object manager to search for an object given the object's name.
- security is called when a process opens or changes the protection of an object.

The Windows 2000 executive allows any object to be given a name. The name space is global, so one process may create a named object, and a second process can then open a handle to the object and share it with the first process. A process opening a named object can ask for the search to be either case sensitive or case insensitive.

A name can be of two types either permanent or termporary. A permanent name represents an entity, such as a disk drive, that remains even if no process is accessing it While some process holds a handls to that object only than a temporary name exist.

Although the name space is not directly visible across a network, the object manager's parse method is used to help access a named object on another systems. the object manager calls the parse method, which then calls a network redirector to find the object when a process attempts, to open an objects that resides on a remote computer.

Like path names in MS-DOS and UNIX, object names are structured. Directories are represented by a directory object that contains the names of all the objects in that directory. The object name space can grow by the addition of object domains, which are self-contained sets of objects. Examples of object domains are floppy disks and hard drives. It is easy to see how the name space gets extended when a floppy disk is added to the system: The floppy has its own name space that is grafted onto the existing name space.

The multiple nicknames or aliases can refer to the same file because UNIX file systems have symbolic links. Similarly, Windows 2000 implements a symbolic link object. One way that Windows 2000 uses symbolic links is to map drive names to the standard MS-DOS drive letters. The drive letters are just symbolic links that can be remapped to suit the user's preferences.

A process gets an object handle by creating an object, by opening an existing object, by receiving a duplicated handle from another process, or by inheriting a handle from a parent process, similar to the way a UNIX process gets a file descriptor. These handles are all stored in the process object table. An entry in the object table contains the object's access rights and states wheter the handle should be inherited by a child processes. Windows 2000 automatically closes all the process open handles when a process terminates.

An access-token object is attached to the user's process. When a user is authenticated by the login process. The access token contains information such as the security id, group ids, privileges, primary group, and default access control list. These attributes determine which services and objects can be used by a given user.

Each object is protected by an access-control list in windows 2000 that contains the scurity ids and access rights granted to each process. When a process attempts to access and object, the system compares the security id in the process access token with the object's access-control list to determine whether access should be permitted. This check is done only when an object is opened, so internal Windows 2000 services that use pointers, rather than opening a handle to an object, bypass the access check.

The access-control list for that object generally determined by the creator of the object. If none is supplied explicity, one may be inherited from the creator object, or a default list may be obtained from the user's access-token object.

One field in the access token controls auditing of the object. Operations that are being audited get logged to the system's audit log with an identification of the user. The audit field can watch this log to discover attempts to break into the system or to access protected objects.

***Virtual-Memory Manager***

The virtual memory (VM) manager is the virtual memory portion of the windows 2000 executive. The design of the VM manager assumes that the underlying hardware supports virtual-to-physical mapping, a paging mechanism, and transparent cache coherence on multiprocessor systems, and allows multiple page-table entries to map to the same page frames. Pages of data that are assigned to a process but are not in physical memory are stored in the paging file on disk.

Each process has a 4GB virtual address space because the VM manager uses 32-bit addresses. The upper 2GB are identical for all processes, and are used by Windows 2000 in kernel mode. The lower 2GB are distinct for every process, and are accessible by both user and kernel-mode threads. Note that certain configurations of Windows 2000 reserve only 1 GB for operating system use, allowing a process to use 3 GB of address space.

The Windows 2000 VM manager uses a two-step process to allocate memory. A portion of the process address space is reserved by the first step. The second step commits the allocation by assigning space in the Windows 2000 paging file. Windows 2000 can limit the amount of paging file space that a process consumes by enforcing a quota on committed memory. A process can uncommit memory that it is no longer using to free up its paging quota. Since memory is represented by object, when one process (the parent) creates a second process (the child), the parent can maintain the ability to access the virtual memory of the child. That is how environmental subsystems can manage the memory of their client processes. For performance, the VM manager allows a privileged process to lock selected pages in physical memory, thus ensuring that the pages will not be swapped out to the paging file.

By getting handles to the same memory object two processes can share memory, since the entire memory space of an object must be committed before either process an access the object so this approach can be inefficient. Windows 2000 provides an alternative, called a section object, to represent a block of shared memory. After getting a handle to a section object, a process can map only the needed portion of the memory. This portion is called a view. The view mechanism also enables a process to access an object that is too large to fit into the process paging file quota. The view to walk through the address space of the object one piece at a time can used by the system.

The use of a shared-memory section object in many ways can controlled by a process. The maximum size of a section can be bounded. Either in the system paging file or by a regular file the section can be backed by disk space. A section can be based, meaning that the section appears at the same virtual address for all processes that access it. Finally, the memory protection of pages in the section can be set to read only, read-write, execute only, guard page, or copy on write. The last two of these protection settings need some explanation:

- A guard page raises an exception if accessed; the exception can be used, for example, to check whether a faulty program iterates beyond the end of an array.
- To save memory, the copy-on-write mechanism allows the VM manager. When two processes want indepenndent copies of an object, the VM manager places only one shared copy into physical memory, but it sets the copy-on-write property on that region of memory. If one of the processes tries to modify data in a copy-on-write page, the VM manager first makes a private copy of the page for that process to use.

Several data structures used in the virtual-address transaction in Windows 2000. Each process has a page directory that contains 1,024 page-directory entries of size 4 bytes. Typically, the page directory is private, but it can be shared among processes if the environment so requires. Each page-directory entry points to a page table that contains 1,024 page-table entries (PTEs) of size 4 bytes. Each PTE points to a 4KB page frame in physical memory. The VM manager will swap out these tables to disk when necessary because the total size of cell the

**page tables for a process is 4MB. See figure for a diagram of this structure.**

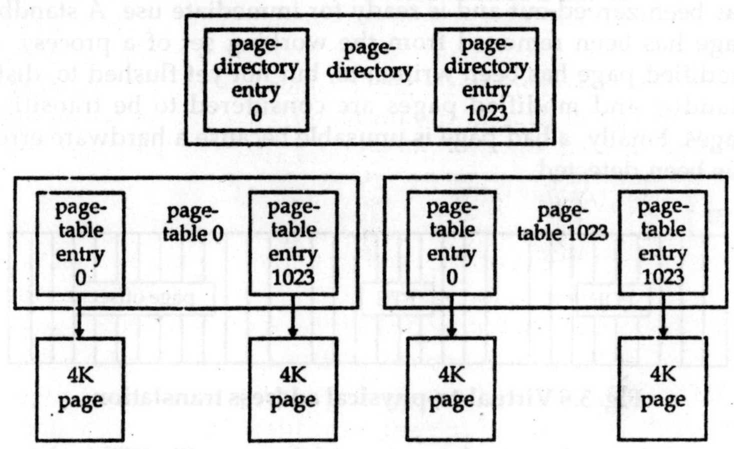


**Fig. 3.5 Virtual-memory layout**

**A 10 bit integer can represent all the values from 0 to 1,023. Thus, a 10-bit integer can select any entry in the page directory, or in a page table.**

**When a virtual-address points is translated to a byte address in physical memory this property is used. A 32-bit virtual-memory address is split into three integers. The first 10 bits of the virtual address are used as a subscript in the page directory. This address selects one page-directory entry, which points to a page table. The next 10 bits of the virtual address to select a PTE from that page table used by the memory management unit (MHU). The PTE points to a page frame in physical memory. The remaining 12 bits of the virtual address point to a specific byte in that page frame. The MMU creates a pointer to that specific byte in physical memory by concatenating 20 bits from the PTE with the lower 12 bits from the virtual address. Thus, the 32-bit PTE has 12 bits left over; these bits describe the page. For the use of the operating system the pentium PTE reserves 3 bits. The rest of the bits specify whether the page is dirty, accessed, cacheable, read only, write through, kernel mode, or valid; thus, describe the state of the page in memory.**

A page can be in one of six states: valid, free, zeroed, standby, modified, or bad. By an active process a valid page is in use. A free page is not referred in PTE. A zeroed page is a free page that has been zeroed out and is ready for immediate use. A standby page has been removed from the working set of a process. A modified page has been written to, but not yet flushed to, disk. Standby and modified pages are considered to be transition pages. Finally, a bad page is unusable because a hardware error has been detected.

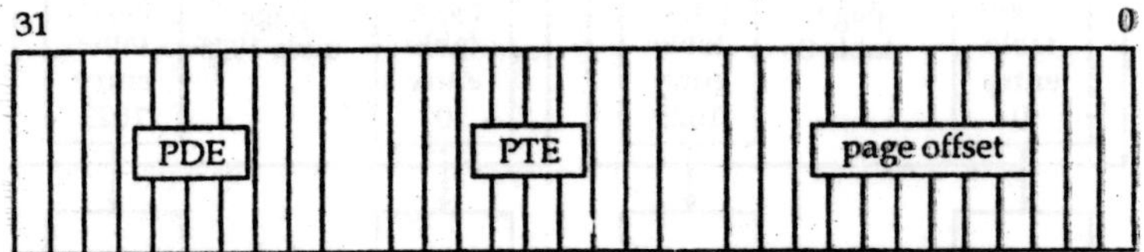


**Fig. 3.6 Virtual-to-physical address translation**

In figure the actual structure of the page-file PTE is shown. The PTE contains 5 bits for page protection, 20 bits for page-file offset, 4 bits to select the paging file, and 3 bits that describe the page state. To the hardware this page-file PTE would appear as an invalid page. Since executabel code and memory-mapped files already have a copy on disk, they do not need space in a paging file. If one of these pages is not in physical memory, the PTE structure is as follows. The most significant bit is used to specify the page protection, the next offset within the file for the page, and the lower 3 bits specify the page state.

If every process has its own set of page tables then it is difficult to share a page between processes, because each process will have its own PTE for the address will have to be stored in the PTEs that belong to each process that shares the page. The protection bits and page-state bits in these PTEs will all need to be set and updated consistently. To avoid these problems, Windows 2000 uses an indirection. For every page that is shared, the process has a PTE that points to a prototype page-table entry, rather than to the page frame. The page-frame address and the protection and state bits included in the prototype PTE. Thus, the first access by a process to a shared page generates a page fault. After the first access, further accesses are performed in the normal manner. If the page is marked read-only, the VM manager does a copy-on-write and the process effectively does not have a shared page any longer. Shared pages never appear in the page file, but are instead found in the file system.

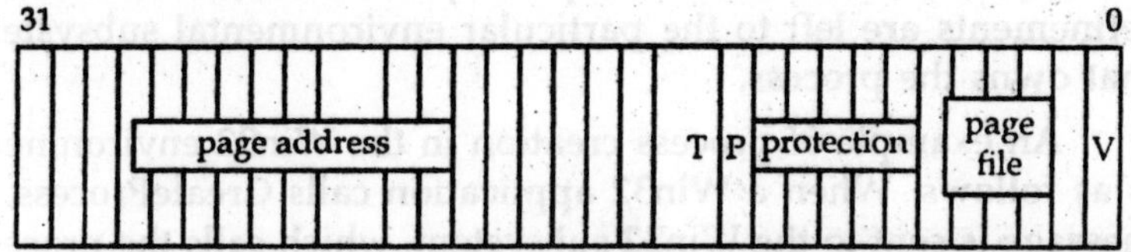


**Fig. 3.7 Page file page-table entry**

In a page-frame data-base the VM manager keeps track of all pages of physical memory. There is one entry for every page frame. The entry points to the PTE that points to the page frame, so the VM manager can maintain the state of the page. Page frames are linked to form, for instance, the list of zeroed pages and the list of free pages.

The VM manager faults in the missing page, placing that page into the first frame on the free list when a page fault occurs. But it does not stop there. Research shows that the memory referencing of a thread tends to have a locality property: When a page is used, it is likely that adjacent pages will be referenced in the near future. (Think of inerating over an array, or fetching sequential instructions that form the executable code for a thread). Because of locality, when the VM manager faults in a page, it also faults in a few adjacent pages. To reduce the total number of page faults this adjacent faulting tends. For more information on locality.

Windows 2000 uses a per process FIFO replacement policy, if no page framed are available on the free list to take pages from processes that are using more than their minimum working-set size. Windows 2000 monitors the page faulting of each process that is at its minimum working-set size, adn adjusts the working-set size accordingly. In particular, when a process is started under Windows 2000, it is assigned a default working-set size of 30 pages. Windows 2000 periodically tests this size by stealing a valid page from the process. If the process continues executing without generating a page fault for the stolen page, the working set of the process is reduced by 1, and the page is added to the list of free pages.

**Process Manager**

Services for creating deleting and using threads and processes provided by the windows 2000. It has no knowledge about parent-child relationships or process hierarchies; those refinements are left to the particular environmental subsystem that owns the process.

An example of process creation in the Win32 environment is as follows. When a Win32 application calls CreateProcess, a message is sent to the Win32 subsystem, which calls the process manager to create a process. The process manager calls the object manager to create a process object, and then returns the object handle to Win32. Win32 calls the process manager again to create a thread for the process, and finally Win32 returns handles to the new process and thread.

# Chapter 4

# UNIX and LINUX

**UNIX is primarily intended for program development and document-preparation environment and it is a time-sharing operating system. Unix is available for a different types of processor classes ranging from microprocessors to super computers due to its high degree of portability. The resulting ability to execute applications written under Unix on vastly different hardware makes the system attractive to both users and software designers.**

**Ten Thompson wrote the first version of Unix and later on joined by Dennis Ditchie. It was a single-user system for the PDP-7 computer written in assembly language. Unix is now commercially available from AT and T, together with numerous variants of the system provided by other vendors. The programmer's workbench, Unix/PWB, and writer's workbench, Unix/WWB are the other specialized versions of Unix which are available.**

**Some of the major features of Unix are as follows:**

**(i) Device independence**

**(ii) Hierarchical file system**

**(iii) Multiuser operation**

**(iv) Portability**

**(v) Tools and tool-building utilities**

**Unix is portable and availabe on a wide range of different hardwares. It is somewhat of a curiosity that portability was not**

one of the design objectives of Unix. Rather, it came as a consequences of coding the system in a high-level language.

### UNIX Application Programming Interface

A simple view of application behaviour is generally a system contain. A typical application reads some data from disk, tape or a terminal and perform some processing. Now output is produced on to disk, tape, terminal or a printer. To support these types of applications such operating systems provides easy handling easy implementation facility.

With memory management hardware and the appropriate communication interfaces unix supports multiple users on suitable installations. In addition to local users, remote users have access to log-in facilities and file transfer between unix hosts in network configurations. The sharing and co-operation among users that is desirable in program development environments is facilited by, among other things, the hierarchical file system. The hierarchical file system of unix spans volume boundaries, virtually stimulating the need for volume awareness among its user this is convenient in time-sharing systems and in network configurations.

### Unix Networking

A complete implementation of the TCP/IP networking protocol is included by the version 4-2 BSD of unix. Systems based on this provides a multi-vender networking capability based on Ethernet networking.

Remort log-in, file transfer, electronicmail and several other features are also supported by it. The unix networking allowed many different types of systems to share and mutually use data. Networs consist of many different systems can be used as a large distributed system.

### File System in Unix

Unix provides a hierarchical file system capable of spanning multiple volumes. In a tree-structured hierarchy of directories, the files are organized. Beginning with the root, which is usually placed at the system boot volume. No cross-links between directories and volumes are allowed, and each directory must be listed in exactly one parent directory. Some of these restrictions were not present in earlier versions of Unix, which allowed arbitrary graphs of directores to exist. Difficulties encountered when processing volume dismounts directories to exist. Difficulties encountered when processing volume dismounts in such systems have led to the current approach of a tree structure of diectories.

**Table 4.1 Some Unix file commands**

| | | |
|---|---|---|
| rm | : | remove (delete) files |
| In | : | link files-used to create aliases |
| mv | : | move files-used to rename files |
| chmod | : | change attributes of files |
| cp | : | copy files |
| cat | : | concatenate one or more files |
| split | : | split a file into more manageable pieces |
| (a) *General file manipulation* | | |
| Is | : | list names of one or more files in directories |
| mkdir | : | make a new directory (subdirectory) |
| rmdir | : | remove a directory (subdirectory) |
| cd | : | change working directory |
| (b) *Directory manipulation* | | |
| mount | : | attach device, add to the tree of directories |
| umount | : | remove the file system contained on a device |
| n/i/dcheck | : | verify integrity of files |
| fsck | : | verify integrity of the file system |
| dump | : | backup devices or files selectively |
| restor | : | restore dumped file system |
| (c) *Volume/media manipulation* | | |

The system maintains several standard directores in addition to user-created directories where programs implementing

UNIX commands, system libraries and standard devices may be found. Files may be specified by full path names, beginning with the root, or by partial path names, beginning with the current working directory. To manipulates files numerous commands are available. Some of those are listed in Table on next page. In addition to the usual range of commands to rename, link, and copy files, Unix has explicit commands for concatenation and splitting of files. A number of standard filters can also be used to manipulate the contents of files. Some examples include comparison identification of differences, elimination of duplicate lines, and printing of a few first and last lines of a file.

By means of a fairly standard set of commands, directories are managed. Some of which are presented in table. The MOUNT command is used to add tree structure of a volume as a leaf of the existing directory tree. The UMOUNT command has the opposite effect. Others commands are also present for the verification of file and volume integrity and also for the backing up and restoring of files and volumes.

With each file an owners ID is associated when it is created in this manner unix provide the file protection. At that time, the owner of the file specifies the modes of access allowed for himself, his group, and for other users of the system. The allowable modes for each individual class of users (owner, group, world) are a combination of 3 bits, 1 each for reading, writing, and execution of the file. This information is recorded as a group of 9 bits. the tenth protection bit, when set, informs the system to temporarily change the user identification to that of the file owner to order to execute the file. This feature, called the set_user_ID, allows privileged programs to use files inaccessible to other users.

To the same file against concurrent access unix does not automatically enforce protection. While some interlocks exist to preserve integrity when two users are creating files in the same directory or deleting each other's files, the system does not prevent two users from simultaneously writing the same file. Although possibly not needed in some program-development environments, the lack of a file-locking mechanism is generally perceived to be a drawback in database applications. For this reason, several Unix variants provide a file-locking mechanism.

Document preparation is closely related to program development unix designers take the view of that. Unix provides a comprehensive set of utilities for document preparation as a result. Among these are the popular NROFF text formatter and the TROFF formatter, which prepares output for typesetting equipment. Other utilities include EQN for mathematical texts and equations, MM for memoranda, and MMT for viewgraphs.

By means of the set of programe available as part of the writer's workbench (WWB) software, preparation of large texts, such as user manuals, may best be handled under unix. WWB is set of programs that help with two-stages of document production : evaluation and editing. Over a dozen programs are available in WWB to analyse prose documents and to suggest improvements. In addition to the usual proofreaders and spelling checkers. WWB software includes programs for punctuation (PUNCT) and detection of split infinitives (SPLTINF), and programs such as STYLE and PROSE for comprehensive analysis of writing style based on linguistic and psychological research. Other input to WWB analysis routines consists of actual documents considered to be exceptionally well written, and of the statistics of the papers analyzed by the system in the past.

The last set of Unix commands discussed in this section is provided for operations between remote Unix hosts. these include CU for remote log-in and UUCP for file transfer. The CU command (call Unix) allows user connected to a Unix host to log-in to a remote host via a communication link. The user can access facilities of the remote host in the same way as its local host ofter invoking the CU command. In addition, the user may temporarily escape to execute a command on its local host, capture on the local host output from operations on the remote host. and send output of local commands to the remote system. The UUCP command, for Unix-to-Unix copy, allows file transfers between two Unix sites. UUCP is actually a collection of utilities for file transfer between Unix sites connected via communication links. A Berkeley variant of Unix also supports networking via the popular Transport Control Protocol/Internet Protocol (TCP)/IP) and introduces the network programmming mechanism called sockets.

**Command-Language User's View of Unix**

By interacting with a command-language interpreter called, the shell unix users invoke commands. The shell is also a programming language suitable for construction of elaborate command files, called shell script. The shell is written as a user process, as opposed to being built into the kernal. When a user logs in, the system invokes a copy of the shell to handle interactions with the related user. Although the shell is the standard system interface, it is possible to invoke any other user-specified process to serve in place of the shell as a system interface, for each particular user. All programs run under the shell start out with three predefined files; standard input, standard output and error output. For example, the command is lists contains of a directory on the standard output. Similarly, from the standard input or from any other file the input to a program are to be taken. For example, the command of < script instructs the program editor to take its input from the file script.

From the command-language users are "point of view, pipes allow standard output of a program which can be used as a standard input of antoher program. We can connect several programs as per our requirements through piping. For example, the command WHO, which lists logged-on users, can be combined with the filter SORT to provide a sorted listing of users.

```
who 1 sort
```

In the above example of a pipe, the output of WHO is piped to SORT.

In order to accomplish more complex task I/D redirection and pipes allow unix utilities built as filters. For example, WHO command can be combined with WC filter, which counts characters, lines and words in a file to obtain the number of logged-on users in the line-count field of the output produced by WC.

```
who 1 wc
```

GREP is an another unix filter which outputs only those lines form its input that contain the specified pattern.

**Implementation of Unix**

Essentially a medium size monolithicmonitor is the unix kernel. As a set of coroutines the system calls are implemented. A kernel coroutine is synchronous to the invoking (user) process. In effect, the system coroutine is viewed as an extension of the calling process, or its different phase unix terminology. Unless preempted by an interrupt, kernel coroutines normally do not give up the processor until they terminate. To process device interrupts some system processes are available.

By means of a data structure that is a partitioned implementation of the process control block, the unix kernel keeps track of user. In particular, information about a process is divided into two parts : one part is permanently resident in main memory, and the other may be swapped out with the rest of the process image. Some of the information maintained in the permanently resident part of a process control block includes the process name, pointers to its memory image, and scheduling information. The swappable part of a process control block contains, among other things, saved CPU registers, a list of files opened by the process and accounting information.

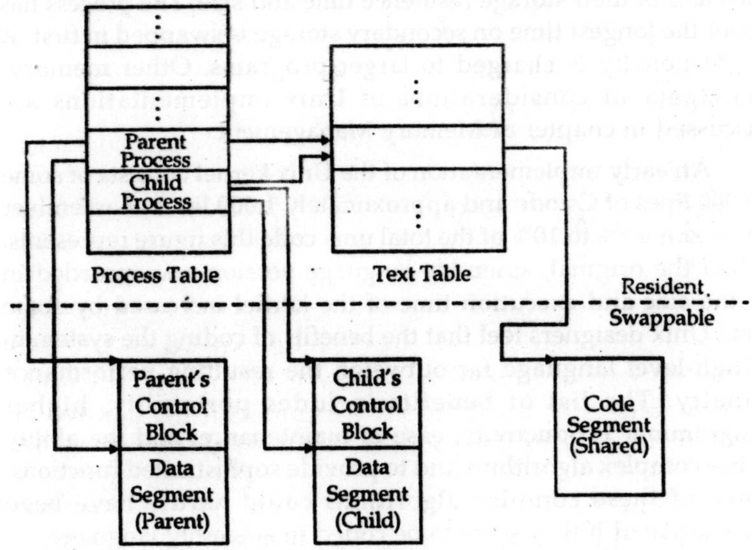


**Fig. 4.1 Process control blocks in Unix**

It simply selects the highest-priority process ready to run, when the unix schedular is invoked. This gives preference to system processes in order to provide acceptable response times to device interrupts. Scheduling is preemptive in the sense that a higher-priority awakened process preempts a lower-priority running one. In effect, a variant of preemptive event-driven scheduling provided to system processes, and an adaptive form of round robin is used for scheduling user processes.

To a seperate kernel process swapping is delegated. When selecting a victim, the swapping process takes into consideration the current status, memory residence time, and size of each resident process. Processes waiting for slow events are most likely to be swapped out, provided that they are of some age. By ensuring that processes just brought into memory are not immediate swapped out consideration of age is intended to prevent thrashing.

For swapping in by consulting the process table the swapping process selects candidates. Ready-to-run processes are ranked on the basis of their storage residence time and size. The process has spent the longest time on secondary storage is swapped in first. A slight penalty is charged to larger programs. Other memory-management considerations of Unix implementations are discussed in chapter of Memory Management.

An early implementation of the Unix kernel consists of some 10,000 lines of C code and approximately 1,000 lines of assembler code. Some 5% to 10% of the total unix code this figure represents. When the original, assembly-language version was recorded in C, the size and execution time of the kernel increased by some 30%. Unix designers feel that the benefits of coding the system in a high-level language far outweigh the resulting performance penalty. The list of benefits includes portability, higher programmer productivity, ease of maintenance, and the ability to use complex algorithms and to provide sophisticated functions. Some of these complex algorithms could hardly have been contemplated if they were to be coded in assembly language.

A tree-structured hierarchy of directories featured by the unix file system that may span volume boundaries. However, each individual file must completely reside on a single volume. Similarly, free blocks on different volumes cannot be pooled together for allocation purposes.

Files in a Unix system can belong to one of the three types : (1) ordinary files, (2) directories, and (3) special files. To access and manipulate I/O devices, the last group of files are used. Directories are stored and manipulated like any other with minimal exceptions. For processing purposes, all files are regarded as featureless arrays of bytes. While sequential access is supported for all files, random access is possible only files stored on block-structured devices.

Disks are normally divided into fixed-size blocks. The root directory of the system also contained by the system volume. Some variants have even larger block sizes. Disk drivers provide an abstraction of disks as linear arrays of blocks numbered from 0 up to the device size. The first few blocks of a disk are normally reserved for the boot block, "super block", and i-list, a list of file definitions. the super block contains volume-specific parameters, such as size, and addresses of other areas on disk. The root directory of the system also contained by the system volume.

Each directory contains at least two entries ; a link to its parent directory and a pointer to itself. Other entries, when used, contain file names and i-numbers. File's i-node contained all other information about a file. An i-node allocated to a file contains the following information :

- The user and group ID of the file owner
- File protection bits
- The physical address of the file contents
- The time of creation, last use, and last modification of the file
- The number of links to the file
- The file type

**Standard Directories**

There are few standard directories in unix file system, where certain types of files can be found. Some standard diectories are as follows :

| | | |
|---|---|---|
| /dev | - | special device files are kept in this |
| /bin | - | executable system utilities like cp, rm, sh are kept |

/etc - where system configuration files and databases are kept

/liv - operating system and programming libraries are kept in this directory.

/tmp - this directory contains temporarly

/usr/local - this is top/level directory for storing application software and data return by local system staff

/usr/man - mannual pages are kept here

**Memory Management**

It sets a certain amount of RAM for itself as well as for all system and user processes, when the unix kernel is loaded into memory. Mainly RASA is divided into five parts.

(i) ***Text :*** This holds the text segment of a running process

(ii) ***Stack :*** This hold the stack segment of the running process

(iii) ***Data :*** This holds the data segment of the running process

(iv) ***Buffer cache :*** All the read and write operations to the file system are cached here first.

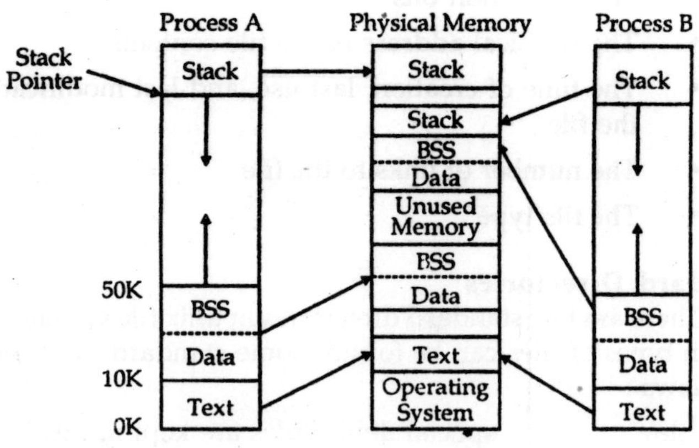


**Fig. 4.2 Memory Management**

## KEY FEATURES OF UNIX

**The key features of UNIX can be explained as :**

**(i) UNIX is highly portable and available for a variety of processor classes and ranging from microprocessors to supercomputers.**

**(ii) UNIX is time-operating system and users round robin CPU scheduling for user processes.**

**(iii) UNIX processes form a family tree and strong ties exist between for user processes.**

(iv) For program development its specialized versions are available.

(v) For document preparation it is also used

(vi) Unix has hierarchical file system that spans volume boundaries

(vii) Unix provides extensive buffering of disk blocks to reduce physical I/O and effective disk access time.

### Linux System

The internal workings of the 4.3 BSD operating system discussed in Appendix A. One of the unix like systems is BSD. Linux is another UNIX-like system that has gained popularity in recent years. We look at the history and development of Linux in this chapter and cover the user and programmer interfaces that Linux presents-interfaces that owe a great deal to the UNIX tradition. The internal methods by which Linux implements there interfaces also discovered in this chapter. However, since Linux has been designed to run as many standard UNIX applications as possible, it has much in common with existing UNIX implementations. We do not duplicate the basic description of UNIX given in Appendix A. A rapidly developing operating system is Linux.

### History

Unix compatibility has been a major design goal of the Linux prefect and Linux looks and feels much like any other Unix system. However, Linux is much younger than most UNIX systems. Its development began in 1991, when a Finnish student, Linus Torvalds, wrote and christened Linux, a small but self-contained kernel for the 80386 processor, the first true 32-bit processor in intel's range of PC-compatible CPUs.

The Linux source code was made available for free on the internet, early in its development. As a result, Linux's history has been one of collaboration by many users from all around the world, corresponding almost exclusively over the internet. The Linux system has grown to include much Unix functional from an initial kernel that partially implemented a small subett of Unix system services.

In its early days, Linux development revolved largely around the central operating system kernel-the core, provileged executive that manages all system resources and that interacts directly with the computer hardware. To produce a full operating system, of course, we need much more than this kernel. It is useful to make the distinction between the Linux kernel and a Linux system. The Linux kernel is an entirely original piece of software developed from scratch by the Linux community. As we know, it today, the Linux system includes a multitude of components. Some written from scratch, others borrowed from other development projects, and others created in collaboration with other teams.

For applications and user programming, the basic Linux system is a standard enviroment. The basic Linux system is a standard environment for application and user programming, but it does not enforce any standard means of managing the available functionally as a whole. There has been a need for another layer of functionally on top of the Linux system, as Linux has matured. A Linux distribution includes all the standard components of the Linux system, plus a set of administrative tools to simplify the initial installation and subsequent upgrading of Linux, and to manage installation and deinstallation of other packages on the system. Tools for managements of file systems, areation and management of user accounts, adminstration of networks are also typically included in a modem distribution.

**The Linux Kernel**

The first Linux kernel released to the public was Version 0.01, dated May 14, 1991. It had no networking, ran on only 80386-compatible Intel processors and PC hardware and had extremely limited device-driver support. For memory mapped files, the virtual memory subsystem was also fairly basic and included no support. However, even early incarnation supported shared pages with copy-on-write. The only file system supported was the Minix file system-the first Linux kernels were cross-developed on a Minix platform. However the kernel did implement proper UNIX processes with protected address spaces.

On March 14, 1994, the next milestone version Linux 1.0, was released. This release culminated three years of rapid development or the Linux kernel. Perhaps the single biggest new feature was networking 1.0 included support for UNIX's standard TCP/IP networking protocols as well as a BSD-compatible socket interface for networking programming. For running IP over an Ethernet or (using PPP or S4P protocols) over serial links or modems device-driver support was added.

Without the limitations of the original Minix file system, the 1.0 kernel also included a new, much enhanced file system, and supported a range of SCSI controllers for high performances disk access. The developers extended the virtual memory subsystem to support paging to swap files and memory mapping of arbitrary files (but only read only memory mapping was implemented in 1.0).

In this release a range of extra hardware support was also included. To include floppy-disk and CD-ROM devices, as well as sound cards, a range of mice and international keyboards, although still restricted to the intel PC plateform, hardware support had grown. Floating point emulation was also provided in the kernel for 80386 users who had no 80386 math coprocessor, and System V UNIX-style interprocess communication (IPC), including shared memory, semaphores, and message queues, was implemented. For dynamically loadable and unloadable kernel moduler simple support was also provided.

At this point, development started on the 1.1 kernel stream, but numerous bug-fix patches were released subsequently against 1.0. For Linux kernels this pattern was adopted as the standard numbering convention. Kernels with an odd minor-version number such as 1.1, 1.3 or 2.1 are development kernels. Updates against the stable kernels are intended as only remedial versions, whereas the development kernels may include newer and relatively untested functionality.

In March, 1995, the 1.2 kernel was released: The same improvement in functionality did not nearly offer by this release as offered by the 1.0 release but it include support for a wider variety of hardware including the new PCI hardware bus architecture. Developers added another PC-specific feature-support for the 80386 CPU's virtual 8086 mode-to allow emulation of the DOS operating system for PC computers. They updated the networking stack to provide support for the IPX protocol, and made the IP implementation more complete by including accounting and firewalling functionality.

The final PC-only Linux kernel was the 1.2 kernel. The source distribution for Linux 1.2 included partially implemented support for SPARC, Alpha and MIPS, CPU, but full integration of these other architectures did not begin until after the 1.2 stable kernel was released.

On wider hardware support and more complete implementations of existing functionality the Linux 1.2 release concentrated. Much new functionality was under development at the time, but integration of the new code into the main kernel source code had been deferred until after the stable 1.2 kernel had been released. As a result, the 1.3 development stream saw a great deal of new funtionality added to the kernel.

This work was finally released on Linux 2.0 in June, 1996. This release was given a major version-number increment on account of two major new capability suport for multiple architectures, including a fully 64-bit native Alpha port, and support for multiprocessor architectures. For the Motorola 68000-serves processors and for sun's SPARC systems the Linux distributions based on 2.0 are also available. A derived version of Linux running on top of the Mach Microkernel also runs on PC and PowerMac systems.

The changes in 2.0 did not stop there. To provide a unified cache for file system data independent of the caching of block deviced the memory management code was subsequently improved. As a result of this change, the kernel offered greatly increased file-system and virtual-memory performance. The file system caching was extended to networked file systems for the first time and writable memory mapped regions also were supported.

Much improved TCP/IP performance and number of new networking protocols including Appletalk, AX 25 amateur radio networking and ISDN support were added and these included by the 2.0 kernel. The ability to mount remote Netware and SMB (Microsoft LanManager) network volumes was added.

Other major improvements in 2.0 were support for internal kernel threads, for handling dependencies between loadable modules, and for automatic loading of modules on demand. Dynamic configuration of the kernel at run-time was much improved through a new, standarized configuration interface. Additional, unrelated new features included file-system quotas and POSIX-compatible real-time process-scheduling classes.

Linux 2.2 was released and continues the improvements added by Linux 2.0, in January 1999. A port for UltraSPARC systems was added. Networking was enhanced with more flexible firewalling, better routing and traffic management, as well as support for TCP large window and selective acks. Acorn, Apple, and NT disks can now be read and NFS was enhanced and a kernel mode NFS daemon was added. Signal handling, interrupts, and some I/O are now locked at a finer level than before to improve SMP performance.

**The Linux System**

The Linux kernel forms the core of the Linux project in many ways, but other components make up the complete Linux operating systems. Whereas the Linux project, much of the supporting software that makes up the Linux system is not exclusive to Linux but is common to a number of UNIX-like operating systems. Linux users many tools developed as part of Berkeley's B3D operating system to partcular MIT's X Window System, and the Free Software Foundation's GNU project.

In both directions this sharing of tools has worked. The main system libraries of Linux were organized by the GNU project, but the Linux community greatly improved the libraries by addressing omissions, inefficiencies, and bugs. Other components such as the GNU's compiler (gcc) were already of sufficiently high quality to be used directly in Linux. The networking administration tools under Linux were derived from code first developed for 4,3BSD, but more recent BSD derivatives such as FreeBSD have borrowed code from Linux in return, such as the intel floatin-point-emulation math library and the PC sound-hardware device drivers.

By a loose network of developers collaborating over the internet the Linux system as a whole is maintained responsibility for maintaining the integrity of specific components. A small number of public Internet file-protocol (ftp) archive sites act as de facto standard repositories for these components. By the Linux community the file system hierarchy standard document is also maintained as a means of keeping compatibility across the various system components. This standard specifies the overall layout of a standard Linux file system; it determines under which directory names configuration files, libraries, system binaries and run-time data files should be stored.

**Linux Distributions**

Anybody can install a Linux system by fetching the latest revisions of the necessary system components from the ftp sites and compiling them. This operation was often precisely the one that a Linux user had to carry out, in Linux's early days. As Linux has matured, however, various individuals and groups have attempted to make this job less painful by providing a standard precompiled set of packages for easy installation.

Much more that is just the basic Linux system these collections or distributions included. They typically include extra system-installation and management utilities, as well as precompiled and ready-to-install packages of many of the common UNIX tools, such as news servers, web browsers, text-processing and editing tools, and even games.

By simply providing a means of unpacking all the files into the appropriate places the first distributions managed these packages. One of the improtant contributions of modern distributions include a package-tracking database that allows packages to be installed, upgraded, or removed painlessly.

The SLS distribution was the first collection of Linux packages in the early days of Linux, that was recognisable as a complete distribution. Although it could be installed as a single entity, SLS lacked the package-management tools now expected of Linux distributions. The Slackware distribution represented a great improvement in overall quality, despite also having poor package management; it is still one of the most widely installed distributions in the Linux community.

A large number of commercial and non-commercial Linux distributions have become available since Slackware's release. Red Hat and Debian are particularly popular distributions from a commercial Linux support company and from the free-software Linux community, respectively. Other commercially supported versions of Linux include distributions from Caldera, Craftworks, and WorkGroup Solutions. A large Linux following in Germany has resulted in several dedicated German-language distributions, including versions from SuSE and Unifix. To list here there are too many Linux distributions in circulation for us. The variety of distributions does not prohibit compatibility across Linux distributions. The RPM package file format is used, or at least understood by the majority of distributions, and commercial applications distributed in this format can be installed and run on any distribution that can accept RPM files.

**Linux Licensing**

Under the GNU General Public License (GPL) the Linux kernel is distributed the terms of which the Linux kernel set out by the free software foundation. Linux is not public-domain software. Public domain implies that the authors have waived copyright over the software, but copyright over Linux code is still held by the code's various authors. The people can copy it, modify it, use it in any manner, they want and give away their own copies. Without any restrictions still Linux is free software.

The main implication of Linux's licensing terms are that anybody using Linux, or creating her own derivative of Linux (a legitimate exercise), cannot make the derived product proprietary. Software released under the GPL cannot be redistributed as a binary-only product. Under the GPL, you must make source code available alongside any binary distributions, if you release software that includes any components covered by GPL. This restriction does not prohibit making-or even selling-binary-only software distributions, as long as anybody who receives binaries is also given the opportunity to get source code too, for a reasonable distribution charge.

**Design Principles**

Linux resembles any other traditional non-microkernel UNIX implementation, in its overall design. With a full set of UNIX-compatible tools. It is a multiuser multitasking system. Linux's file system adherest to traditional UNIX semantics, and the standard UNIX networking model is implemented fully. The internal details of Linux's design have been influenced heavily by the history of this operating system's development.

Linux was developed exclusively on PC architecture, although it runs on a wide variety of platforms. A great deal of that early development was carried out by individual enthusiasts, rather than by well-funded development of research facilities, so from the start Linux attempted to squeeze as much functionality as possible from limited resources. Today, Linux can run happily on a multiprocessor machine with hundreds of megabytes of main memory and many gigabytes of disk space, but it is still capable of operating usefully in under 4 MB of RAM.

As PCs became more powerful and as memory and hard disks became cheaper, the original minimalist Linux kernels grew to implement more, UNIX functionality speed and efficiency are still important design goals, but much of the recent and current work on Linux has concentrated on a third major design goal standardization. One of the prizes paid for the diversity of UNIX implementations currently available is that source code written for one flavor may not necessarily compile or run correctly on another. It is not necessary that same system calls are present on two different UNIX systems. The POSIX standards comprise a set of specifications of different aspects or operating system functionality and for extensions such as process threads and real time operations. With the relevant POSIX documents Linux is designed to be compliant. at least two Linux distributions have achieved official POSIX certification.

Linux presents few surprises to anybody familiar with Unix, because it presents standard interfaces to both the programmer and the user. We do not detail this interfaces under Linux. The sections on the programmer interface and user interface of 4.3BSD apply equally well to UNIX semantics, rather than to BSD behaviour. A separate set of libraries is available to implement BSD semantics in places where the two behaviour are significantly different.

Many other standards in the UNIX world exist, but full certification of Linux against them is sometimes slowed because they are often available only for a fee, and the expense involved in certifying an operating system's compliance with most standards is substantial. However, supporting a wide base of applications is important for any operating system, so implementation of standards is a major goal for Linux development even if the implementation is not formally certified. Linux currently supports the POSIX threading extensions and a subset of the POSIX extensions for real-time process control in addition to the basic POSIX standard.

## Components of a Linux System

The Linux system is composed of three main bodies of code, in line with most traditional UNIX implementations:

1. *Kernel:* For maintaining all the important abstractions of the operating system, the kernel is responsible, including virtual memory and processes.
2. *System libraries:* The system libraries define a standard set of functions through which application can interact with the kernel, and that implement much of the operating system functionality that does not need the full privileges of kernel code.
3. *System utilities:* The system utilities are programs that perform individual specialized management tasks. Some system utilities may be invoked just once to intialize and configure some aspect of the system; other-known as daemons in UNIX terminology-may run permanently, handling such tasks as responding to incoming network connections, accepting logon requests from terminals, or updating log files.

Figure illustrates the various components that make up a full Linux system. Between kernel and everything else the most important distinction is here. All the kernel code executes in the processor's privileged mode with full access to all the physical resources of the computer. Linux refers to this previleged mode as kernel mode. No user mode code is built into the kernel, under Linux. Any operating system-support code that does not need to run in kernel mode is placed into the system libraries instead.

Linux retains UNIX's historical model-the kernel is created as a single monolithic binary although various modern operating systems have adopted a message-passing architectures for their kernel internals. The main reason is to improve performance: Because all kernel code and data structures are kept in a single address space, no context switches are necessary when a process calls an operating-system function or when a hardware interrupt is delivered. Not only the core scheduling and virtual-memory code occupies this address space; all kernel code, including all device drivers, file systems, and networking code, is present in the same single address space.

It does not mean there is no scope for modularity just because all the kernel shares this same melting pot. In the same way that user applications can load shared libraries of run time to pull in a needed piece of code, so the Linux kernel can load (and unload) modules dynamically at run time. The kernel does not necessarily need to know in advance which modules may be loaded-they are truly independent loadable components.

| system management programs | user processes | user utility programs | compilers |
|---|---|---|---|
| system shared libraries | | | |
| Linux kernel | | | |
| loadable kernel modules | | | |

Fig. 4.3 Components of the Linux system

The core of the Linux operating system formed by the Linux kernal. It provides all the functionality necessary to run processes, and it provides system services to give arbitrated and protected to hardware resources. The kernel implements all the features required to qualify as an operating system. On its own, however, the operating system provided by the Linux kernel looks nothing like a UNIX system. It is missing many of the extra features of UNIX, and the features that it does provide are not necessarily in the format in which a UNIX application expects them to appear. To running applications is not maintained directly by kernel the operating system interface visible. Rather, applications make calls to the system libraries, which in turn call the operating system services as necessary.

Many types of functionality provided by the system libraries. They allow applications to make kernel-system-service requests at the simplest level. Making a system call involves transferring control from unpriviledged user mode to privileged kernel mode; the details of this transfer vary from architecture to architecture. The libraries take care of collecting the system-call arguments and if necessary, arranging those arguments in the special form necessary to make the system call.

More complex versions of the basic system calls may also provided by the libraries. For example, the C language's buffered file-handling functions are all implemented in the system libraries, providing more advanced control of file I/O than the basic kernel system calls. The libraries also provide routines that do not correspond to system calls at all, such assorting algorithms, mathematical functions, and string-manipulation routines. In the system libraries all the function necessary to support the running of UNIX or POSIX applications are implemented.

A wide variety of user-mode programs are included by the Linux system. The system utilities include all the programs necessary to initialize the system, such as those to configure network devices or to load kernel modules. Continually running server programs also count as system utilities, such programs hands user login requests, incoming network connections, and the printer queues.

Not all the standard utilities serve key system-administration functions. The UNIX user environment contains a large number of standard utilities to do simple everyday tasks, such as listing directories, moving and deleting files, or displaying the contents of a file. More complex utilities can perform text-processing functions, such as sorting textual data or performing pattern searches on input text. Together, these utilities form a standard toolset that users can expect on any UNIX system; although they do not perform any operating system function, they are an important part of the basic Linux system.

# Chapter 5

# Internet

You will read in this chapter that what really is the Internet, its functions, uses and how has it made so much of a difference? Here is some basic information about the net and the associated terminology.

A global network of thousands of computers which communicate to each other by using a common language is called the Internet, like the international telephone network. As a large network it works and no one company owns the network. A large number of Internet server computers works on the Internet and each one contains different information or services.

Word Wide Web (WWW) the part of internet recently has made the Internet more popular due to the advances in the graphical and easy to use interface. WWW contains graphics, text, photos, videos, sound that's why people like it. Internet becomes an interesting means of communication by it. Hundreds and even thousands of "websites" can be contained on one server; on the other hand, a single "website" could be contained on numerous server computers. A web site may contain a single page, several pages and even thousands of pages. It is not easy to measure the number of user on Internet. Approximately over 80 million people access the Internet worldwide. However, these are loose estimates that change on a daily basis. Around the globe more and more people are able to get online through Internet.

Now, business is becoming a major player on the web and changes are occurring with greater frequency. To interconnect the different types of networks and to allow the information to move freely among users the Internet was designed.

## HISTORY

During the 1960s the Internet had its origins in the cold war between Russia and America. The US air-force needed about the survicability of its communications in the event of a nuclear strike to ensure that it could still communicate with its forces. The RAND corporation proposed a system with no centralized authority, as any centralized system would be a target of any possible attack.

Paul Baran, suggested a decentralized system that would still operate even if parts of it were destroyed and developed the proposed system. All interconnections in the network could send and receive messages, forwarding them onto other interconnection points (called nodes) until the message reached its destination. Information would be sent in little packets., each packet would be self-contained and have its own address information. Packets would travel from node to node, each node deciding how to send the packet to the next available node. Even if some nodes were destroyed, an alternative route could still send the message. In this way, the network would withstand a nuclear strike. After implementing the network in 1969, it was known as ARPANET (Advanced Research Projects Administration Network), and used by the US Department of Defence (DOD) and US universities with one computer at California and three at Utah. Later on other universities and R & D institutions were allowed to connect to the Network, ARPANET quickly grew to encompass the entire America continent and became a huge success. To become a part of ARPANET each university to the country wanted because of that the network was broken into 2 smaller parts, one for managing military sites the MILNET and second for managing non-military sites ARPANET. Around 1980, NSFNET (National Science Foundation Network) was created. With the advancement of modern communication facilities, other computers were also allowed to be linked up with any computer of NSFNET. By 1990 many computers were hooking up to NSFNET. It has evoloved in to the Internet, as more and more connections were made gradually.

Some people termed Internet as the world's largest democracy with no governement, and to control it, it has no state of head. With no head of state, no bosses, no board of directors, no official censors, the Internet is a rare example of a large democracy. Nobody controls the Internet and in principle, any computer can speak to any other computer, as long as it obeys the technical rules of the TCP/IP protocol. This freedom of Internet helped it to move out of its original base in military and research institutions, into elementary and high schools, colleges, public libraries, commercial sectors even into the shop of a vegetable vendor.

**The Inside Story**

The Internet is a global connection of computers as you read earlier, via a huge network of telecommunication links these computers are connected. How do these interconnected computers communicate with each other? What is their "language" so to speak? What is the meaning of the terms that you often hear in the context of the Internet? You shall look at the answers to all these questions in this section.

A whole resource of data and information stored at different sites (called hosts or servers) and locations all around the world the Internet allows you to access. In Internet there is huge resource of information. Information in every field starting from education, science, health, medicine, history, and geography to business, news, etc. can be retrieved through Internet. You can also download programs and software packages from anywhere in the world.

As a transport mehcanism for electronic transactions the Internet is now beirg used. For many years it has been transferring data, from email messages, to programs and data files. Data has largely been sent unencrypted over the Internet.

**Functioning of Internet**

The Internet consists of a number of computers called hosts and interconnecting equipment such as routers and telecommunication links that interconnect routers and hosts together.

A computer on the Internet is called a host and each host is act as a provider of information like files, images, document etc. A host can also access information on another host if it has the required permissions to do so.

A router is a device that joins telecommunications links and groups of computers together. It provides a mechanism for determining a route (or path) between the two computers that want to exchange information.

Server is a host computer that provides information for others. A server is a computer or computer program that offers a service to other computers on the network by responding to commands sent by the client computer. The server transfers the file when a client computer sends a request for a file on the server. For instance, when you enter a URL (Universal Resource Locator) or more commonly, a web address, into your web browser's addres box, your client computer sends a request to a server computer that responds by transmitting the web page that corresponds to the address back to your browser.

A computer or computer program that request and accesses network resources from a server as called a client. The client and the server use a common method for communicating and for transferring data from one computer to another.

A server or a client computer is a computer workstation or PC that connects to the Internet. Web servers, file servers, mail servers and news servers are the examples of servers.

How does information get transferred on the net?

In Internet terminology any message to be transferred is divided into small chunks of data called packets. The complet address of the destination contained by the each packet. The packets are sent out from one node to the other through the subnetwork and at each node a routing decision is taken for the packet. Different packets formed from the same original message and intended from the same source to the same destination may proceed along different routes because the routing decidion for each packet is taken independently. To indicate the path that the packet should take served by the address of the destination node.

But how is the address of the node assigned in the first place?

**Addresses on the Internet**

Internet is not a governmental organization. The Internet society is the ultimate authority of the Internet. To promote global information exchange Internet is a voluntary membership organization. Internet has nore than one million computers attached to it. Each host computer is identified in two ways. Firstly, each computer on the Internet has a unique assigned name, such as host1.cit.ac.nz that is referred to as its domain name. Secondly, TCP/IP address is the unique numerical address of the each computer on the Internet. This is a group of numbers joined by dots. For example, the computer known as host1.cit.ac.nz could have a TCP/IP address of 156.59.20.49. This is a 32-bit binary number that uniquely identifies a computer on the Internet to other Internet computers, for the purpose of communication through the transfer of data packets. As mentioned above, each data packet that is transferred over the Internet contains the IP address of the sending computer and that of the receiving computer. Using IP addresses, routers move the packets across the Internet until they reach their destination.

**Domain Names**

According to geographical location servers or host computers are arranged except the USA all countries in the world have a country suffix. Suffix for India is in. Typically, the domain name of a host computer looks like.

- server name
- organization name
- type of organization
- country name

For instance, the server www.yahoo.com defines it as a host called www, belonging to an organization called yahoo, which is a commercial organization located in the United States. .com is an abbreviation that is used to designate all the commercial organizations.

Some common abbreviations are:

| *Abbreviation* | *Meaning* |
|---|---|
| ac | Academic |
| co | Company |
| com | Commercial |
| edu | Educational |

| | |
|---|---|
| gov | Government |
| govt | Government |
| mil | Military |
| net | Large Internet service provider |
| org | Non-profit organization |

Some common country names are:

| *Abbreviation* | *Meaning* |
|---|---|
| au | Australia |
| bc | Belgium |
| ge | Germany |
| jp | Japan |
| mx | Maxico |
| nz | New Zealand |
| uk | United Kingdom |
| in | India |

For the world wide allocation of domain names and IP addresses Inter NIC is responsible.

## Connecting to Internet

Various types of connectivities are there to get on to Internet which can be broadly classified into the following catagories-

### *(i) Gateway Access*

It is the access to the Internet from a network, which is not on the Internet. As level one connection Gateway Access is also known the two different types of networks allows by the Gateway to 'talk' to each other. But the users of the Gateway Internet have limited access to the Internet. They might not be able to use all the tools available on Internet. The local Internet Service Provider (ISP) normally defines this limitation.

### *(ii) Dial-up Connection*

A level two connection is 'Dial-up connection'. Through dial-up terminal connection this provides connection to Internet. The computer, which provides Internet access is known as 'Host' and the computer that receives the access. is 'Client' or 'Terminal'. The client computer uses modem to access a 'host' and acts as if it is a terminal directly connected to that host. So this type of connection is also known as 'Remote Modem Access' connection. By a full time connection, the host to which the client gets connected is actually connected to the Internet.

Host carries all the commands that you type on a client machine and forwards them to Internet in dial-up connection to Internet. It also receives the data or information from the internet on behalf of the 'Client' and passes it to them. The client computer acts as a 'dumb' terminal connected to remote host.

This type of connection can further be divided into two categories.

*(a) Shell Connection*

You get only textual matter of a web page in this type of Internet connection. This connection does not support Graphics display. However you are able to surf the Internet, do FTP, receive mail. Shell Accounts were the only type of Internet access available for many years before the Internet entered the world of graphics and became more users friendly.

*(b) TCP/IP Connection*

With multimedia sound and pictures today's graphical WWW to browsers provide easier access. The major difference between Shell and TCP/IP account is that, shell account can only display text and does not support graphics display, whereas TCP/IP can display both. Hence, it is a more popular Internet connection. Shell accounts have almost phased out from the Internet scenario.

You need the following things to access any of these dial-up accounts-

- Computer
- Modem
- Telephone Connection
- Shell or TCP/IP account from the ISP
- Internet client software or Browser such as explorer or Netsacape Navigator

***(iii) Leased Connection***

As Direct Internet access or level three connection the leased connection is called. It is the secure, dedicated and most expensive level of Internet connection. With leased connection, your computer is dedicatedly and directly connected to the Internet using high-speed transmission lines. It is on-line twenty-four hours a day, seven days a week. To large corporations and universities, the leased Internet connections are limited who can offord the expense.

## Internet Service Providers

The companies that provide others the access to the Internet are called Internet Service Providers (ISP's). This can be via dial-up connection using a modem, or using an ISDN or permanent high-speed connection. Various charging levels may exist, but a popular method for home users is flat rate (per month unlimited time and data amount). These charges are continuously coming down in India.

Through connection on an existing network or via a modem from a remote site such as a private residence each user can access the Internet. The data and information that can be accessed on the Internet comes in numerous different formats and there are wide range of applications that interpret the information for the user.

## Common Protocol of the Internet

Transmission control protocol, Internet protocol which is known as TCP/IP is the common protocol. A protocol is a set of rules for the exchange of data. In the political world, protocol refers to how you are polite (diplomatic) and tactful to your adversaries. In the network world, a protocol refers to the method used to encode and exchange information between two computers.

TCP/IP is like a transport protocol. It is just like a bus that transports information from the source to a destination. Other protocols can reside on top of TCP/IP because it does not really care what it carries in the bus. Just as a passenger gets on the bus and is transported from one place to another, other protocols can use TCP/IP to send data from one point to another. You will learn more about this is s course on Computer Networks.

## SERVICES PROVIDED BY INTERNET

The Internet provides for a wide range of services. Some of these are listed in the table below.

| *Service* | *Description of Service* |
|---|---|
| EMAIL | Electronic mail. Permits the sending and receiving files from one computer to another. |
| FTP | File Transfer Protocol. A means of sending and receiving files from one computer to another. |
| GOPHER | An early form of representing information as graphical icons or symbols, that could be displayed in a window and then diwonloaded. It has been replaced by the WWW. |
| USENET | A number of discussion groups that allow users to post questions and replies, sorted by topic. |
| WWW | World Wide Web. Accessed using a web browser such as Netscape Navigator or Internet Emplorer, a means of locating and displaying information located on the Internet. |

You shall now look at these in more detail.

### Email

Email stands for electronic mail. You will find this term being referred to variously as email, Email, E-mail or e-mail. Whatever be the term used they all refer to the same. In this text you shall be using the simplest form i.e. email.

The most heavily used feature of Internet is probably the email. To exchange the text messages and computer files on the Internet with any one who has an email address it is used. The biggest advantage of using email is that it is cheap, especially when sending messages to other states or countries, it is quick and at the same time it can be delivered to a number of people around the world.

Formatted text, images, video clips, sound files can transferred by the modern email programs. Here data are transmitted through Internet and , therefore, within minutes the message reaches the destination may it be anywhere in the world. Thus, the mailing system is excessively fast. It is not uncommon to send a mail to another part of the world from India and receive the reply within an hour. The speed of this mail has made the cynics rename the ordinary post office based mail as "snail-mail" to reflect its comparatively much slower speed. The receiver does not get the mail until logging on to the server and retrieving it, where as the email is sent immediately.

**What are email addresses?**

Writing a postal letter and an email is almost same, just like the letters it also have a header or address portion. For example, you write the name of the person and where he lives on the envelope. This information is used by the postal services to ensure your letter is delivered to the correct destination.

In the same way, email has a header or address portion, which is used by routers and other devices on the Internet to determine the correct destination. Email is created using a mail program.

You are identified by a name and a location in the real world just like it in the electronic world of Internet you have an assigned name given to you by the network administrator or ISP. This identifies your name. The other portion is your address, which is a server on the Internet that holds your mail (its like your physical mail box). These two portions are linked together using the @ (called at) sign.

For example,

erbrij@yahoo.co.in

this identifies the username as erbrij on amail server at yahoo.co.in. Many organizations now offer you the chance to open a email account (such as hotmail.com.yahoo.com and usa.net).

**Features of email**

Some important features that have made email an extremely efficient and cost-effective form of communication are as follow:

- One-to-one or one-to-many communications.
- Instant and inexpensive communications.
- Physical presence of recipient is not required.
- Most inexpensive mail service, 24-hours a day and seven days a week.
- Encourages informal communication.
- Not restricted to text alone-can send video, photographs, audio etc. also.

**World Wide Web (WWW)**

Tim Berners-Lee invented the WWW in 1991 by creating a method that combined a new way to share and find information on the Internet. The web began when Berners-Lee wrote a small computer program for his own personal use. This program allowed pages, within his computer, to be linked together using keywords. It soon became possible to link documents in different computer, as long as they were connected to the Internet. To link documents, the document formatting language is used which is called HTML (Hypertext Markup language).

Until 1992 the web remained primarily text based. A new computer program called the NCSA Mosaic was developed by Marc Anderson who was the first web browser. The browser made it easier to access the different websites that had started to appear. Soon websites contained more than just text, they also had sound and video files.

So, what is the WWW today? Essentially, the WWW is a collection of host machines that deliver documents, graphics and multi-media to users via the Internet or an Intranet. Pages or files are stored on Web Servers. Users access these pages using a graphical browser like Netscape Navigator or Internet Explorer. Pages can include graphics, sound, movies and other media rich content, as well as references to other pages on the same site or other sites.

The following events take place when client requests a document or file from a www server:

- A connection is made to that computer using the HTTP (Hyper Text Transfer Protocol).

- The WWW server services the request, locates the information, and sends it back to the client.
- The connection between the client and the WWW is released.
- The Client browser software interprets the retrieved HTML document and formats it on the client computer's screen.

**Hyperlinks**

To another document or resource a hyperlink is a clickable link. In blue underline it is normally shown. When a user clicks on this link, the client will retrieves the document associated with that link, by requesting the document from the designed server upon which it resides.

**Uniform Resource Locator (URL)**

For any resource on the Internet or an Intranet URL is a means of specifying the pathname. It consists of three parts:

- a protocol part
- a host part
- a document name

For instance, the following URL

http://www.cit.ac.in/smac/csware.htm

specifies the protocol as http, the host or WWW server as www.cit.ac.in and the document as /smac/csware.htm.

Internet browser or browser is the tool used to view these web pages on Internet. It is a software program specifically developed to extract information on user request from the Internet and present it as a Web Page. There are several browsers available in the market. However, the most popular are Internet Explorer from Microsoft and Netscape from Netscape inc. To view information on Internet, the process of using browser is known as browsing or surfing.

**What is web page?**

A web page is a document that contains information (text, images, sound, video and links) to be displayed and instructions on how to format that information on the screen. The format instructions are called HTML, tags, and are simple instructions that inform the web browser as to how the information should be displayed.

By the web browser HTML tags are net displayed by using a simple text editor a web page can be written such as Notepad by incorporating the formatting information using HTML tags. The page is then saved and stored on a web server. When you access that page on a web server by entering the URL of the page, it is downloaded by your web browser and then all the HTML tags are interpreted and the information displayed accordingly.

The beginning document of a website is normally called default. htm or index. htm and a web page typically has the file extention .htm.

**What do you use to write a web page?**

As described above, a web page can be written using a simple text editor such as Notepad. You have to know the HTML command tags inorder to specify how the information is to be formatted this is the problem using Notepad. There are other editors that allow you to write HTML web pages in WYSIWYG (what you see is what you get, pronounced whiz-ee-wig) format, such as Microsoft Word, Frontpage express and Frontpage 2000, Dreamweaver and Hotmetal Pro.

To produce HTML pages much quicker than using Notepad is the advantage of using a sophisticated editor and many of these editors can produce complex HTML code simply and quickly.

**What is HTML?**

A series of tags enclosed in <and> brackets to HTML. For example, <HEAD> is an HTML tag that defines a head section of an HTML document & <> are the reserved characters which are interpreted as HTML codes. Each HTML page adheres to a basic structure.

**What are the advantages of the WWW?**

By using clickable links the WWW allows users to link documents together. The browser automatically displays the documents correctly formatted along with the graphic images or additional multimedia components that the author of the page wishes to incorporate.

Some of the advantages of the WWW are:

- Easy linking of documents to other documents.
- Content is simple to create and make available for use.
- Support for mixed multimedia components in a single documents (such as text, images, sound).
- Open standards.
- Accessible to anyone connected to the Internet with an appropriate web browser.
- Facilitates the publication, dissemination and sharing of information on a global basis.

**Usenet News**

To post and reply to messages in certain categories by the users usenet news is a large discussion type service. It is great way to ask questions and communicate with people of similar interests.

News is held on a news server and is connected to the Internet and from other new servers it gets news articles. Any new messages that local users write are forwarded from the local news server to the next level up, and so on, until the message propagates to all other news servers in the world.

As you might expect, this can generate a large amount of information traffic. For the organization of news, these articles are placed into groups. There is a hierarchy of groups, illustrated below:

| | |
|---|---|
| alt | alternate lifestyles |
| biz | business companies |
| comp | computers |
| misc | miscellaneous |
| rec | recreational |
| soc | social issues |

In addition, there are also country specific and organization specific news groups. To read news you require a news-reader client and access to a news server. NMTP protocol that runs on top of TCP/IP is used by the news.

**File Transfer Protocol (FTP)**

An Internet utility software use to upload and download files is called file transfer protocol (FTP). On remote computers it gives access to directories or folders and allows data software and text files to be transferred between different hide kind of computers. FTP works on the basis of same principle as that of Client/Server. FTP "Client" is a program running on the your computer that enables you to talk to, and get stuff from, remote computers. The FTP client takes FTP commands and sends them as requests for information from the remote computer or known as ftp servers. To access remote FTP server it is required but not necessary to have an account in the FTP server. FTP server asks for the identification in terms of user login name and password, when the FTP client gets connected. If you do not have an account in the remote FTP server, you can connect to the server using anonymous login.

Using anonymous login anyone can login in to an FTP server and can access public file archives, anywhere in the world, without having an account. One can easily Login to the FTP site with the username anonymous and e-mail address as password.

The important features of FTP are:

- For useful files and programs FTP servers provide a storage place.
- You can login on to these servers and download the files to your local computer.
- You have to know the server name and where the file is located (subdirectory and filename).
- It is driven by the command such as-open, bye, get.
- It is hard to see the general structure or layout of any FTP server.

The basic objectives of FTP session are:

- To give flexibility and promote sharing of computer programs, files and data.
- To transfer data reliably and more efficiently over network.

- To encourage implicit or indirect use of remote computers using internet.
- To shield you from variations in file storage systems among hosts.

The basic steps in an FTP session are:

- Start up your FTP client; by typing FTP on your system's command line/'C>' prompt (or, if you are in a Windows, double-click on the FTP icon).
- Give the FTP client an address to connect to. This is the FTP server address to which the FTP client will get connected.
- Identify yourself to the FTP remote site by giving the Login Name.
- Give a password to the remote site.
- To allow the FTP client to acces its files remote site will verify the Login Name/password.
- Look directory for files in FTP server.
- Change Directories if required.
- Set the transfer mode (optional);
- Get the file(s) you want; and
- Quit.

**Telnet**

To login and run programs on a remote server on the Internet Telnet is a service allows yout to do that. On the Telnet server this requires a user account (name and password). On the user computer, a Telnet client application is run, similar to the FTP command interface discussed earlier.

The general features of Telnet are:

- You login using a specific account and password.
- You run programs on the host computer.
- On your own computer you see the program output.
- Telnet is interactive.
- You must know the commands and what programs are available.

To the host computer all commands you type are sent and executed there to which you are connected. On your local computer you can see the programs output. In this way, it is possible for you to run programs on a much more powerful computer than your own, or run software which may not be present on your own local computer.

The followings steps are required for a Telnet session.

- Start up the TELNET program;
- An address should be given to the TELNET program; to connect to (some really nifty TELNET packages allow you to combine steps 1 and 2 into one simple step!);
- Make a note of what the "escape character" is;
- Log onto the remote computer;
- Set the "terminal emulation";
- Play around on the remote computer; and
- Quit

## Using Internet Explorer 5.5

A web browser produced by the Microsoft Corporation is Internet Explorer.

## The Main Browser Window

The main screen of the program will appear when IE 5.5 is first opened up on your computer. This main window has many parts to it, these parts are described in detail below:

The main screen of the program will appear when IE 5.5 is first opened up on your computer. this main window has many parts to it, these parts are described in detail below:

1. **"Title Bar"** at the very top of the window tells you what the title of the page you are viewing is and what IE application is currently active.
2. **"Main Menu Bar"** has many different sub-menus that control all options, functions and commands for the entire IE program. In these sub-menus some of the browsing controls can also be found.

"**Internet Explorer Toolbar**" contains all of the most frequently used commands and all of the browsing functions.

3. "**Address Bar**" tells you the exact TTTP/URL location of the page you are currently viewing. You can also type a Web address directly into this bar and then press enter to got to that site.
4. "**Link Bar**" takes you to pages at Microsoft's main home site where they have applications and information specifically designed for your easy use.
5. "**Main Browser Window**" displays all of the information that is located at the Web site you are currently located at. In this window any text, animation, movies, images, links or any other application files will be shown. the scroll bars located on the right side and on the bottom of this window allow you to continue viewing the page you are located at even when the page is too large to fit in your screen.

**The Toobars**

At the top of the browser window IE 5.5 has two toolbars. These toolbars contains short cuts for menu commands in the form of buttons. They make browsing faster and easier.

**Menu Bar**

Contains menu items that open up dropdown lists for related options. Among the items are options for printing, customizing IE 5.5, copying and pasting text, managing Favorites, and accessing Help.

**Internet Explorer Toolbar**

This tool bar is also called the navigating tool bar. It contains icons for a variety of features including navigating among Web pages, searching the Web using a selection of search tools, accessing and managing Favorites, viewing a History of visited pages, printing, and accessing email and newsgroups.

(i) **Back**-If you want of view the pages which you previously viewed it lets you to do that, beginning with the recently visited. With IE 5.5, right-click the Back button and select from a list of recently visited sites.

(ii) **Forward**-Lets you move forward through pages you've viewed using the Back button. With IE 5.5, right-click the Foward button and select from a list of recently visited site.

(iii) **Stop**-While a page is in the process of loading the circle containing the X will stop a page. This is useful of a page is not successfully or speedily retrieving. Try downloading it again or browse elsewhere.

(iv) **Refresh**-the square containing the two curved arrows re-retrieves the page you are currently viewing. If the page does not load successfully or completely this button is useful. It updates any Web page stored in your disk cache with the latest content when you return to a page that you've visited. This saves download time.

(v) **Home**-Returns you to your home page. You can designate any Web page as your home page.

(vi) **Search**-Displays a choice of popular Internet search engines in the left pane. Your search results appear in the left pane, too. The page appears in the right pane, when you click a link so you don't lose right of your search results.

(vii) **Favorites**-Favorites contains the websites that you have visited that you would like to store for easy access. It recently displays a list of the sites-and, with IE 5.5, the folders, files, and servers-that you've saved as Favorites. To directly go to the item click any item. You can add, delete and organize your Favorites.

Click on the favorites and then Add to add the current web page. To choose the folder where you want to store this listing, click on Create in and choose the destination folder. At this point, you also have the option to create a new folder.

To delete a Favorite, simply right click on the item and choose Delete. Or, you can choose Organize, select the desired item, and click on the Delete button.

Click on organize to move a favorite to another folder and select the desired item & click on move to folder. Select the folder in the pop-up window where you would like to store this listing.

(viii) **Print**-Prints the page you're viewing.

(ix) **Font**-Lets you display text in a larger or smaller font with IE 5.5.

(x) **Mail**-Connects you to the Microsoft Outlook@ Express messaging and collaboration client so you can read e-mail and newsgroup messages.

(xi) **Edit**-For the page you're viewing open a file in the MS Word word-processor that contains the HTML code so you can see ad even edit it.

(xii) **Customize**-A pop-up window called "Customize Search Settings" will appear. If you choose to "Use the Search Assistant for Smart Searching", broad search topics will be displayed and the appropriate search tool will be queried. You can also opt to have IE 5.5 remember your last 10 searches so that you can easily repeat them.

## How to access resources on the Web with IE 5.5

***(i) If you have the URL (address) of a Web page***

To go directly to the page type URL. There are two ways given by IE 5.5 for doing this.

Type the URL in the Address bar at the top of the screen. To accomplish this click on the Address bar to highlight the current URL. Then type in the new URL and press the Enter key.

***(ii) If you are on Web page***

Click on

- The images or words on which the mouse pointer change their shape from an arrow to a hand and when an URL appears on the bottom of screen.
- The blue words presents on the display screen.

- The purple words on the display screen (the purple color indicates that the resource has been recently accessed on your terminal).

**Note:** The default color for text that contains a link is blue and the default color for text representing a link is purple. Today, designers of web page uses all sorts of colours to colour their links. The best way to figure out which text represents a link is to position your mouse over the words and see if the pointer shape changes from an arrow to a hand. A link is represented by the hand.

**Useful options on the menu bar**

At the top of the screen the menu bar includes some useful options:

**File/New/Window:** By using this feature you can open up a second copy of IE 5.5. To visit more than one page at a time this option allows you.

**File/Edit with:** By using the HTML editor of your choice, you can edit the current web page. Choose the editor by going back to the Menu Bar and choosing.

**Tools/Internet Options/Programs:** Software installed on your computer determined your choices.

**Edit/Find (on This Page):** To do a text search of the document on your screen IE 5.5 allows you.

**Tools/Show Related Links:** The pages that are related to the current page IE 5.5 will display.

**Saving Web documents for later use:** How to download, email, and print

***(i) Download***

1. A pop-up window will appear when you click on file/ save as (top left of screen).
2. Save in: To choose the desired drive.
3. File/Save as type: If you want to save the useful file or page you can use this option. You will need a web browser or HTML to view it, if you save the page as web page. In a word processing program such as word or Word Perfect a text file (txt) can be viewed.
4. Click on Save.

***(ii) To email***

1. On top left of the screen click on File/Send.
2. You may insert the link to the current page with in an email message or you may send the current page as an email message. Your email software will open once you make your selection. You can change the default software by going to the Menu Bar and choosing Tools/ Internet Options/Programs. You choices will be determined by software installed on your computer.

***(iii) To PRINT***

To print the whole document

1. Click on the Print icon on the Tool Bar.
2. Click on OK.

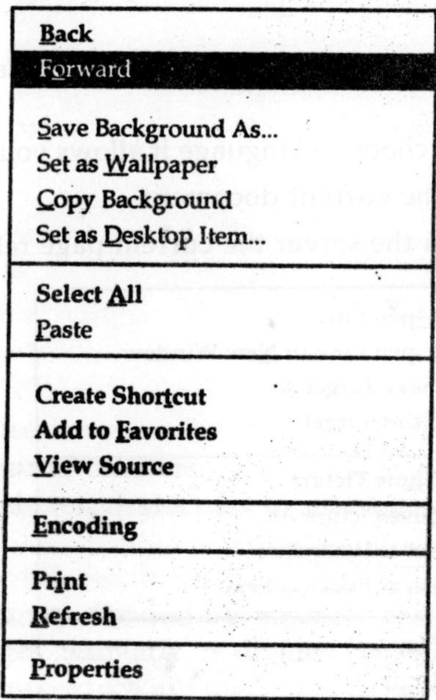


**The Right Mouse Button**

If you are using a PC a number of useful features provided by the right mouse button. Press down on the right mouse button and hold to view the possibilities. In a pop-up window options will display.

The following is a selected list of right mouse button options.

***(i) When the mouse pointer is on the screen (but not on a link or an image).***

**Back:** The previously visited page appears on the screen from your history list.

**Forward:** Moves forward to the next page in your history list.

**Select All:** All the text be selecting on the page for copying and pasting.

**Create Shorcut:** On your desktop it creates a shortcut to the current web page.

**Add to Favorites:** The current web page will added to your favorites.

**View Source:** Brings up the HTML source code of the current page.

**Encoding:** To choose a language it allows you.

**Print:** Prints the current document.

**Refresh:** Form the server the current page reloaded.

| Open Link<br>Open Link in New Window<br>Save Target As...<br>Print Target |
|---|
| Show Picture<br>Save Picture As...<br>Set as Wallpaper<br>Set as Desktop Item |
| Cut<br>Copy<br>Copy Shortcut<br>Paste |
| Add to Favorites... |
| Properties |

***(ii) When the Mouse Pointer is over a link***

**Open Link:** Opens the page.

**Open Link in New Window: The link will be opened in a new copy of IE 5.5.**

**Save Target As:** The link will be saved of IE 5.5.

**Print Target:** Prints the link.

**Copy Shortcut:** Copies the URL to the Clipboard into a text editor or word processing program.

**Add to Favorites:** The selective page will added to your favorites.

| |
|---|
| Open Link<br>Open Link in New Window<br>Save Target As...<br>Print Target |
| Show Picture<br>**Save Picture As...**<br>**Set as Wallpaper**<br>**Set as Desktop Item** |
| Cut<br>**Copy**<br>Copy Shortcut<br>Paste |
| **Add to Favorites...** |
| **Properties** |

***(iii) When the Mouse Printer is over an Image***

**Save Picture As:** To disk drive of your choice it saves the image.

**Set as Wallpaper:** Uses the image as your desktop wallpaper.

**Set as Desktop Item:** Sets the image as an Active Desktop item.

**Copy:** For pasting into a graphics aditing program it copies the images to the clipboard.

**Add to Favorites:** Adds the selected images to your Favorites.

### Tips for performing Web searches efficently

To find something on the web when you are using a search engine, it helps to find ways to narrow your search, so that it is faster and more efficient. The following are the most commonly used operators and a brief description of each. Into a search engine these would supplied along with a keyboard or phrase.

- Quotes (" "): To find the match in exact sequence in the words quotes are used around a set of words.
- Wildcard Use (*): Attaching an * to the right-hand side of a word will return partial matches to that word.
- Using Plus (+): Attaching a + in front of a word requires that the word be found in every one of the search results.
- Using Minus (–): Attaching a-in front of a word requires that the word not be found in any of the search results.

### Pine

In the university of washington pine was created it is an email program.

### Characteristics of Pine

- Across the bottom of each screen On-screen menus available options are displayed.
- Whenyou need a warning or information On-screen messages appear.
- Online help within Pine.

### Pine-Getting Started

**To start:** From menu of choices select pine or type pine as a command at the using prompt. The Main menu screen appears after starting Pine. Each Pine screen has a similar layout: the top line tells you the screen name and additional useful information, below that is the work area on the Main Menu Screen, the work area is a menu of options, then the message/prompt line, and finally the menu of commands.

**To quit:** Press Q (Quit) when you want to leave pine.

### The Main Menu

Pine's main options are the main menu lists. To enter your choice you must type the key or keys to the life of each option or command name. You do not need to press (return) and you can usually type either uppercase or lowercase letters.

From the Main Menu you can select following options:

(i) read online help.

(ii) compose and send a message.

(iii) look at an index of your mail messages.

(iv) open or maintain your mail folders.

(v) update your address book.

(vi) configure Pine and

(vii) quit Pine.

There are additional options listed at the bottom of the screen as well.

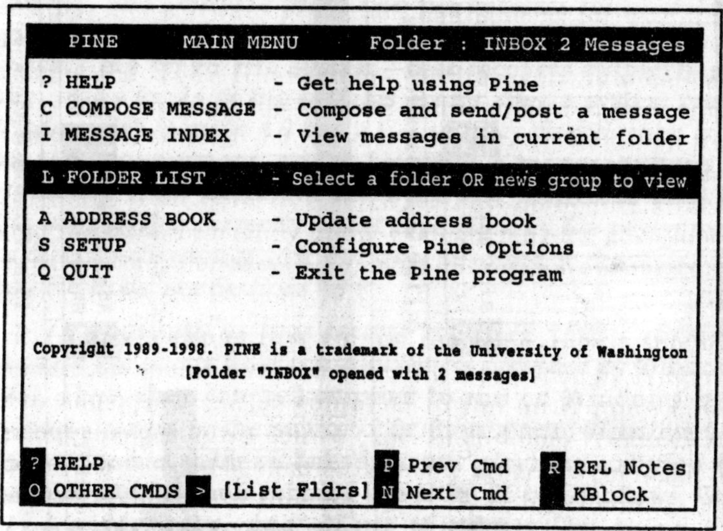


**A Pine Main Menu Screen**

## Getting Help in Pine

Use the Help command at the bottom of each screen to read the online help. For example, at the Main Menu screen press ? (Help). The help text is context-sensitive. Press E (Exit help), to exit the on line help.

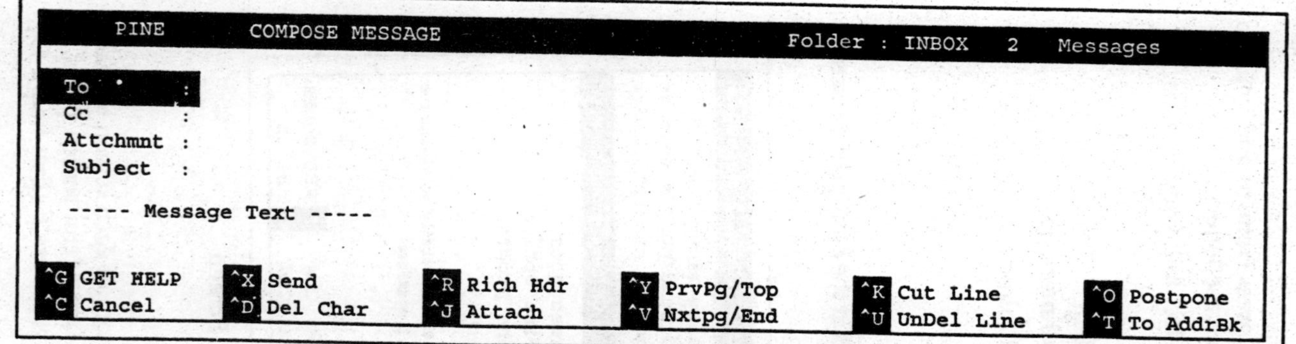


A Pine Compose Message Screen

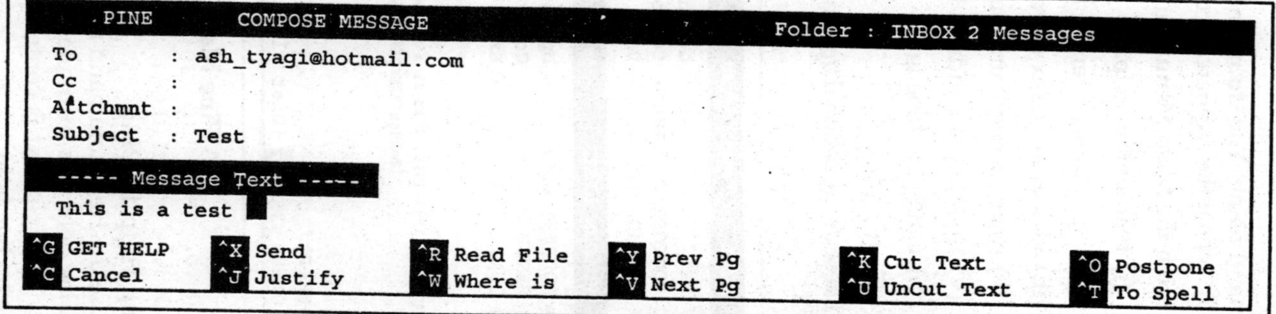


A Pine Compose Message Screen

***(ii) Writing a Message in Pine***

Press C (Compose) to write a message.

The character is used to indicate the control key in the above command menu. This character means you must hold down the Control Key while you press the letter for each command.

When your cursor is in different fields on this screen, different commands are available. Type <Control> G(Get help), to see additional commands available when your cursor is in the Message text field. To move around, use the arrow keys or <Control>N (Next line) and <Control>P (Previous line); to correct typing errors, use <Backspace> or <Delete>.

**Writing and Sending a Text Message**

To write and send a test message:

1. Press C (Compose). You see the Compose Message screen.
2. In the To field, type email address of reciepient and press <Return>.
3. In the Cc field, press <Return>.
4. In the Attachment field, press <Return>.
5. In the Subject field, type Test and press <Return>.
6. Below the Message Text line, type This is a test.

   The completed screen would look like the following example:
7. Type <Control> (send), to send your message.

   You are asked:

   Send message?
8. Press <Return> or press Y (yes).

A copy is saved to your sent mail folder and the message is sent. (If you press n (no) the message is not sent, and you can continue to work on it).

Of course there are other options that you can use as you compose a message. As you compose a message, you can type <Control>G (Get Help) at any time to see details about your current task.

**Hints for Writing a Message**

**To:** Type the mail addresses of your recipients in this field. Separate the addresses with commas. Press <Return> when you have finished.

**Finding and Formatting Addresses:** The best way to get a person's email address is to ask him or her for it. Type <Control>G (Get Help) for more information on finding and formatting email addresses on local and remote computers, while your cursor is in the To field.

**Using the Pine Address Book:** In both the To and the Cc fields, you can enter a person's email address as shown above, or you can use an entry from your pine address book.

**Cc:** In this field, type the email addresses of the persons to whom you want to send copies. Separate their addresses with commas. When you are finished, or if you do not want to send any copies, press <Return>.

**Attchmnt:** This is an advanced Pine feature that allows you to attach files, including word processing documents, spreadsheets, or images that exist on the same computer where you are running Pine. Press <Return> if you do not want to attach a file to your message.

**Subject:** Enter an on-line description of your message. Recipients appriciate a short, pertinent description, since this is what they see when they scan their index of messages. Press <Return> when finished.

**Message Text:** Type your message. Use the cursor keys to move around, Press <Backspace> or <Delete> to delete a character. Type <Control>K to delete a line. To justify text, type <Control>J. (To immediately undelete a line or to unjustify text, <Control>U). to check the spellin, type <Control>T. To see other editing commands, type <Control>G (Get Help).

**Sending a Message:** Type <Control>X, after your message is composed and then press <Return> or press Y. A copy is saved to the sent-mail folder and your message is sent. If a message cannot be delivered, it eventually is returned to you. If you want to re-send a message, you can use the F (Forward) command.

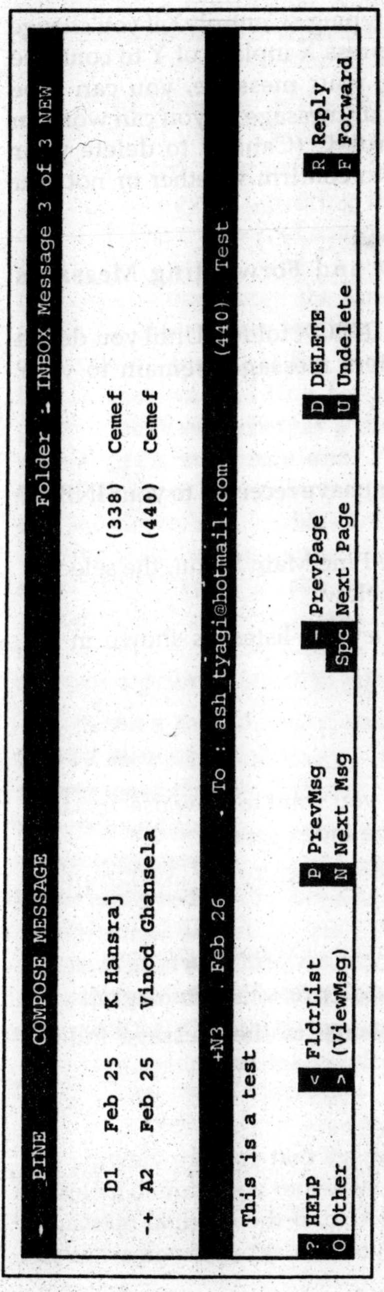

```
-  PINE      COMPOSE MESSAGE                    Folder - INBOX Message 3 of 3 NEW

   D1   Feb 25   K Hansraj                  (338)  Cemef
-+ A2   Feb 25   Vinod Ghansela             (440)  Cemef

        +N3  Feb 26      To : ash_tyagi@hotmail.com      (440)  Test
 This is a test

? HELP     < FldrList    P PrevMsg     - PrevPage    D DELETE     R Reply
O Other    > (ViewMsg)   N Next Msg  Spc Next Page   U Undelete   F Forward
```

**A Pine Message Index System**

**Changing Your Mind:** After typing <Control>X if you change your mind to send a message or press X inplace of Y to continue to work. While you are writing your message, you can type <Control>O (Postpone) to hold your message so you can work on it later, or you can type <Control>C (Cancel) to delete your message entirely. You are asked to confirm whether or not you want to cancel a message.

### Listing, Viewing, Replying to, and Forwarding Messages in Pine

Pine stores messages in your INBOX folder, Until you delete them or save them in other folders messages remain to your INBOX.

### Listing Messages

To see a list of the messages you have received to your INBOX folder:

Press I (Message Index) at the Pine Main Menu, the selected message is highlighted as shown below.

If you have any messages, they are listed as shown in the following example:

### Viewing a Message

To view a message:

(i) To highlight the message you want to view use, use this arrow keys at the message index screen.

(ii) To read a selected message press V(view msg) or press <Return>.

(iii) Press N(Next msg) to see the next message.

(iv) To see the previous message, press P (PrevMsg).

(v) To return from your message to the Message index, press I (Index).

### Replying to a Message

Press R(Reply) to reply to a messge that you are viewing or that you have selected. You are asked whether you want to include the original message in your reply. Also, if the original message was sent to more than one person, you are asked if you want to reply to all recipients.

### Forwarding a Message

At the Message Index screen to forward a message that you have selected or that you are viewing:

(i) Press F (Forward). A copy of the message opens and the To field is highlighted.

(ii) Enter the address of your recipient and send the message as usual.

### Message Index Screen

Details about the message index screen

- The selected message is highlighted.
- If the message was sent directly to you the first column on the left is blank as shows a "+", it is not a copy.
- The second column may be blank, or it may contain:
  - (i) "N" if the message is new (unread).
  - (ii) "A" if you have answered the message (using the Reply command).
  - (iii) "D" if you have marked the message for deletion.

The rest of the column in the message line show you the:

- Message number,
- Date sent,
- Sender,
- Size, and
- Subject.

### Pine folders

Just like the messages in your INBOX a folder is a collection of one or more message that are stored, so that you can access and manage them.

### Organizing Messages With Folders

Your email messages can organize into different folders by:

- topic,
- correspondent,
- date, or
- any other category that is meaningful to you.

Pine automatically provides three folders:

(i) INBOX folder-In this folder messages sent to you are listed.

(ii) Saved-messages folder-Unless you save the copies of messages to other folders which you create yourself these are stored in this folder.

(iii) Sent-mail folder-copies of messages you send are stored in this folder.

Of course, you can create your own folders as well.

## Saving a Message

Saving a Message to the Saved-Messages Folder

To save a message to your saved-messages folder.

(i) Use the arrow keys to highlight the message you want to save at the message screen or press S(save) at the message text screen as you view a message. You are asked if they want to save the message to the saved-messages folder or to another folder.

SAVE to folder in <Mail.....> [saved-messages]:

(ii) To choose the default folder (saved-messages) press <Return>.

## Saving a Message to a Folder You Specify

To create additional folders for storing message on particular subject you will find it useful. To save a message to a folder you specify:

(i) At the Message Index screen, use the arrow keys to highlight the message you want to save, or, at the Message Text screen as you view a message, press S(Save) to save a message. You are assked if you want to save it to the saved-messages folder or to another folder.

SAVE to folder in <Mail.....> [saved-messages]

(ii) Press <Return> and type a folder name. For example, to save a message to a folder named "deepprakash" type deepprakash and press <Return>. You see the message, if this is the first time you have named this folder.

Folder "deepprakash" in <Mail.....> doesn't exist. Create?

To create the folder press y or press <Return>. Once you have created the folder, or whenever you type the name of a folder that already exists, you see a message like this one:

[Message # copied to "deepprakash" in <Mail....> and deleted]

**Deleting a Message**

To deleting a messages there are two types:

Marking it for deletion and then expunging it.

To mark a message you do not want for deletion.

(i) Select and open the folder that contains the message you wish to mark for deletion.

(ii) Select the message. At the message screen that you want to mark for deletion or view the message.

(iii) Press D (Delete).

**Undeleting a Message**

To remove the deletion mark use the U(Undelete) command to any time before you expunge a message. After you expunge a message, Pine cannot get it back.

**Expunging a Message**

Until you expunge it a message that is marked for deletion remains in Pine. You can expunge a message that is marked for deletion at any time, or you can wait until you quit Pine. Once you have a few messages marked for deletion, you may want to expunge them before you continue to work.

To expunge a message:

(i) At the Message Index screen, press X(eXpunge). You are asked:

Expunge # message(s) from "foldername"?

(ii) Press Y(yes) or press <Return>. Messages marked for deletion disappear.

### Printing Messages

For printing Pine provides different options.

### Printing an Email Message

To print a message:

(i) From either the Message Index screen or the Message Text screen, press %(Print). You are asked to confirm your choice.

(ii) Follow the instructions. Type <Control>G if you still need help.

### Pine's Printing Options

There are three printing options in Pine which are available under S(Setup), P(Printer) on Pine's Main Menu screen.

1. Printing Using a Printer Attached to PC.
2. Printing Using a Standard Unix Print Command.
3. Printing Using a Personally Selected Print Command.

### Other features:

For sending, receiving and filing Internet electronic mail messages and bulletin board (USENET) messages. Pine has other useful features which make it an easy to use program.

Press S(Setup) at the Pine Main Menu to see them. You see a message asking you to choose one of the following tasks:

(i) P (Printer) to select a printer.

(ii) N (Newpassword) to change your account password.

(iii) C (Config) to allow advanced users to set different Pine configurations.

(iv) S (Signature) to create an email signature.

(v) A (AddressBooks) to work with your Address Books.

(vi) L (collectionList) to work with your Collection List.

# Chapter 6

# Programming and C

Before starting serious programs in C. First we find out what is C, how it is developed and how it is useful or beneficial as compare to other languages. In this chapter we would briefly outline these issues.

There are the three kinds of building blocks that we will discuss in this chapter which make the three important aspects of any language the 1st one, it the way of storing data, 2nd how it accomplishes input and output and the 3rd one the operators to transform and combine data. Of course, in a single chapter we can't present every aspect of each of these topics; much will remain to be said in the later chapters. However, what we discuss here will be enough to understand it well.

In the following chapters we will put these building blocks to use exploring the control statements of the language: decision, loop and case.

## WHAT IS C

In 1972 at AT & T's Bell laboratories of USA C programming language is developed. Dinnis Ritchie was designed and developed this language. In late seventies more familiar languages like PL/I, ALGOL etc. are start replaced by C. No one pushed C. It wasn't made the 'official' Bell Labs language. Thus, without any advertisement C's reputation spread and its pool of users group. So many programmers preferred C over the older languages like FORTRAN or PL/I or over the newer ones like Pascal and APL, Ritchie was surprised by this.

C is simple, easy to use and reliable that why C became so popular. Out of so many languages, PASCAL held the prize of purity, which is called the C's pretty sister. C wasn't meant to win prizes; it was meant to be friendly, capable and reliable. Therefore, some of the programmers switched to C after using PASCAL for a long time.

**Historical Development of C**

After 1960 a number of computer languages start began into seen everyone for a specific purpose. For example, COBOL was being used for Commercial Applications, FORTRAN for Engineering and Scientific Applications and so on. People started thinking at this stage whey not use only one language which can program almost all possible applications instead of using and learning separate languages for different functions. Therefore, an international committee was set up to develop such a language. A new language called ALGOL 60 was developed by this committee. However, ALGOL 60 never really became popular because it seemed too abstract, too general. To reduce this abstractness and generality, a new language called Combined Programming Language (CPL) was developed at Cambridge University. To bring ALGOL 60 down to earth CPL waas an attempt. However, CPL turned out to be so big, having so many features, that it was hard to learn and difficult to implement.

To solve this problem by bringing CPL down to its basic good features Martin Richards at Cambridge University developed the Basic Combined Programming Language (BCPL). But unfortunately it turned out to be too less powerful and too specific. As a further simplification of CPL Ken Thompson at AT & T's Bell Laboratories wrote another language called B. But like BCPL, B too turned out to be very specific. Ritchie inherited the features of B and BCPL, added some of his own and developed C. The restoration of the lost generality in BCPL is the main acheivement of Ritchie and still keeping it powerful.

C's compactness and coherence is mainly due to the fact that it's a one man language. PASCAL LISP and APL are the one man language. Counter examples include many headed monsters like PL/I, ALGOL 60 and ADA. Figure 6.1 shows the various stages in evolution of C language.

| *Year* | *Language* | *Developed by* | *Remarks* |
|---|---|---|---|
| 1960 | ALGOL | International<br><br>Committee | Too general, too abstract |
| 1963 | CPL | Cambridge University | Hard to learn, difficult to implement |
| 1967 | BCPL | Martin Rechards at Cambridge University | Could deal with only specific problems |
| 1970 | B | Ken Thompson at AT & T | Could deal with only specific problems |
| 1972 | C | Dennis Ritchie at<br><br>AT & T | Lost generality of BCPL<br>and B restored |

**Fig. 6.1**

### Where C Stands

Now we compare C with other programming languages. All the programming languages can be divided into two categories.

(a) Problem oriented languages or High level languages: To give a better programming efficiency these languages have been designed, i.e. faster program development. FORTRAN, PASCAL and BASIC etc are the languages falling in this catagory.

(b) Machine oriented languages or Low level languages: To give a better machine efficiency these languages have been designed, i.e. faster program execution. Machine language and Assembly Language are the languages falling in this catagory.

'C' is often called a middle level language because it stands between these two catagories. Since it was designed to have both: a relatively good programming efficiency (as compared to Machine oriented languages) and a relatively good machine efficiency (as compared to Problem oriented languages).

## Getting Started with C

Speaking a language which also understand by the computer is the main point to start communication with the computer which immediately rules out English as the language of communication with computer. In between learning C language and learning English language there is a close analogy. The classical method of learning English is to first learn the alphabets or characters used in the language, then learn to combine these alphabets to form words, which in turn are combined to form sentences and sentences are combined to form paragraphs. Learning C is similar and much more easy.

Firstly we must know what numbers, alphabets and special symbols are used in C and then how using these alphabets, variables constants and keywords are formed by combining these and finally how the instructions are constructed rather then learning straight how to write programs in 'C'. A group of instructions would be combined later on to form a program.

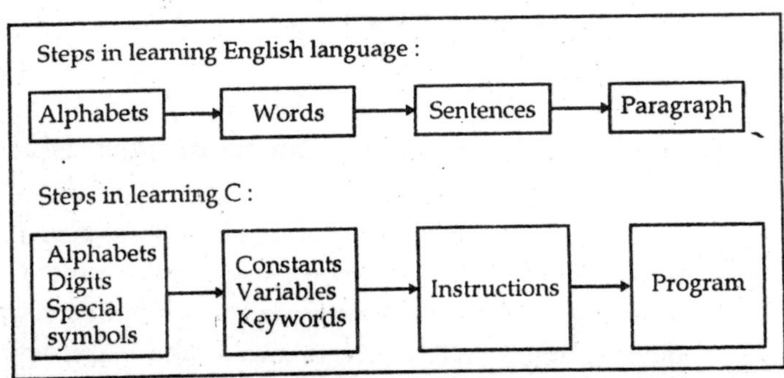


**Fig. 6.2**

## The C character Set

Any alphabet, special symbol or digit used to represent information denotes a character. Following table shows the valid alphabets, numbers and special symbols allowed in C.

## Constants, Variables and Keywords

Constants, variables and keywords are formed when the alphabets, numbers and symbols are properly combined. Let us see what are 'constants' and 'variables' in C. A constant is a quantity that doesn't change. In the memory locations of the computer these quantities can be stored. A variable can be considered as a name given to the location in memory where this constant is stored. Naturally the contents of the variable can change. For example in the equation.

5X+Y = 30

Since 5 and 30 cannot change, they are called constants, where as the X & Y can vary so they are called variables.

| Alphabets | A, B, ....., Y, Z<br>a, b, ....., y, z |
|---|---|
| Digits | 0, 1, 2, 3, 4, 5, 6, 7, 8, 9 |
| Special Symbols | ~ ' ! @ # % ^ & * () _ - + =<br>\| \ {} [] : ; " ' < > , . ? / |

**Fig. 6.3**

To be able to write error free programs, we will now take up a detailed discussion about the different fundamental elements of C language, viz. constants, variables and keywords. Possibly, and absolutely clear. The single most important factor contributing towards writing error programs is the understanding about the constants, variables and keywords and their interactions.

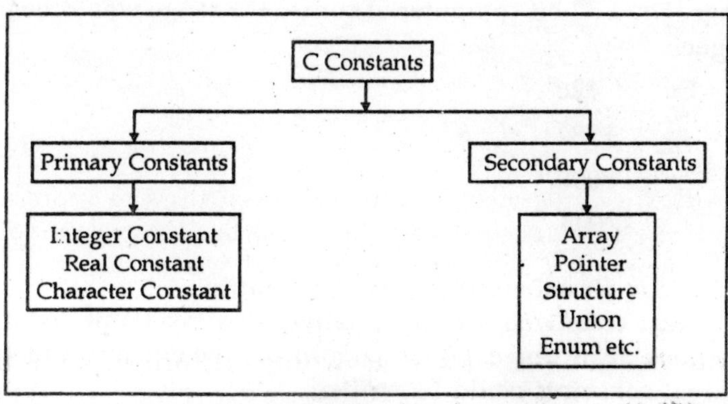


**Fig. 6.4**

## Types of C Constants

In to two major catagories C constants can be divided:

(a) Primary Constants

(b) Secondary Constants

To only primary constants, namely, Integer character and Real constants we would restrict our discussion at this stage. Let us see the details of each of these constants. Certain rules have been laid down for constructing these different types of constants. These rules are as under:

## Rules for Constructing Integer Constants

(a) An integer constant must have at least one digit.

(b) It must not have a decimal point.

(c) It could be either positive or negative.

(d) It is assume to be positive if no sign precides an integer constant.

(e) With in an integer constant no commas or blanks are allowed.

(f) The allowable range for integer constants is-32768 to + 32767.

Because the IBM compatible micro-computers are usually 16 bit computers which cannot support a number falling outside the above range so the Integer constants must fall within this range. For a 32 bit computer of course the range would be much larger.

Ex : 426

+782

-8000

-7605

## Rules for Constructing Real Constants

Real constants are often called Floating Point constants. Fractional form and exponential form are the two forms in which the real constants could be written.

While constructing real constants expressed in fractional form following rules must be observed.

(a) A real constant must have atleast one digit.

(b) It must have a decimal point.

(c) It could be either positive or negative.

(d) Default sign is positive.

(e) No commas or blanks are allowed within a real constant.

Ex.:+325.34

426.0

-32.76

-48.5792

If the value of the constant is either too small or too large then the exponential form of representation of real constants is usually used. It however doesn't restrict us in any way from using exponential form of representation for other real constants.

The real constant is represented in two parts in exponential form of representation. The part appearing before 'e' is called mantissa, whereas the part following 'e' is called exponent.

During construction of real constants expressed in exponential form following rules must be observed.

(a) The mantissa part and the exponential part should be separated by a letter e.

(b) The mantissa part may have a positive or negative sign.

(c) Default sign of mantissa part is positive.

(d) The exponent must have at least one digit which must be a positive or negative integer. Default sign is positive.

(e) Range of real constants expressed in exponential form is-3.4e38 to 3.4e38

**Rules for Constructing Character Constants**

(a) A character constant is either a single alphabet, a single digit or a single special symbol enclosed within single inverted commas. Both the inverted commas should point to the left. For example, 'A' is a valid character constant whereas 'A' is not.

(b) The maximum length of a character constant can be 1 character.

## Types of C Variables

A variable is a quantity which may vary during program execution. In the memory of computer variable names are names given to locations where different constants are stored. These locations can contain integer, real or character constants. On the types of constants that it can handle the types of variables that it can support depends, in any language. This is because a constant stored in a location with a particular type of variable name can hold only that type of constant. For example, a constant stored in a memory location with an integer variable name must be an integer constant, one stored in location with a real variable name must be a real constant and the one stored in location with a character variable name must be a character constant.

For constructing different types of constants the rules are different. However, for constructing variable names of all types the same set of rules apply. These rules are given below.

## Rules for Constructing Variables Names

(a) A variable name is any combination of 1 to 8 alphabets, digits or underscores. Some compilers allow variable names whose length could be upto 40 characters. Still, it would be safer to stick to the rule of 8 characters.

(b) An alphabet must be the first character in the variable.

(c) Within variable name No commas or blanks are allowed.

(d) In a variable name no special symbol other than an underscore can be used.

For all the types of primary and secondary variables these rules remain same. Naturally, the question follows....how is C able to differentiate between these variables? This is a rather simple matter. By making it compulsory for you to declare the type of any variable name which you wish to use in a program C compiler is able to distinguish between the variable names. This type declaration is done at the beginning of the program.

An enormous number of variables names can be constructed using the afore-mentioned rules since the maximum length of a variable name is 8 characters. It is good practice to exploit this enormous choice in naming variables by using meaningful variable names.

Thus, if we want to calculate simple interest, it is always advisable to construct meaningful variable names like prin, roi, noy to represent Principle, Rate of interest and Number of years rather than using the variables a,b,c.

## C Keywords

The words whose meaning has already been explained to the C compiler are called the keywords. The keywords cannot be used as variables names because if we do so we are trying to assign a new meaning to the keyword, which is not allowed by the computer. To construct variables names which exactly resemble the keywords some compilers allow you. However, it would be safer not to mix up the variable names and the keywords. The keywords are also called 'Research words'.

In C there are only 32 keywords, here is the list of keywords used in C. A detailed discussion of each of these keywords would be taken up in later chapters wherever their use is relevant.

| | | | |
|---|---|---|---|
| auto | double | if | static |
| break | else | int | struct |
| case | enum | long | switch |
| char | extern | near | typedef |
| const | float | register | union |
| continue | far | return | unsigned |
| default | for | short | void |
| do | goto | signed | while |

**Fig. 6.5**

## C Instructions

After gaining knowledge about the different types of constants, variables and keywords the next step is to learn their combination to form instructions. These are basically four types of instructions in C:

(a) Type Declaration Instruction

(b) Input/Output Instruction

(c) Arithmetic Instruction

(d) Control Instruction

The purpose of each of these instructions is given below:

| | | |
|---|---|---|
| (a) Type declaration instruction | - | to declare the type of variables used in a C program. |
| (b) Input/Output instruction | - | to perform the function of supplying input data to a program and obtaining the output results from it. |
| (c) Arithmetic instruction | - | to perform arithmetic operations between constants and variables. |
| (d) Control instruction | - | to control the sequence of execution of various statements in a C progam. |

The type declaration and the arithmetic instruction are usually contained by the elementary C programs so here we discuss only these two instructions. The other types of instructions would be discussed in detail in the subsequent chapters.

### Type Declaration Instruction

To declare the type of variables being used in the program this instruction is used. Before using it in any statement any variable used in the program must be declared. The type declaration statement is usually written at the beginning of the C program.

## ALGORITHMS

The method of solving a given problem as a sequence of well-defined steps is called an algorithms. The steps must be such that they can be easily implemented in a computer program, in case of a computer algorithm. The sequence has to be rigorously followed. Otherwise, the solution will not be correct.

You have to code it in a computer programming language once you know the algorithm. You can provide it to the processor for execution because this is now a computer program. Errors in solution of the problem arise either when you do not perform the right steps or you do not perform them in the correct sequence.

**Consider the following problem:** On a knock out basis a tournament is being played. In this tournament there are 16 teams. How many matches are played?

- A little arithmatic shows that there are 15 matches this can be calculated as follows: 16 teams will be divided into eight pairs for the first round. So there will be eight matches.
- After this eight teams (winners) shall remainl. So in the next round there will be four matches.
- Then two and then one.

So there will be fifteen matches. Similarly, for 32 teams there are 31 matches. You might have guessed that for a teams, there will be n-1 matches. How do you prove this? One way of proving this is by mathematical induction. After each match one team gets out this is the another way to recognize it. Only one team remains when this tournament is over. Therefore, there are n-1 matches. This insight makes it very easy to solve the problem.

For performing a particular task there may be several algorithms. Some of them are more useful than the others. For a given a problem a programmer is one who is able to identify the best possible algorithm. No amount of coding expertise can really offset the bad performance of an unsuitable algorithm.

It must terminate in a finite time is the important features of an algorithm. Every computational procedure is not an algorithm. Consider the following problems:

(i) Find the smallest integer that cannot be represented as a sum of squares of three integers.

(ii) Find the smallest integer that cannot be represented as a sum of squares of four integers.

The answer to (i) can easily be found. Start from 1 and work upwards and find how each number can be represented as a sum of squares of three numbers by trying various combinations possible for each number. You would find that 7 is the smallest such number. But if the same method is tried for the (ii) then the procedure does not terminate. You will not be able to find any number satisfying the requirement posed. The reason is that it can be shown that no such integer exists. It may be a well-defined step-by-step procedure but every computational procedure is not an algorithm.

The important features of an algorithm are:

(i) **Definiteness:** An algorithm must have a single output for a particular input.

(ii) **Specified input:** The input to the algorithm must be clearly specified.

(iii) **Specified output:** The output of the algorithm must be clearly specified.

(iv) **Finiteness:** The algorithm must terminate in a finite time.

(v) **Correctness:** The algorithm must provide the correct answer for the problem for which it is designed.

In the overall programming effort the importance of algorithm developed cannot be overemphasised. Before you actually write the code you must take sufficient care to come up with a suitable logic and proram design. Do not worry over the time spent by you in understanding the problem and coming up with a suitable and efficient algorithm for its solution. This effort would be paying for itself many times over in terms of the simplified code development and program maintenance. To make the task of visualising the aalgorithm for any problem easier, several methods and tools have been developed. You shall now learn some of these methods.

## FLOWCHARTS AND FLOWCHARTING

For the solution of a given problem flowcharts are a convenient way of expressing the alogrithm. They are easy to understand because they are a pictorial representation. Thus, they serve the purpose of documentation as well as aid understanding of the allgorithm.

A general chart to reveal the overall purpose and structure of the application is created in developing application software which is usually called system flowchart or application flowchart.

To describe how each program is to be developed more detailed flowcharts are created. This type of flowchart is called a program flowchart.

Some standard symbols are used as per convention for describing the various steps is a flowchart. the sue of standard symbols aids in understanding of the steps as their role is known.

## FLOWCHART SYMBOLS

**Terminal**

The terminal symbol, is used to indicate the starting (BEGIN), stopping(END), and pause(HALT) in the program logic flow. It is the first and also the last symbol in the program logic. In addition, if the program logic calls for a pause in the program, that is also indicated with a terminal symbol.

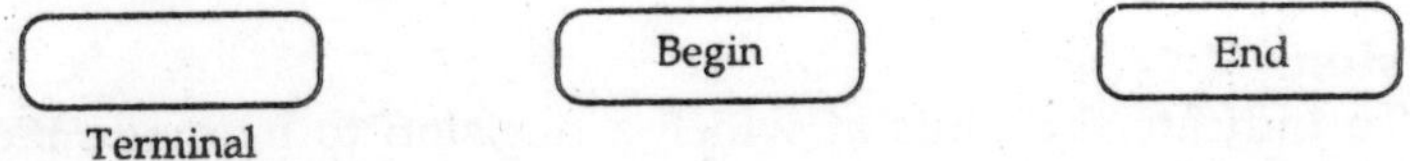

Terminal

**Input/Output**

To denote any function of an input/output device in the program the input/output symbol is used. If there is a program instruction to input data from any input device, the step will be indicated in the flowchart using an input/output symbol. Similarly, all output instructions, are indicated in the flowchart using an output symbol.

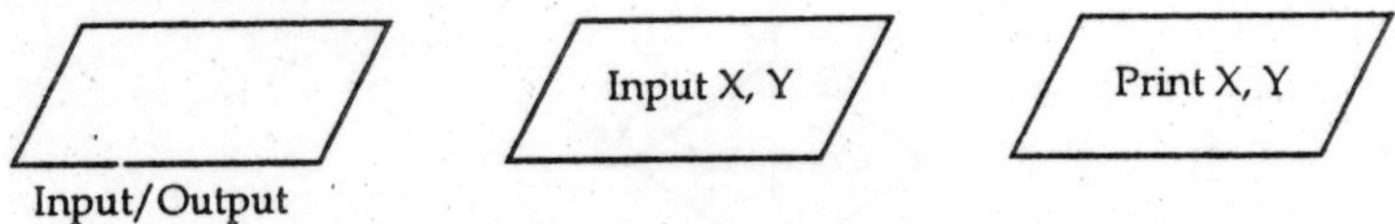

Input/Output

**Processing:** To represent arithmatic and data movement instructions a processing symbol is used in a flowchart. By a processing symbol, all arithmatic processor such as addition, substraction, multiplication adn division are shown. The logical process of moving data from one location in the memory to another is also shown by this symbol. When more than one arithmatic and data movement instructions are to be executed consecutively, they are normally placed in the same processing box and they are assumed to be executed in the order of their appearance.

**Flowlines:** To indicate the flow of operations flow-lines with arrowheads are normally used, that is, the exact sequence in which the instructions are to be executed. The normal flow of flowchart is from the top to bottom and from the left to right. When the normal top to bottom flow is not be followed only then arrowheads are required. However, as a good practice to avoid confusion, flowlines are usually drawn with an arrowhead at the point of entry to a symbol. The flowlines should not cross each other is a good practice and such intersections should be avoided.

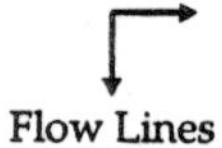

Flow Lines

## Decision

To indicate the pints at which a decision to be made the decision symbol is used as well as where the text or more althernatives are possible. The criteria for making the decision are indicated within the box. Moreover, the condition upon which each of the possible exit paths well be executed are identified and all the possible paths are accounted for. The appropriate path is followed during execution depending upon the result of the decision.

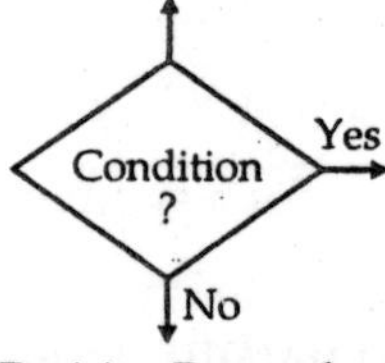


Decision Demand

## Connector

The flow lines begin to crisscross each other if a flowchart becomes very long. This causes confusion regarding the actual program flow and reduces the readability of the flowchart. Further, if the flowchart is so long that it does not fit in a single page, it is not possible to use flowlines to show the program flow. As a subsitute for the flowlines in each of these cases it is useful to use the connector symbol. The symbol represents an entry from or an exit to another part of the flowchart. A connector symbol represented by a circle and to indicate a the link a letter or a digit is placed within the circle. To indicate a continued flow when a flowline is confusing a pair of indentically labelled connector is used. So two connectors with the same label serve the same purpose as a long flowline. that is, they show an exit to some other chart section, or they show an entry from some other chart section. How do you know whether the connector is an entry point or an exit point? If an arrow enters but does not leave a connector, it is used as an exit point and the program control is transferred to an identically labelled connector. You must realize that the connectors are used only for improving the clarity and do not indicate any processing.

There can be various levels of detail in both program and system flowcharts. A flowchart that shows less detail is a macroflowchart whereas a flowchart that shows more detail is called a microflowchart.

There are a number of general guidelines recommended by the ANSI (American National Standards Institute) while programmers and systems analysts have a good deal of freedom, to help standardise and flowcharting process. These are used by convention to make the flowcharts more readable and easily understandable.

Some of these are:

(i) Go from left to right and from top to bottom of the page in constructing the flowchart.

(ii) When a reference for a symbol is needed, place it above the symbol.

(iii) If a new flowcharting page is needed, break the flowchart as an input or an output file.

(iv) Use an annotation symbol when a more detailed explanation is needed.

(v) Words in the flowchart symbols should be common English words and easy to understand.

(vi) Maintain a consistant level of detail for a given flowchart.

(vii) Keep the flowchart as simple as possible and avoid flowcharting lines that cross or loop.

(viii) Be consistent in using names and variables in a flowchart.

Flowcharts were originally developed to help programmers and analysis design and document computer programs. Flowcharts became more difficult to implement as programs became larger. The flowcharts that have been drawn in this book to illustrate the process of drawing and using them are quite small and easily fit in a single page of the book. Thus, they are not very difficult to draw or read. But imagine that you were required to develop a detailed flowchart for a program that contains over 50,000 lines of code. It is clear that it is very difficult to draw due to its containts cover several pages and the process become lethargic. Further, its utility is questionable because no one would be able to make sense out of such a long document of lines and boxes. To depict the logic which can be described in a few symbols the flowcharts are used e.g. for depicting the algorithm within a particular module.

**Other Tools for Program Design and Development**

For designing and developing programs for a given application, there are several standard tools. In developing the program logic for your problem you can use these with advantage. You shall now look at some standard terms that are used in this context.

(i) Structural design.

(ii) Structural Programming.

(iii) Structural Flowcharts.

(iv) Pseudo-code.

(v) Top down approach.

(vi) Bottom up approach.

*(i) Structural Design*

To find the best way to develop better software is the objective of structured design. This software should cost less to develop and maintain and should be easy to modify over time. The approach of structured design is to break a large and difficult problem into smaller problems that are simple enough to manage and handle but independent enough to solve separately.

Programmer productivity can also improved by structured design a number of specific advantages are possible with structured design over the more traditional approaches to application development. These advantages include:

(a) Better ability to meet customer or user needs.

(b) More reliable total project cost estimates.

(c) More reliable total project completion date.

(d) Improved project scheduling and planning.

(e) Less expense in implementation and testing.

(f) Less expenses in maintenance.

(g) More reliability and flexibility.

*(ii) Structured Programming*

A way of standardising using the existing computer programming languages and not a new language is structured programming. One of the objectives of structured programming is to untangle computer programs. You might have learnt to program in BASIC or COBOL in school. To comprehend the concepts outlined in this section in such a case would be easier for you. Even if you have not programmed in any language and the material in this section is difficult to comprehend at this stage you can always come back after having read the subsequent chapters.

The main problem was the extensive use of goto statement to control the flow of program in the desired fashion with the BASIC, COBOL and FORTRAN. To execute the next statement to the statement mentioned in the goto statement this is used. It is very difficult to discern the control flow or the sequence in which the statements in the program are written and executed because they seen as criss-cross forward and backwards in the code. There will be a lots of arrows showing where to go next in case a conditioned is fullfilled or not fullfilled in terms of the flowcharts that you have seen above. In fact, it will remind you of tangled web of noodles and is also referred to as "spaghetti code". It is very difficult to comprehend the logic of such a flowchart.

This causes lot of difficulty in program maintenance, as the person attempting the maintenance cannot fathom the extent of code that would be affected by the changes that he makes. The use of programming technique in which the use of goto is reduced encouraged by the structured programming.

A program can be broken down into independent groups of statements with only one entry and one exit point from the group is the basic idea behind structured programming. These groups are formed according to their functional and there is no restriction or size that how many statements can be in a group. One group may read the data while another may perform a certain processing task.

The statements must confirm to a certain standardised pattern or structure when using structured programming approach. There are only one entry point into a block of statements to begin with and only one exit point. Therefore, you cannot branch to or from a structured group of statements. To debug the programs much easier this restriction eliminates many programming errors. Furthermore, there should not be any groups of statements that cannot be reached or executed. Each group can be tested separately by using the structured programming approach. What structures or patterns are allowed when using structured programming approach? There can be only three types-sequence, decision and loop.

There must be starting and ending point in the sequence structure. The program statements are executed one after another until all the statements in the sequence have been executed after starting the sequence. Then the program continues another sequence.

The control to branch allowed by the decision structure depending upon certain conditions. Only two possible branches are present there. As we know, there is a starting and ending point with all decision structures. The ending point is same regardless of which branch is taken.

Loop is the final structure. There are two commonly used structures for the loop. One of them is do....while and other is do...until structure both are used for the same thing. In the do...until structure, the loop is executed until a certain condition is met. For the do..while structure, the loop is executed while a certain condition exists.

The syntax rules of programming construction are designed to ensure that only those programs are construct which follow the rules of program construction, in modern programming language. For example, when you look at the constructs that C provides you shall see that its programming constructs are primarily of the three types outlined above. Thus, you, as a programmer, are constrained to write programs that are structured to a large extent. To enable you to have the flexibility desired by you, there are a few exceptions e.g. to terminate the program on certain exceptional conditions.

***(iii) Structured flowcharts***

For constructing flowcharts that is especially suited for the structured programming, structured flowcharing is the way. The structured flowchart has a definite starting and end point first like in structured programming. Furthermore, there are three basic forms of drawing the structured flowcharts that correspond to the sequence, decision and loop structure.

***(iv) Pseudo-code***

It is very tedious process for creating flowcharts containing several steps. In such a situation, it is preferable to express the program logic in a form that is very similar in structure to the constructs in programming described above but containing more English-like statements that are easier to understand. As a tool in the program development stage to express the problem logic and as a tool for effective program documentation this type of description is called pseudo code and is very useful. The primary advantate of pseudo-code is the flexibility of level of detail and the ease with which you can create and understand it.

Consider that you are required to compute the average of 10 given numbers. The logic for solving this problem can be expressed in the form of pseudo-code as follows:

(i) Read the 10 numbers. Let them be Xi, i = 1, ....., 10.

(ii) Sum the Xis, i = 1, ....., 10. Let the sum be called SUM.

(iii) Average, AVG = SUM/10.

(iv) Output the result as AVG.

If you have not yet learnt any programming language you can very early understand the above pseudo-code. To describe the algorithm in a cryptic but easily understandable manner you are expressions that you are familiar with. You use expressions that you are familiar with to describe the algorithm in a cryptic but easily understandable manner. More importantly, the description is clear and unambiguous although it has the look and feel of natural language.

Professional programmers and the scientific community find the pseudo-code a very effective means of communicating amongst themselves. It is very important that you know how to create and understand pseudo-code. It would be instructive for you to write the pseudo-code for all the examples given in the section on flowcharts.

*(v) Top down approach*

It is much better to "divide and conquer" by breaking the selection of a large problem into small pieces as mentioned in structured design whose solution can be visualized individually and easily coded in any programming language. The individual pieces are referred to as modules.

To start with the main module describing the overall problem solving steps and then working downwards for specifying the details of how each of these steps is to be performed is a good approach to writing a large program. This approach is called the top-down approach. this concept is simple but can prevent a lot of problems that could surface later when you are developing the code or when you are debugging.

In this approach, you begin by writing the main module. At the next level the modules are written, until all the modules are written this procedure is continued.

The top-down approach is used with advantage even in program testing and debugging in addition to coding. It is tested and debugged after the first or the main module is developed.

But the main module sends the computer to the modules at the second level, which have not been written yet. Thus, dummy modules at the second level are needed to send the execution back to the main module so it can be fully and completely tested. If any errors are found in the main module they are immediately corrected. When the main module is working satisfactorily, the dummy modules at the second level are discarded, and the actual modules at the second level are written. If one or more modules at the second level send the execution to the third level, it will be necessary to develop and use dummy modules at the third level. To use the modules at the second level the main module is necessary, the main module is again automatically tested, when the second level modules are tested and debugge. Indeed, when you test a module at any level, all of the modules above it are tested again.

The top-down approach is a very common method of implementing a structured design due to its advantages. Some of these are:

(a) The most important modules are written and tested first.

(b) It is easier for the users or the customers to see the progress being made in the project.

(c) Testing and debugging are easier and more efficient.

(d) The use of computer resources is more evenly distributed over the entire project.

(e) The implementation is normally smoother and shorter.

(f) It is easier to detect and correct time delays and cost overruns.

***(vi) Bottom-up approach***

To the top-down approach Bottom-up approach an alternative. The bottomlevel modules are written first in this approach. To test these modules, dummy driver modules are written. After the lower-level modules are written, tested and debugged, the next lowest level modules are written, tested and debugged. This process continues until all the modules have been completed. Thus, the approach is exactly opposite of what is done in the top down approach. This approach encourages the reuse of a lot of code that may be available for small functions thats why this is very useful. This is especially true with the availability of a lot of programming libraries.

## NEED FOR LANGUAGES

For aiding the programmers various developments have taken place in the compiling environments. These developments have been motivated by the necessity of making the task of the programmer more and more simple and less error-prone. To create larger and error free programs the programmer is now provided with better and better tools. So much so that error rates of one error per million lines of code have been achieved by programming teams strictly adhering to the prescribed standard practices.

An important variety of developments is in the form of the changes in the programming languages used by the programmers. The languages have developed through four generations.

### First generation languages or Machine languages

Programming in these languages was hard and the programs harder to debug as they were merely sequences of 1s and 0s or worse the computers were programmed by physically establishing the desired connections. There was virtually no support for the programmer. In order to get his work done he interacted directly with the hardware available.

### Second Generation languages or Assembly languages

In this generation easier to remember words called Mnemonics replaced the hard to remember and code machine level commands. Programming was still tedious and programs in assembly language processor dependent and, therefore, not portable.

### Third Generation Languages or High Level Languages (HLLs)

These languages are called Procedural languages because you not only have to specify in the program what is to be done but also how it is to be done. HLLs include languages like PASCAL, BASIC, COBOL, FORTRAN, C LISP, PROLOG etc. These languages are machine independent, this the main advantage over the assembly language programming and the program written for one machine can be easily transferred to another machine. Further, the syntax of the programming language reflects the terminology of the application that predominantly influenced its design. This enables the programmer to express the problem solution logic of terminology that he is more familiar with. For example:

**Common Business Oriented Language (COBOL)**

Designed for Business applications

**PASCAL:** for teaching structured programming concepts.

C: for systems programming but now ubiquitous as a general purpose programming language.

**FORMULA TRANSLATION (FORTRAN):** for numerical application.

**LISP & PROLOG:** designed for AI application.

To represent the solution of this problem in the form of a computer program the design of these languages only makes it more easy for the programmer i.e. improves the programmer's productivity. It does not in any way enhance the capability of the machine in solving the problems. It is not possible to say anything about its original language once on HLL program is converted to a machine level language by its compiler i.e. the source language in which the code was originally written.

**Forth Generation Languages (4GLs)**

The 4GLs are also called as Non-procedural languages. You only need to specify what is to be computed in these language and not hwo it is to be done. To include the details of how the task it to be done the language constructs are big enough. These are typically special purpose languages that are used as Query languages in databases and other database and simulation languages.

The languages provide building blocks that are joined together to create th programs is an important observation that can be made regarding the overall development of languages. As you go towards the 4GLs you find that the blocks are becoming larger and larger and constructing the programs and debugging them is becoming simpler and simpler. However, this is at the cost of generality and speed. Even today speed critical applications need to be coded in assembly language or at least in a middle level language like C that offers the speed and efficiency of an assembly language. 4GLs are designed for the domain in which they are easily used and not for general purpose like C. Thus, for every domain its 4GL has to be separately mastered.

Each language fulfills a certain need in its own niche area that why they coexist peacefully in the computing scenario. You, the programmer, can pick a language of your choice for your particular application. Of course, some languages like C and C++ have become more popular than the others. This is because they have features that are desired by more people. You shall now see what C language is.

"C"

**A brief history of C:** You would benefit from knowing a little about the history of C language. this would give you insight into why a particular feature of the language is the way it is. After all, there is nothing sacred about any feature that the language has. Because it fulfills a certain need so the feature has been provided. For appretiating this relationship knowledge of history of C helps you.

C is a third generation programming language or a High Level Language (HLL). It was called C as it was the next step after and influenced by Ken Thompson's 'B'. B was typeless language in which the variables were simply words in the memory. This language served the needs in its times but as software tasks grew more demanding, it became clear that something better had to be invented. To use integers ......programmers needed a structured programming language with data types. Systems programmers, especially, needed the efficiency of the assembly language without the associated coding hassles and machine dependence.

To these requirements C provided the answer. Dennis Ritchie developed it on a DECPDP 11 that used the UNIX O.S. Later on in C Unix itself was rewritten completely. Thus, C literally grew up with UNIX. But, since then, it has left the environs of UNIX to become available on a large variety of environments and a variety of machines.

In 1978, C blossomed into what was to become the most popular computer programming language ever. A book that established the standard by which all C compilers were judged written by Brian W. Kernighan and Dennis M. Ritchie (K & R) entitled "The C programming language". This language soon was a smash hit among the programming community. It was originally designed for a small subset of programmers i.e. the system programmers but the features it provided were so well liked by the programmers that the language has become the standard compilers were developed that loosely adhered to the standard as established by the K&R a program written for one computer required only minor changes to be transferred or ported to another system. To the language's next and more formal stage C's widspread use and the relative compatibility among its implementations led directly.

The American National Standards Institute charged the C Programming Language Committee to adopt a rigorous standard for the C implementation to follow in 1983.

The standard that all the compilers faithfully incorporate while adding newer and newer libraries to attract the customers remained by ANSI C which was adopted in 1988. this implies that any code developed using only the features specified in the ANSI C is sure to be portable any code that takes advantage of the additional features provided by any particular implementation is not necessarily portable.

**Special Features of C**

**1. A middle level language:** It combines elements of HLLs with the functionality of an assembly language. The incorporation of the elements of the HLLs helps the programmers to code their logic in a simple way and, thus, increases the programmer's efficiency. C code may approach the speed of the assembly language because of its efficient generation of machine code. C allows manipulation of bits, bytes and addresses-the basic elements with which the compiler functions. With assembly language routines it can also interface, due to this C is called as middle level language.

The C code is very portable as compilers are available for C over a wide range of machines.

Like any other HLL C supports data types. But it is not a strongly-typed language like PASCAL. In fact, it allows almost all type conversions.

C performs no run-time error checking such as array-bounds checking or argument type-compatibility checking. These checks are the responsibility of the programmer.

C has only 32 keywords.

2. **A structured Language:** Due to structural similarities to ALGOL & PASCAL and modula-2 C is called a structured language.

However, since C does not allow the creation of functions within functions, it is not really block-structured.

3. **The Programmer's Language:** The real working programmers created, influenced and field tested the C.

C gives you, the programmer, what you want: few restrictions, few complaints, stand alone functions and a compact set of keywords.

For system programming C was initially used. Because of its speed and other unique features it is used for all purposes now. These include graphics programming, DBMS development, scientific computations etc.

**Some myths about C and their clarification**

Because of lack of proper information or misrepresentation of facts some ideas about C and its features gained prominace in due course of time. At the very outset it is necessary to clear these myths regarding C that are encountered often. Of course, these issues are quite debatable. It is not necessary that everybody agree upon the viewpoint presented below. What is important for you is to form your own conviction regarding it.

***(i) C is more prestigious as a programming language than other languages.***

About any programming language there is nothing "Prestigious". C has become a very popular language and is being used for a variety of applications. But every language is designed for a particular application and is best for that application. So, there are languages like Simulation languages or Database Query languages that may be much more suitable for the task that they are designed for. So, a programmer cannot attempt to stick to C even for these applications just because he regards C as a "prestigious" language. The myth probably owes its origin to the fact that the language first became popular with the systems programmers. With a wide variety of programmers C has become extremely popular and is now the lingua franca of the Computer Science community. C is definitely popular but not "prestigious".

***(ii) Learning C is more difficult than learning other languages.***

There is nothing more difficult about C that is different from any other language. Because of the nature of C compiler this myth has propagated. C has been designed with the philosophy that the programmer knows what he is doing. This is because it was designed for use by systems programmers who are well trained in computer science and programming. Therefore, the compiler allows a lot of flexibility in writing the code and also several types of short hand notation etc. This flexibility is a double-edged sword. It means that the compiler accepts code with whatever syntax and interprets it appropriately even when it was not intentionally written the way it was! This makes it more difficult to predict the outcome of the program and hence debugging is sometimes more difficult. There is no reason to believe that programming in C is more difficult in comparison to other languages is such errors are avoided in the first place.

***(iii) Since C is portable language, a program that is developed in one C programming environment can be easily transferred to some other environment.***

The American National Standard Institutes 'C give the standard which is referred as ANSIC. This standard is fully implemented by TURBO C and is a fast efficient compiler which provides an integrated programming environments. It also provides a host of library functions that can be directly used by the user by including them in his program. There are other efficient and popular compilers for C also. However, all these compilers provide support for the ANSI C. Where they do differ is in the libraries that they offer. As long as only the features supported by ANSI C are used the program can be run with the help of any C compiler. However, if the program is developed in a particular environment and the special library functions provided by the a particular environment library are used, then the program will not longer be portable to other compiler environments. The special library functions is not a problem free blessing because of ease provided by programming.

### General Structure of a C Program

One or more subprograms or functions included by all C programs. The only function that must be present is called main( ). It is the first function that is called when program execution begins. The basic structure of a C program is as follows:

**The structure of a complete C program**

```
    preprocessor directives, if any
    global declarations, if any
    main ( )
    { local variables
     statements sequence
    }
/* other functions will follow. if any */
    f1( )
    { local variables
     statements sequence
    }
    f2( )
    { local variables
    statements sequence
    }
    .
    .
    fN ( )
    { local variables
     statements sequence
    }
```

The first item in the C program structure shown above is the set of preprocessor directives. To perform some required action these are commands to the preprocessor. A wide variety of preprocessor commands are available in C. You will learn about these later. For now it is sufficient to understand that the preprocessor expands the code written in the program according to the directives issued to it and then the expanded program is passed to the compiler. The compiler produces the object code of the program that is input to it. There may be references to library functions or user-defined functions that are compiled into object modules separately because of that the object code is not yet ready to run at this stage. These and the system library are linked together by the linker by resolving the references to each other and integrating them, thus creating an excutable file that can be run.

The type of every variable that is used in program declared in C because the compiler needs to be told about the global variables are declared in the program after the preprocessor directives. This enables the compiler to reserve the space meant for the variables in the memory. The type of the variable has to be specified so that compiler knows how much space is to be reserved. The global variables are so called because they can be accessed throughout the program. In contrast, the local variables declared within the main function are available only within that function. You shall learn more about this point in due course.

The algorithm designed for the problem at hand because the statements written within the main function and the other functions code. The advantage of breaking up the code into several small functions is that it improves the redability of the program. Further, the functions can be written and tested individually. As each function has only a small amount of code as compared to a program in which there is only one function called main this makes the job much easier and it has the complete code required for the program at hand.

**Summary of major points**

The main points dealth with in this section are:

- At main ( ) program execution begins.
- In lower-case keywords are written.
- With a semi-colon statements are terminated.
- Text strings are enclosed in double quotes.

- C uses lower-case and trynot to capitalize variable names thats why it is case sensitive.
- \n means position the cursor on the beginning of the next line.
- To display text to the screen print of ( ) can be used.
- The beginning and end of a program block defined by the curly braces.

You are now familiar with the basic structure of the C program and its interpretation. Before you can really begin programming on your own there are a lot of details that have to be learnt. These details shall be explained in the forthcoming chapters. Before that, however, there are a few things that you need to learn in order to be able to start using a computer to run C programs on your own.

**Preparing and Running a Complete C Program**

The development of various programming languages suitable for particular applications has made it simpler for the programmer to develop code for his problem. But this is only part of the task in running the programs. The other part is keying in the program into the machine and getting it urn to produce the results. To aid the programmer in this task several software tools have been produced. These are:

Editors

Assembles

Compilers

Interpreters

Loader and Linkers

Debuggers

Profilers

Integrated Development Environments (IDI)

The generic name of Language Processors includes Compilers, Interpreters etc.

**Editor** helps you key in the program and save it in the disk so that it may be retrieved later as per requirement.

**Assemblers** covert a program in assembly language into its equivalent machine language program.

**Compilers** are programs that covert an HLL program into its equivalent machine language program (excutable program). A C compiler reads the statements written in C language and translate these statements into machine language code in the context of C programming so that the processor understands on which the program is to be run. This process is called compilation. After compilation, the program runs as an independent application from an operating system like DOS or Windows. Professional programmers prefer to use compiled language like the C language because it lets them write high-level statements that the human can understand, but produce compiled low-level code that runs quickly on a computer.

**Interpreters** are programs that do not produce any executable file of the HLL program. Interpreter decode the HLL program line by line and for executing it provide necessary information to the processor. They are useful at the program development stage as it is possible to verify the veracity of individual instruction. However, interpreted programs are slower than the programs that are executed from the excutable file. the executably file is typically prepared and run once the program development is over.

**Loaders and Linkers** are programs that help in putting the program into the appropriate place in the RAM so that it can be executed. The connection between the modules prepared separately established by the linker. The corresponding addresses of the modules are placed in the other module and , then, they are run together as one program.

**Debuggers** are programs that help in finding the errors in the code that is being executed. With the help of debugger program runs step by step. The values of the different variables after the execution of each step are monitored and any discrepancy is noted to find out the statement that has the error.

**Integrated Development Environment** offers the services of all the above in a single program. For example to provide a unified interface to the user a compiler a debugger and editer etc. are integrated seamlessly in TURBO C which is an integrated development environment.

Apart from the above software the Operating System is a large collection of programs that provides a secure environment in which youcan execute your programs without coming in each others way and providing better utilisation of the system resources. In the first section of this book you have already locked at several OSs.

Following steps take place when you enter your C program in an integrated development environment and then run it by using run command:

(i) Your HLL program is compiled to yield the executable code.

(ii) The linker establishes the connection with the other functions or portions of code.

(iii) The executable code is loaded into the RAM.

(iv) The processor through its fetch-decode-execute cycles runs it.

### A few important terms

You shall encounter some terms repeatedly in our discussion on C programming. It is important to understand the significance of these terms at the very outset so that you are sure what you should make out when you see these terms in the subsequent sections.

- Keywords are words that are reserved by a programming language. You cannot use them in any other way that they defined in language because these words are reserved C reserves only few keywords unlike the massive keywords list that some other languages have. You would see their purpose as you go along in this book.
- Syntax refers to the rules that you must follow when writing the code. These rules are just like the grammer rules of the language. You must strictly follow the rules just as in the case of natural languages like English. However, you need not fear, as the compiler would tell you if you make up some syntax mistake. It would issue the proper message telling you about the error so that you can rectify the error and start over again.

- Semantics refers to the meanings behind C's rules of syntax. The purpose of this book is not only to tell about the syntax rules of C but also its semantics so that you can learn how to apply the language for writing the programs that perform specific tasks.
- Algorithms are best defined as "methods of solution". The step-by-step description of the solution to the problem is called an Algorithm. There are several ways of expressing an algorithm in a proper way to aid the coding effort. You have already looked at some of these in this chapter. Algorithms are usually written in pseudo-code-informal description of a program's steps that resemble actual programming which programmers can translate more or less directly into C statements.
- Library functions extend a programming language's native capabilities. Hundreds of ready-made functions for mathematics tasks included by the standard library functions provided with any C compiler string handling, file processing, date and time operations, memory management, and many other tasks.
- Source code files contain the program's statements in plain ASCII text form. You may create and edit source code files using any of the editors provided along with the modern operating systems or more easily by using the editors provided by programming environments. To identify the source code files as having C code given the extension.
- Object code files contain the program's raw instruction codes. The compiler reads one or more source code files, processes any statements that it finds, and generates object code, storing the results in files ending with the filename extensions .obj.
- Executable code files are created by linking one or more object code files, producing a new file ending with extension. EXE. Execution refers to the Running of a program. At the DOS prompt type the name of the executable file to run the program. Some programming environment also provide a means of running a program from within the environment itself.

- Compile-time refers to the time during which the compiler reads the source code files and generates the object code. A mistake in the syntax of the code being compiled is a compile-time error discovered by the compiler. The compiler in such a case issues a remark stating the error and you can then rectify it before attempting to compile the code again.
- Run-time refers to the time during which a program runs i.e. the machine code of the program is being executed by the processor. A run-time error is an error that occurs at this time and is due to a mistake in the program's logic. These errors may cause abrupt termination of the program or worse may cause the system to hang. The compiler's role is over before the run-time phase starts and so it typically cannot warn about these errors before their occurrence.
- Debugging is the process of locating and fixing errors in a program. These errors are historically called bugs. This is somewhat of a misnomer as the situation is different from an inadvertent bug creeping in from somewhere. Programming errors-plains and simple are called bugs in programs. To run the program currectly these have to be deleted and rectified and for this purpose there are several tools are present to help the programmer called debuggers that have been developed to aid the programmer in this endeavour. Some are stand-alone programs whereas other share integrated into the programming environment. You are strongly advised to pick up the manual of your environment and learn how to use the debugger as you begin to learn programming. This is because you will soon see that writing a piece of code gets pretty quickly once you have mastered a few constructs. To produce the desired results the real challenge is in getting the code.

You will be looking at different concepts and programming constructs in C in the subsequent chapters. The text is liberally interspersed with programs to enable you to comprehend the material in a better way.

# Chapter 7

# Elements of C

Some grammatical rules and basic elements are present in every language. It is must to know the basics elements of C language before understanding programming. These basic elements are character set, variables, datatypes, constants, keywords (reserved word), variable declaratin, expressions, statements etc. To construct a C program all of these are used.

### C Character Set

The characters that are used in programs are given below-

***Alphabets***

A,B,C................Z.

a,b,c..................z.

***Digits***

0,1,2,3,4,5,6,7,8,9

***Special character***

Some special characters are also used besides these characters which are as follow-

| *Character* | *Meaning* | *Character* | *Meaning* |
|---|---|---|---|
| + | plus sign | ~ | tilide |
| - | minus sign (hyphen) | ( | left parenthesis |
| * | asterisk | ) | right parenthesis |
| % | percent sign | { | left braces |
| / | forward slash | } | right braces |

*Contd.*

<table>
<tr><th>Character</th><th>Meaning</th><th>Character</th><th>Meaning</th></tr>
<tr><td>\</td><td>backward slash</td><td>[</td><td>left bracket</td></tr>
<tr><td><</td><td>less than sign</td><td>]</td><td>right bracket</td></tr>
<tr><td>></td><td>greater than sign</td><td>!</td><td>exclamation sign</td></tr>
<tr><td>#</td><td>hash sign</td><td>|</td><td>vertical bar</td></tr>
<tr><td>^</td><td>caret</td><td>$</td><td>dollar sign</td></tr>
<tr><td>&</td><td>ampersand</td><td>,</td><td>comma</td></tr>
<tr><td>'</td><td>single quotes</td><td>.</td><td>(dot)</td></tr>
<tr><td>"</td><td>double quotes</td><td>:</td><td>colon</td></tr>
<tr><td>@</td><td>at the rate</td><td>?</td><td>question mark</td></tr>
<tr><td>;</td><td>semi colon</td><td></td><td></td></tr>
</table>

### Execution Character/Escape Sequence

Some characters such as new line, tab, backspace cannot be printed like other characters which are printed on screen through keyboard. C support the combination of (\) with the C character set to print these characters.

The combination of these characters are called escape sequences which are separated by two characters. The first character is "\" and the second character is from the C characters set. Some escape sequences are as given below-

| *Escape sequence* | *Meaning* | *ASCII Value* | *Result* |
|---|---|---|---|
| \b | backspace | 008 | Move the cursor to the previous position of the current line |
| \a | bell (alert) | 007 | Produce a beep sound for alert |
| \r | carriage return | 013 | Move the cursor to beginning of the current line |
| \n | newline | 010 | Move the cursor to the beginning of the next line |
| \f | form feed | 012 | Move the cursor to the initial position of the next logical page |

*Contd.*

| *Escape sequence* | *Meaning* | *ASCII Value* | *Result* |
|---|---|---|---|
| \0 | null | 000 | Null |
| \v | vertical tab | 011 | Move the cursor to next vertical tab position |
| \t | horizontal tab | 009 | Move the cursor to the next horizontal tab position |
| \\ | backslash | 092 | Present a character with backslash (\) |

## Trigraph Characters

There is a possibility that the keyboard doesn't print some characters. To print these characters C support the facility of "trigraph sequence". Three characters are present in these trigraph sequence. First two are '??' and third character is any character from C character set. Some trigraph sequence are as given below-

| *Trigraph sequence* | *Symbol* |
|---|---|
| ??< | { left brace |
| ??> | } right brace |
| ??( | [ left bracket |
| ??) | ] right bracket |
| ??! | \| vertical bar |
| ??/ | \ backslash |
| ??= | # hash sign |
| ??- | ~ tilde |
| ??' | ^ caret |

## Reserved Words/Keywords

For doing specific tasks there are certain words are reserved known as keywords. These keywords have standard, predefined meaning in C. There are only 32 keywords available in C which are given below-

auto break case char

const continue default do

| | | | |
|---|---|---|---|
| double | else | enum | extern |
| float | for | goto | if |
| int | long | register | return |
| short | signed | sizeof | static |
| struct | switch | typedef | union |
| unsigned | void | volatile | while |

**Delimiters**

In C for syntactic meaning delimiter is used. These are as given below-

| | | |
|---|---|---|
| : | colon | used for label |
| ; | semicolon | end of statement |
| ( ) | parenthesis | used in expression |
| [ ] | square bracket | used for array |
| { } | curly braces | used for block of statements |
| # | hash | preprocessor directive |
| , | comma | variable delimeter |

**Variable/Identifiers**

To store values variable can be used. These variables can take different values but one at a time. During execution these values can be changed.

Variable names may be consist of uppercase character, lowercase character and underscore (-) Rules to giving the name to the variable are as-

1. First character should be a letter or underscore (-)
2. The variable names can not be a keyword.
3. Usually variables are in lowercase but uppercase and lowercase are significant for eg.-CODE, Code and code are different variables.

A variable can be arbitrarily long. Some implementations of C recognize only the first eight characters. Though most implementations recognize 31 characters. 31 characters are recognized by ANSI standard.

It is useful to give a meaningful name to the variable. As example-

value

code

grade

rec_no

some example of valid variables-

value

a

net_pay

rec]

-data

some examples of invalid variable-

| *Variable* | *Remark* |
|---|---|
| 5bc | First character should start with letters or underscore (-) |
| int | int is a keyword |
| rec# | # is a special character |
| avg no | blank space is not permitted |

## Data Types

C support different types of data In memory storage representation of these data types are also different. There are four fundamental datatype in C, which are int, char, float and double.

To store any simple character 'char' is used, to store the integer value 'int' is used, for storing floating point 'float' is used and for storing long range of floating point 'double' is used. Size and range of some data types are given below-

| *Data types* | *Size (bytes)* | *Range* |
|---|---|---|
| char or signed char | 1 | -128 to 127 |
| unsigned char | 1 | 0 to 255 |
| int or signed int | 2 | -32768 to 32767 |

*Contd.*

| *Data types* | *Size (bytes)* | *Range* |
|---|---|---|
| short int or signed short int | 1 | -128 to 127 |
| unsigned short int | 1 | 0 to 155 |
| long int or signed long int | 4 | -2147483648 to 2147483647 |
| unsigned long int | 4 | 0 to 4294967295 |
| float | 4 | 3.4E-38 to 3.4E+38 |
| double | 8 | 1.7E-308 to 1.7E+308 |
| long double | 10 | 3.4E-4932 to 1.1E+4932 |

## Constants/Literals

A value that can be stored in the memory is called constant, during execution of program that can be changed. These are a three types of constants-

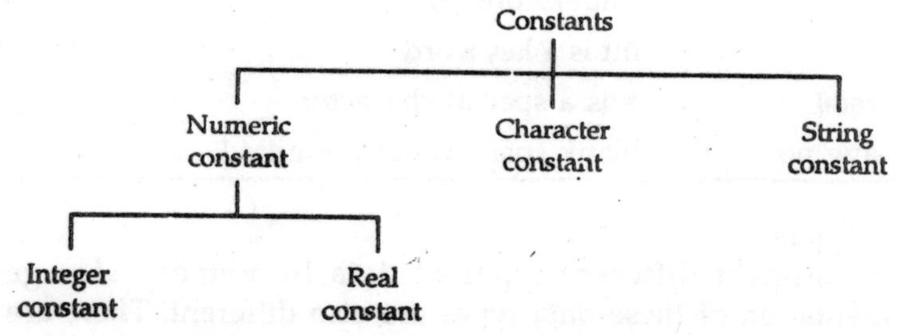


## Numeric Constant

The numeric digits which may or may not have decimal point are called numeric constants. These are the rules for defining numeric constant.

1. Numeric constant must have at least one digit.
2. No comma and space are allowed within the numeric constant.
3. Numeric constants can either be positive or negative but default sign is always positive.

There are two types of numeric constant.

***1. Integer Constant***

The whole number which has no decimal point called integer constants. Three types of integer constants are present in different number systems.

Decimal number-0,1,2,3,4,5,6,7,8,9 (base 10)

Octal number-0,1,2,3,4,5,6,7 (base 8)

Hex decimal number-0,1,2,3,4,5,6,7,8,9,A,B,C,D,E,F (base 16)

Some valid integer constants are-

0

123

3705

837590

Some invalid decimal integer constants are-

| ***Invalid*** | ***Remark*** |
|---|---|
| 2.5 | illegal character (.) |
| 3#5 | illegal character ( # ) |
| 9.85 | No blank space allowed |
| 0925 | First digit can not be zero |
| 8,354 | Comma is not allowed |

The first digit must be 0 in octal integer constant for eg.-

0

05

077

0324

The first character should be O× in hex decimal integer constant for example-

0×

0×23

0×515

0×A15B

0×FFF

2. *Real (floating point) constant*

The numbers which hold the decimal point are floating point constants.

Some valid floating point constants are-

0.5

5.3

4000.0

0.0073

5597.

39.0807

**Character Constant**

A single character that is enclosed with in single quotes ('') is a character constant for example-

'9'

'D'

'$'

' '

'#'

A unique integer value is associated with every character. These are ASCII (American Standard code for Information Interchange) value for each character of the character set. As example-

| | |
|---|---|
| A-Z | ASCII value (65-90) |
| a-z | ASCII value (97-122) |
| 0-9 | ASCII value (48-57) |
| ; | ASCII value (59) |

**String Constant**

Zero, one or more than are character represent a string constant which is enclosed in 'double quotes' (" "). At the end of string \0 is automatically placed.

Some example of string constants are-

"Parul"

"593"

"8"

" "

"S"

**Symbolic Constant**

We can use symbolic constant if we want to use certain unique constant several times. A symbolic constant is a name that substitutes for a sequence of characters. The character may represent a numeric constant, a character constant or a string constant.

At the beginning of the program this is generally written. This is written as a define name value.

Here name is the symbolic name, this can be written in uppercase letters. Value can be numeric, character or string constant.

Some example of symbolic constant are as-

```
# define MAX 100
# define PI 3. 14
# define CH 'y'
# define NAME "HEMANT"
```

**Declaration of Variable**

Before it is used in the program it is must to declare the variables. The variable name can store the value of this datatype because we declare the variable with datatype. C computer distinguishes all these variable names which are declared. Declaration of variable can be done as-

datatype variablename;

int, float, char, double are the datatype here. Some examples of declaration of variable are-

```
int basic;
int a,b,c;
```

Here basic, a,b,c are the variable name which are declared as data type int.

With the declaration of variable initialization of variables can also be done.

int a=5;

int b,c=10;

Some other examples-

float height;

float a=5.5;

float b=3. 5,c=4. 9;

double no=0. 15197e-7;

char ch;

char type,b,c;

char ch='y';

Here ch is a character variable which has the value 'y'

## Expressions

An expression is a data item, such as number or character. This is a combination of operators, constants, variables and functions.

The expression can be arithmetic, logical or relational.

Some examples are as-

| | |
|---|---|
| x+y | -arithmetic operation |
| a=b+c | -use two operator (=) and (+) |
| a>b | -relational expression |
| a= =b | -logical expression |

## Statements

A set of declaration or steps in a sequence of actions represented by statements. To carry out some action a statement causes the computer. All the statements end with semicolon and executed in sequence. These statements are given below-

### *Assignment Statements*

We use the assignment operator (=) for assigning the value to the variable in this type of statement. This can be written as-

variable name = value;

Some examples are as-

```
basic=1200;
flag=0;
```

We can also use the multiple assignment statement as-

```
x = y = z =];
```

***Null Statement***

Null statement is a statement that has only semicolon. As example-

```
; (null statement)
```

***Expression Statement***

An expression statement consists of expressions. These expression can be arithmetic, logical or relational. As example-

```
x=5;
x = y-z;
fun (a,b);
```

***Block of Statements***

Several statements enclosed with in a pair of curly braces ({ }) made a block of statements. The statements can be expressions, assignment statement or control statement. As example-

```
{
1=4,
b=2;
area = 1 * b;
}
```

**Comments**

For understanding the program later comments are used and they also used for documentation. Comments are given by starting with / * and ending with * /. It can be of one or many number of lines. As example-

```
/ * This is a C program * / (-one line)
/ * a = 3;
```

```
b = a + c;
c = a /-b ; * /
```

### Operators & Expression

An operation to be performed specified by an operator that yields a value. To form an expressions variables, constant can be joined by various operators. An operand is a data item on which an operator acts. Some operations require two operands, while others act upon only one operand. Several different categories are present of number of operators in C which are as-

1. Arithmetic operator
2. Relational operator
3. Logical operator
4. Assignment operator
5. Ternary operator
6. Bitwise operator
7. Increment or Decrement operator

### Arithmetic Operators

Several different categories are present of number of operators in C. They are of two type-

***1. Unary arithmetic***

It requires only one operand.

Ex-

+x-y

Here '-' changes the sign of the operand y.

***2. Binary arithmetic***

There are two operands and five operators required for binary arithmetic.

| *Operator* | *Meaning* | *Purpose* |
|---|---|---|
| + | plus | addition |
| - | minus | subtraction |
| * | asterisk | multiplication |

*Contd.*

| *Operator* | *Meaning* | *Purpose* |
|---|---|---|
| / | slash | division |
| % | percent (modulus) | gives the remainder in integer division |

With floating point number % (modulus operator) cannot be applied. In C there is exponent operator. However there is a library function (pow) to carry out exponent.

a+b

a-b

a/b

a*b

a%b

Here 'a' and 'b' are two operands.

***3. Integer arithmetic***

Integer arithmetic is the arithmetic operation in which both operands are integer.

Ex-

Let us take two variables a and b. The value of a=17 and b=4. Then the result of these operations are-

| *Expression* | *Result* |
|---|---|
| a+b | 21 |
| a-b | 13 |
| a*b | 68 |
| a/b | 4 (decimal part truncates) |
| a%b | 1 (Remainder after integer division) |

After division operation the decimal part will be truncated and result is only integer part of quotient (Remainder part of integer division will be the result after modulus operation).

It is necessary for division and modulus operation that second operand must be nonzero.

```
/* Program to understand the integer arithmetic
operation */
# include<stdio.h>
main ( )
(
int a=17, b=4;
print £    ( "After addition : %d \ n" , a+b);
print £    ( "After subtraction : %d \ n" , a-b);
print £    ( "After multiplication : %d \ n" , a*b);
print £    ( "After division : %d \ n" , a / b);
print £    ( "After modulus : %d \ n" , a %b);
```

**Output:**

After addition : 21

After subtraction : 13

After multiplication : 68

After division : 4

After modulus : 1

*4. Floating point arithmetic*

Floating point arithmetic is the type of arithmetic operation in which both operands are of float type.

Ex-

| *Expression* | *Result* |
|---|---|
| a+b | 15.5 |
| a-b | 9.3 |
| a*b | 38.44 |
| a / b | 4.0 |

With floating point numbers the modulus operator % cannot be used.

```
/* program to understand the floating point arithmetic
operation */
# include<stdio.h>
main ( )
{
float a = 9.6,b = 1.6;
print £    ( "After addition : %£ \ n" , a+b);
```

```
print £    ( "After subtraction : %£ \ n" , a-b);
print £    ( "After division : %£ \ n"  , a / b);
print £    ( "After multiplication : %£ \ n" , a+b);
```

**Output:**

After addition : 11.2

After subtraction : 8.0

After division : 6.0

After multiplication : 15.36

*Relational Operator*

To compare two values depending on their relations relational operators are used which requires two operands.

Relational expression is an expression that contain the relational operator. If the relation is true then it returns the value 1, if the relation is false then it returns the value 0. These operators are-

| *Operator* | *Meaning* |
|---|---|
| < | less than |
| <= | less than or equal |
| = = | equal |
| != | Not equal |
| > | Greater than |
| >= | Greater than or equal |

Ex-

Let a=9 and b=5, then the operation with relational operators are-

| *Expression* | *Result* |
|---|---|
| a < b | False (0) |
| a <= b | False (0) |
| a = = b | False (0) |
| a !=b | True (1) |
| a > b | True (1) |
| a >= b | True (1) |

```
/* program to understand the use of relational operator
*/
# include<stdio.h>
main ( )
(
int a, b;
print £   ( "First number :" );
scan £ ( " %d , & a);
print £   ( "Second number :");
scan £ (" %d , &b);
if ( a < b ) /* relational operator with ££ (in control)
statement) */
print £   ( "%d is less than %d \ n", a, b);
if ( a< =b )
print £   ( "%d is less or equal to %d \ n", a, b);
if ( a = = b)
print £   ( "%d is equal to %d \ n", a, b);
if ( a ! = b )
print £   ( "%d is not equal to %d \ n", a, b);
if ( a > b)
print ( "%d is greater than %d \ n", a, b );
if ( a > = b)
print ( "%d is greater or equal to %d \ n", a, b);
)
```

After run

First number : 12

Second number : 7

12 is not equal to 7

12 is greater than 7

12 is greater or equal to 7

***Logical or Boolean Operator***

A logical expression is an expression that combines two or more expression. We use the logical operator for combining these expression. After testing the value of the condition (which is true or false), it gives the logical status (true or false) as a net result.

The operands may be constants, variables and expression C has three logical operators-

<table>
<tr><th>Operator</th><th>Meaning</th></tr>
<tr><td>&&</td><td>AND</td></tr>
<tr><td>| |</td><td>OR</td></tr>
<tr><td>!</td><td>NOT</td></tr>
</table>

***And (&&) Operator***

**If the condition have the true value than this operator gives the net result true otherwise result will be false.**

**Boolean Table**

| *Condition 1* | *Condition 2* | *Result* |
|---|---|---|
| false | false | false |
| false | true | false |
| true | false | false |
| true | true | true |

Ex-

Let a = 10 and b = 5

The logical expression is-

Because both the conditions a = = 10 and b<a is true then this gives the result true.

OR ( | | ) operator-

**If both the conditions have the value false then this operator gives the net result false otherwise it gives the result true**

**Boolean Table**

| Condition 1 | Condition 2 | Result |
|---|---|---|
| false | false | false |
| false | true | true |
| true | false | true |
| true | true | true |

Ex-

Let us take the value of two variables a = 7 and b = 12

The logical expression is-

a < = b | | b > 15

this gives the result true because one condition is true and gives the net result true.

Not ( ! ) operator-

This is a unary operator. This negates the value of the condition. If both the conditions have the value false then this opertor gives the net result false.

**Boolean Table**

| *Condition* | *Result* |
|---|---|
| false | true |
| true | false |

Ex-

Let us take any variable a = 10

Then logical expression is

! ( a = = 10 )

The value of the condition is true NOT operator negates the value of the condition. Hence the result is false.

## Assignment Operator

With the use of assignment operator a value can be stored in variables. For assignment statement this assgnment operator "=" is used which is also discussed in chapter 2.

For updation statement assignment statement is also used.

Ex-

x = x + 5 can also be written as-

x + = 5

Similarly

x = x-5 is equivalent to x-= 5

x = x / 5 is equivalent to x / = 5

x = x % 5 is equivalent to x % = 5

**Ternary Operator**

Ternary operator ( ? and : ) requires three operand. This is written as-

Condition ? operand 1 : operand 2

First the condition is tested if the result is true then the value of the operand 1 is taken otherwise value of operand 2 is taken.

Ex-

maximum = a > b ? a : b

First the condition a > b is evaluafed, if the value is true then the value of 'a' is taken by maximum, otherwise value of 'b' is given to the maximum.

```
/* Program to print the largest between two number with
the use of ternary operator */
# include<stdio.h>
main ( )
{
int a, b, max;
print f    ( "Enter the first number :" );
scan f ( "%d" , & a );
print f    ( "Enter the second number :" );
scan f ( "%d" , & b );
max = a > b ? a : b /* ternary operator */
print f    ( "Largest between %d and %d os %d", a, b, max
);
}
```

After run

Enter the first number : 12

Enter the second number : 7

Largest between 12 and 7 is 12

**Bitwise Operator**

At the bit level to support the manipulation C has the ability. For opertions on bits bitwise operator are used. Bitwise operators are operated on only integer. The bitwise opertors are as given below-

| Bitwise operator | Meaning |
|---|---|
| & | bitwise AND |
| \| | bitwise OR |
| ~ | one's complement |
| << | left shift |
| >> | right shift |
| ^ | bitwise XOR |

These bitwise operators are discussed later in chapter 12.

## Increment and Decrement Operator

Increment (++) and decrement (--) are two useful operators which C has, these operate on only single operand so they are unary operators.

The increment operator (++) increment the value of the variable by 1 and decrement operator (--) decrement the value of the variable by 1. We can write this as-

++a or a = a + 1

--a or a = a-1

*1. Prefix increment / decrement*

The value of variable is first incremented/decremented and then for operation the value of variable is taken.

Ex-

Let us take the value of a = 3

then the statement b = ++a; means first increment the value of 'a' by 1, then 'b' takes the value of 'a'.

Hence a = 4 b = 4

the statement b =--a; means first decrement the value of 'a' by 1 then 'b' takes the value of 'a'

Hence a = 3 b = 3

```
/* Program to understand the use of prefix increment /
decrement */
# include , stdio.h>
main ( )
(
```

```
int a = 3;
print £  ( "a = %d\n", a );
print £  ( "a = %d\n", ++ a ); /* prefix increment */
print £  ( "a = %d\n", a );
print £  ( "a = %d\n",--a ); /* prefix decrement */
print £  ( "a = %d\n", a );
```

Output:

a = 3

a = 4

a = 4

a = 3

a = 3

2. ***Postfix increment / decrement***

For operation first the value of variable is taken and then it is incremented/ decremented.

Ex-

a++

a--

Ex-

Let us take the value of a = 3

Then the statement b = a++, means first 'b' takes the value of 'a' then increment it by 1.

Hence a = 4 b = 3

The statement b = a--means first 'b' takes the value of 'a' then decrement it by 1.

Hence a = 3 b = 4

```
/* program to understand the use of postfix increment /
decrement */
# include < stdio.h>
main ( )
(
int a = 3;
print £ ( "a = %d\n", a );
print £ ( "a = %d\n", ++ a ); /* postfix increment */
print £ ( "a = %d\n", a );
print £ ( "a = %d\n",--a ); /* postfix increment */
```

```
print £ ( "a = %d\n", a );
```

Output:

a = 3

a = 3

a = 4

a = 4

a = 3

**Comma Operator**

To appear in situations where only one expression would be used the comma operator (,) is used to permit two different expressions. The comma operator separates the expressions. Since comma operator for using this operator. For example-

sum = ( a = 8, b = 7, a + b);

First 8 is assign to the variable a, then 7 is assign to the variable b and after this resultant value a + b = 15 is assigned to the variable sum.

```
/* Program to understand the use of comma operator */
# include<stdio.h>
main ( )
(
int a, b, sum;
sum = ( a = 8, b = 7, a + b ); /* Use of comma operator
*/
print £ ( "Sum = %d \n", sum );
)
```

Output

Sum = 15

The value of two variables can also be changed.

temp = a, a = b, b = temp;

```
/* Program to interchange the value of two variable with
the use of comma operator */
# include<stdio.h>
main ( )
( inte a = 8, b = 7, temp;
print £ ( "a = %d, b = %d \n", a, b );
temp = a, a = b, b = temp;
print £ ( " a = %d, b = %d, \n", a, b);
```

```
)
```

Output

a = 8, b = 7

a = 7, b = 8

## Type Casting

Type casting is used for converting the value of an expression to a particular data type. This is written as-

(datatype) expression;

Into particular datatype the result of expression is converted here.

```
/* Program without use of type casting */
# include<stdio.h>
main ( )
(
float a;
int b = 5, c = 2;
a = b / c;
print £ ( "a = %£\n", a );
)
```

Output:

a = 2.000000

Here, first the operation b/c is evaluated, both are integer hence after division decimal value is truncated and integer value 2 is taken by variable a. Since a is float type hence 2 is converted into 2.000000.

We use the type casting for solving this type of difficulties.

```
/* Program without use of type casting */
# include<stdio.h>
main ( )
(
float a;
int b = 5, c = 2;
a = b / c;
print £ ( "a = %£ \n", a );
)
```

Output:

a = 2.500000

**Data Type Conversion**

For mixing the different type of variable in expression C has the facility. One data type is converted into another data type in this type of operation. There are some rules for data type conversion. Which are as-

| *Operand 1* | *Operand 2* | *Result* |
|---|---|---|
| char | char | char |
| char | int | int |
| char | float | float |
| char | double | double |
| *Operand 1* | *Operand 2* | *Result* |
| int | char | int |
| int | int | int |
| int | float | float |
| int | double | double |
| *Operand 1* | *Operand 2* | *Result* |
| float | char | float |
| float | int | float |
| float | float | float |
| float | double | double |
| *Operand 1* | *Operand 2* | *Result* |
| double | char | double |
| double | int | double |
| double | float | double |
| double | double | double |

```
/* Program to understand the data type conversion */
# include<stdio.h>
main ( )
(
int a;
float £, g;
a = 6, 4;
```

```
/* only integer value assign to a that is 6 */
print £ ( a = %d\n", a );
£ = a;
/* ' £ has the value 6.0*/
print £ ( "£ = %£\n", £ );
g = ( £ + a ) / a;
print £ ( " g = % £\n", g );
)
```

Output:

a = 6

f = 6.000000

g = 2.000000

/* Program to understand the dat type conversion */

```
# include<stdio.h>
main ( )
( char C;
int a:
a 97;
print £ ( "a = %d\n", a);
c = a;
/* Now c has the character which has ASCII value 97 */
print £ ( "c = %c\n", c);
c = 'z';
a = c;
/* Now a has ASCII value of z which is 90 */
print £ ( "a = %d\n", a );
)
```

Output:

a = 97

c = a

a = 90

*Precedence of Operator and Associativity*

It must be necessary to give the precedance to each operation if the expressions has more than one operator to each operator C has the facility for giving the precedence. Sometimes there is problem for evaluating the expression when two operators has some precedence. C has the facility to provide the associativity to each operator for solving this problem. Precedence and associativity of each operator are given below:

| *Operator* | *Description* | *precedence level* | *Associativity* |
|---|---|---|---|
| ( ) | Function call | | |
| [ ] | Array expression | 1 | left to right |
| | structure operator | | |
| | structure operator | | |
| + | unary plus | | |
| - | unary minus | | |
| ++ | increment | | |
| — | decrement | | |
| ! | Negation | | |
| ~ | one's complement | 2 | right to left |
| & | address | | |
| * | value at address | | |
| sizeof | size in bytes | | |
| (type) | type cast | | |
| * | multiplication | | |
| / | division | 3 | left to right |

# Chapter 8

# Control Statements in 'C'

To specify the order in which the various instructions in a program are to be executed by the computer the 'control instructions' enable us. In other words the control instructions determine the 'flow of control' in a program. In C there are four types of control instructions. They are:

(a) Sequence Control Instruction

(b) Selection or Decision Control Instruction

(c) Repitition or Loop Control Instruction

(d) Case Control Instruction

The instructions are executed in the same order in which they appear in the program ensured by the sequence control instruction. Decision and Case control instructions allow the computer to take a decision as to which instruction is to be executed next. To execute a group of statements repeatedly the loop control instruction help the computer.

**Types and Type Declarations**

C has only a few built-in types. Here they are:

*char*-a byte which is usually eight bits is capable of storing a single character.

*int*-an integer is usually the size of the basic unit of storage for the machine.

*float*-a single precision floating point number.

*double*-a double precision floating point number.

To modify the basic types additional qualifier are used These qualifiers include:

***short***-modifies an int, and usually produces a variable size that is smaller than the normal int. For example, on a 32-bit machine, an int might be 32 bits and a short int could be 16 bits.

***Long***-modifies an int, and usually produces a variable size that is larger than the normal int. For example, on a 16-bit machine, an int might be 16 bits, and a long int could be 32 bits. Long can also modify a double to specify an extended *precision floating point number.*

***Singned-modifies the type char or int and producers a rang of numbers that contains both positive and negative numbers. For example, if the type char is 8 bits, a signed char can contain*** the range of numbers-128 to +127. Default for char and int is signed when they are declared.

***Unsigned***-modifies the type of char or int and produces a range of numbers that are positive only. For example, if the type char is 8 bits, an unsigned char can contain the range of numbers 0 to +255.

There are other qualifiers that can be used. These qualifiers will be desicussed later in the text. With the qualifiers short or long it is not neccessary to include the type int. Thus, the following statements are the same.

```
Long int a,c;
Short int d;
```

and

```
Long a,c;
Short d;
```

A space is allocated in memory when a variable is declared for its storage. Especially for micro controller the basic variable size is implementation dependent. You will find that this variability will show up when you change from one microcomputer to another.

Before it is being used each variable must be declared. A variable may be declared at the beginning of any code block, and *the variable's scope is the block in which it is declared. The variable goes out of existence when the block in which the* variable is declared is exited. The variables can be declared with the same name in different blocks. The computer will make-certain that these variables do not get mixed up in the execution of code.

**Global or External Variables**

Global or external variables are the variables declared outside the program blocks and the entire program is the scope for these variables. A Global variable can directly accessed by any function contained in the file which contains a global declaration. If there is a global variable that is declared in one file that is to be accessed by a function defined in another file, the function must notify the compiler that the variable is global with the use of the keyword extern. The followingis an example of such an access.

In file 1:

```
int able;
void main (void)
(
long quickstart (void);
long x;
*
*
*
able = 17;
isquickstart ( );
*
*.
)
```

In file 2:

```
long quickstart (void)
(
extern int able;
*
*
*
return result;
)
```

The memory is allocated for its storage when file 1 is compiled and the variable able is marked as global. When the file 2 is compiled, the variable able is recognized to be global because of the extern keyword, and no memory is allocated for the variable. the address of able that was defined in file 1 will be assigned when the link phase of compilation is completed are address references to able in file 2.

**Storage Classes**

Storage classes are the addition of modifiers which designate where a variable is to be stored and how it is initialized. auto, register and static are the storage classes.

The default storage class is auto for local variables defined with in a function. An automatic variable has the scope of the block in which it is defined, and it is uninitialized when it is create. Automatic variables are stored on the program stack, so space for the variable is created when the function is entered. All variables stored on the stack are deleted whem stack is cleaned up prior to return at the end of function.

As we saw in our first program example, variables can be initialized at the time of declaration by assigning the variable an initial value.

```
int rupt = 17;
```

Each time the block in which the variable is declared is entered an automatic variable will be assigned its initial value. If the variable is not initialized at declaration, it will contain the contents of uninitialized memory which can be any value.

Sometimes you might want to assign a value to a variable and have it retain that value for later function calls. Such a variable can be created by calling it static at its declaration. static variables have a scope of the function in which they are defined, and they are intialized to 0 when they are created. Inside of a function, the following declaration is made:

```
static int keep = 1;
```

Keep is stored in a static data memory area not in the stack. Keep is initialized to the value 0 when the program is loaded being a static variable. The first time that the function is entered, the value 1, is assigned to keep. Therefore, each time the function is entered, keep will not be intialized and it will retain the value assigned to it the time the function was executed.

Register is another automatic storage class. Integer variables can be declared to be stored in register by a declaration like:

```
register int roter = 10;
```

These variables can be long, short, or char. The compiler will attempt to store it in an available computer register when a variable is declared to be register. Such variables can be accessed quicker than variables stored in memory, so variables used in tight loops might best be register variables. Of course, register space in computers is limited, especially in small microcontrollers. For data storage registers will not often be available. When the compiler senses that there is no available register for data storage, it makes the variable a normal automatic variable and provides for its storage in memory.

When the program is loaded global variables are initialized to zero. For the entire program these variables have the scope. Global variables act like static variables in that their values will be intialized either to zero or an initially assigned value when created. Subsequent change in a global variable will be the result of a specific programmed assignment.

Global variables can be designed as static. A global variable that is static is similar to a conventional global variable with the exception that it can be accessed only from the file in which it is declared. The example above in which the declaration

```
extern int able;
```

allowed access to able from the file 2 will not work if able had been declared as follows in file 1:

```
static int able;
```

An additional qualifier is const. An initialization value must be declared when const is used as a qualifier on the declaration of any variable. This value cannot be changed by the program. Therefore the declaration

```
const double PI = 3.14159265;
```

will create the value for the mathematical constant pi and store it in the location provided for PI. Any attempt to change the value of PI by the program will cause compiler error.

Conventions for writing constants are straightforward. int is an simple number with no decimal point. You must suffix it with an l or an L to make a number long. For example, 6047 is an int and 6047L is a long. The u or U suffix on a number will cause creation of a proper unsigned number.

A decimal point or an exponent or both is contained by a floating point number. The numbers 1.114 and 17.3e-5 are examples of floating point numbers. All floating point numbers are of the type double unless a suffix is appended to the number. Any number suffixed with an £ or an F is a single precision floating point number, and a suffix of 1 or L on a floating point number will generate a type long double.

Octal (base 8) and hexadecimal (base 16) numbers can be created. Any number that is prefixed with a 0-a leading zero-is taken to be an octal number. Hexadecimal numbers are prefixed with a 0x or a OX. To octal and hexadecimal numbers the rules for L and U can also apply.

**Character Constants**

The data that can be stored in memory locations the character constants or escape sequences are designated as char. By A backslash preceding the character character constant is identified. We have seen the use of the character constants '\n' and '\t' in previous examples. Several of these escape sequences shown in the following table have predefined meanings.

| *Escape* | *Meaning* |
|---|---|
| Sequence\a | bell character |
| \b | backspace |
| \f | form feed |
| \n | new line |
| \r | carriage return |
| \v | vertical tab |
| \t | horizontal tab |
| \ \ | back slash |
| \ ' | single quote |
| \ " | double quote |
| \000 | octal number |
| \ xxx | hexadecimal number |

The constants must be identified by quotes if they are used with in a program. The new line character was a part of a string in the earlier example. Therefore, it effectively was contained in quotes. If a single character constant is to be generated, the constant must be included in single quotes. For example, a test might include a statement like.

```
if (c! = '\t')
• • • •
```

This statement causes the variable c to be compared with the constant '\t', and the statement following the if will be executed if they are not the same.

# define is another preprocessor command. You can define a character sequence that will be placed in your code sequence with # define command whenever it is encountered. If you have character constants that you wish to use in your code, these constants can be identified as

```
# define CR '\x0d'
# define LF '\x0a'
# define BELL '\x07'
# define NULL '\x00'
```

and so forth.

We'll discuss the # define preprocessor command further later. The use of an escape character shown by the following program.

```
/* Count lines of text in an input */
# include <stdio.h>
void main (void)
(
int c,nl = 0; /* the number of lines is in nl */
while ( (c = getchar ( ) ) ! = EOF)
if (c = = '\n')
nl + + ;
print f ( "The number of lines is %d\n", nl );
)
```

Often you will want to leave "clues" as to what the program or kind of code is supposed to do. This documentation provided by comments within the code. A C comment is delimited by

```
/* . . . . . . . . . */
```

and the comment can contain anything except another comment. In other words, comments may NOT be nested. In the above program first line of code is a comment and both code and a comment is present in sixth line. The compiler ignores all information inside the comment delimiters.

Two integer variables c and nl used in this program. The variable c is the temporary storage location in which input data are stored, and no is where the number of input lines are counted.

A complicated argument contained by the while statement. It can be stored in a specified location at any point in a C program when a value is calculated. For example in the while expression.

```
while ( (c = getchar ( ) ) ! = EOF)
```

the inner expression

```
c = getchar ( )
```

causes the function getchar ( ) to be executed. The return from getchar ( ) is a character from the input stream. To the variable c this character is assigned. The result returned from getchar ( ) is compared with the constant EOF means end-of-file after this operation is completed and when a program tries to read beyond the end of the data stream then it is the value returned by getchar ( ). It is defined in the file stdio.h. The symbol ! = is read "is not equal to". Therefore, the argument of the while will be TRUE so long as getchar ( ) does not return an EOF and the statement following the while will be continually executed until an EOF is returned.

Operators in an expression that have the higher precedence will be executed before the lower precedence operators. In the expression

```
c = getchar ( ) ! = EOF
```

Higher precedence will be given to the ! = operator that the = operator. So the logical portion of the expressions will be evaluated first and the result of the logical evaluation either true or false will be assigned to the variables when this expression is evaluated. This result is of course incorrect. To avoid this problem use.

```
(c = getchar ( ) ) ! = EOF
```

as the while argument. In this case, the parenthesis group the c = getchar ( ) expression and it will be completed prior to execution of the comparison. As returned from the input stream the variable c will have the correct value. The value that was returned from the input stream is tested to determine if it is a new line character if the above expression is logically true. If a new line character is found, the counter nl is incremented. Otherwise, the next character is read in and the sequence repeated until an EOC is returned from the getchar ( ).

The final statement in the program

```
print f ( *The number of lines is %d\n" , nl );
```

The number of new line character detected in reading the input file printed.

The name enum is used in C in a manner similar to the # define preprocessor command. The enum call

```
enum state ( OUT, IN );
```

produces the same result as

```
# define OUT 0
# define IN 1
```

Here, the name state is called the tag name. In this case OUT will be given a value of 1 and IN a value 1. The members will be given successively increasing values and the first will be given a value 0. In enum ( ) form, unless specifically assigned. Values can be assigned by an enum ( ):

```
enum months (Jan = 1, Feb, Mar, April, May, June, July,
Aug, Sept, Oct, Nov, Dec ):
```

will cause Jan to be 1, Feb 2, and so forth up to Dec which will be 12. A different value can be assigned to each member but the values assigned to the variables following will be successively increase whenever the programmer assignments stop. These values are, by default, of the int type. Another example is

```
enum (FALSE, TRUE, Sun = 1, Mon, Tues, Wed, Thur, Fri,
Sat );
```

will result in FALSE being 0, TRUE 1, SUN 1, Mon 2, and so forth to Sat 7. To assign a tag name to an enum is not necessary.

An enum can be typed at declaration time. Therefore, the values created by an enum are indeed numerical values. This differs from the # define because the statement.

```
# define FALSE 0
```

will cause the character '0' to be inserted into the code whenever the label FALSE is encountered. As such, the #define construct is a character substitution technique or a macro expansion. The result of an enum is a numerical substitution.

Being a simple character substitution the # define construct has no typing attached to its arguments. Constants created by an enum can be typed, and therefore, will avoid many of the potential hazards of dealing with untyped variables.

## Operators and Expressions

Operands are the variables and constants discussed in the previous section. They are values or objects that are operated upon by a program. The operations that take place are specified by operators. This section contains a discussion of several types of operators.

Operators abound in C. Operators are all of the symbols involved in the language. Each has a precedence and an associativity. This section is concerned with how operators and operands are put together to interact in a manner desired by the programmer.

### *Arithmetic Operators*

The arithmetic operators are those used to perform arithmetic operations. These operators are:

- +
- -
- *
- /
- %

Because these operators are always used with two operands hence they are called binary operators. These operands are placed on either side of the operator.

The symbol + designates arithmetic addition, and the-symbol designates substraction. The symbols * and / designate multiplication and division respectively. For different variable types these operators are clearly different and for the operand types involved the compiler understands these differences and creates correct code. The modulus operator % returns the remainder after an integer division. The modulus operator works only on integer types-int, char, and long. It cannot be applied to types long or double.

+ and-are two unary operators. These operators are of higher precedence than the normal arithmetic operators. They called unary because they operate on only the operand written to be right of the operator. The unary minus sign causes the negative value of the operand to be calculated, and the unary positive sign causes no calculation to take place.

Among the binary operators, *, /, and % have equal precedence, which is higher that of + and-. The unary operators + and-have a higher precedence than *, /, or %.

With any of the arithmetic types the arithmetic operators will work. Because the operations needed to an integer operation differ those needed for the corresponding double operation. To perform the specified operation the compiler will place the proper arithmetic routines in the code.

To an integer type the concept of a fraction is almost unknown. The result is rounded down if a division of two inters is executed. Therefore, the result of 1/2 is 0 as is 9999/10000. This characteristic is often used in programming.

The only way that you can handle fractions with integer operations is to make use of the modulus operation. The result of a % b is the remainder that is left over after a is divided by b. The modulus operation can provide insight into fractional value of what is left over after an integer divide.

***Relational or Logical Operators***

The relational operators are all binary operators. The program will evaluate the left operand and then the right operand when contained in an expression. These operands will be compared, and if the comparison shows that the meaning of the operator is correct, the program will return 1. Otherwise, the program will return a 0. In the vocabulary of C, FALSE is always zero. If calculated by a logical expression, TRUE will always be one. However, if the argument of a conditional expression is anything but zero, it will respond as if the argument is TRUE. FALSE is always zero and TRUE is anything else in other word.

The relational operators are:

- < (less than)
- <= (less than or equal to)

- > (greater than)
- >= (greater than or equal to)

These operators all have the same precedence, which is slightly higher than the following equally operators:

- == (is equal to)
- != (is not equal to)

&& and || are the logical operators. The first operator indicates a logical AND and the second a logical OR. A logical AND will return TRUE if both of its operands are TRUE, and a logical OR will return TRUE if either of its operands is TRUE. The logical OR has lower precedence than the logical AND. The precedence of the logical AND is lower than the precedence of the relational operators and the equality operators.

The program starts on the left side of expression and evaluates the expression until it knows in the evaluation of long logical expressions whether the whole expression is true or false, and it then exits the evaluation and returns a proper value. For example, suppose there is a character C, and it is necessary to determine if this character is letter. In such a case, the following logical expression might be used:

```
if ( c >= 'A' && c <= 'Z' || c >= 'a' && c <= 'z' )
```

The relational expressions will be evaluated prior to the && operations because the logical and operator && has lower precedence than any of the relational operators. If upon entering this expression, c is equal to the character '5', which is arithmetically smaller than any of the letters, the first term c >= 'A' will be FALSE. Therefore, the result of the first logical and expression is known to be FALSE without evaluating the term c <= 'Z'. The evaluation will then skip to the third term c >= 'a', and the term c <= 'Z' will not be evaluated. In this case, the character '5' will be smaller than the character 'a' so that the second and expression will also be FALSE. Rather than having to evaluate all four of the terms the logical value will be known after evaluation of only two of the logical terms of the argument.

***Type Conversions Within Expressions***

Different data types not only occupy different width in memory implied in our earlier discussions on variable types but when attempting to execute operations involving mixed data types some may be completely in compatible. In earlier languages, it was up to the programmer to guarantee that the data types involved with an operation were the same. C resolves this problem, and the compiler will select the proper data type to complete operations on mixed date types.

Each data type has an implied width. The widths of the two types are evaluated when an operation is to be executed on mixed data types and to execution of the operation the lesser width operand is promoted to the type of the greater width operand. Thus, if the program called for d = a * b, where d is of type long, a is type int, and b is type long, a will be converted to the type long prior to the multiplication.

To mixing of float and double types as well this logic carries over. If for example a program called for the division a/b where a is of the type int and b is of the type double, the program would convert a to the type double before execution of the divide.

There might be times when the programmer will want to change the type of a variable. To convert the type of a variable to a different type C provides a cast operator which forces the program. This unary operator has the form.

```
(type name) expression
```

where the results of the evaluation of expression will be converted to the named type contained wihtin the parenthesis preceding the expression.

***Bitwise Operators***

Bitwise operators are the operators that work on the individual bits within a variable. Following is a table of all these operators:

| | | | |
|---|---|---|---|
| * & | bitwise AND | * >> | right shift |
| * \| | bitwise Inclusive OR | * << | left shift |
| * ^ | bitwise Exlusive OR | * ~ | one's complement |

The first three bitwise operators are traditional binary operators. These binary operators operate in integer type (char, int, long. etc.) operands, and the two operands must be of the same type.

If a bitwise AND is executed, those locations in the result where both operands have bit values of 1 will have a value of 1. All other locations will be 0. Each bit in the result will be 1 when either or both operand bits are 1 for a biwise inclusive OR. All locations where both operand bits are 0 will be 0. The exclusive OR is similar to an addition with no carry. The result bit will be 1 whenever the bits in the operands are different. If both operand bits are the same, either both bits 1 or both bits 0, the result will be 0.

The right shift operator and the left shift operator are also binary operators. Here the types of the operands need not be the same the expression.

```
x >> 3
```

causes the variable x to be shifted to the right by three bits prior to its use. Likewise,

```
y << 5
```

will cause y to be shifted to the left by five bits. In all number systems, a left shift by one digit corresponds to a multiplication by the number base. Similarly, a shift to the right by one digit causes a division by the number base. A shift left by one bit causes the number to be multiplied by two because we are using the binary system. The binary system allows the sign of the number to be contained in the binary representation of the number itself unlike most number systems.These considerations lead to two different types of shifts for a system of binary numbers. A shift in which bits vacated by the shift are replaced by zeors is called logical shift. All left shifts are logical shifts. As the shift progresses toward the left, bits that fill the number from the right will all be zero. Bits that shift out of the number on the left side are lost. A right shift can be either a logical or an arithmetic shift. If the type being shifted is signed, the sign bit-which is the leftmost bit-will propagate, retaining a number of the same sign. This is an arithmetic sign. Zeros are filled into the number from the left as the shift proceed if the number being shifted is unsigned. In all cases, bits shifted out of a number by a shift operation will be lost.

The one's complement operator-is a unary operator that causes the bits in a variable to be reversed. Every 1 is replaced by a 0, and every 0 is replaced by a 1.

Zeros are filled into the number from the left as the shift proceed if the number being shifted is consigned. Suppose that we have a character variable r, and we wish to turn the least significant three bits off. Try

```
x = r & ~ 7;
```

In this case, the number 7 has each of the least significant bits turned on or1. Therefore, the term-7 has all of the bits in the number but the least significant turned on and these three bits are turned off or 0. When this mask is ANDed with r, all of the bits of r, with the exception of the least significant three bits, will be ANDed with a 1, and these bit values will remain unchanged. The result in these three bits will be 0 if the least significant three bits will be ANDed with 0.

The bitwise OR will turn bits on. Suppose you wanted to turn bits 2 and 3 of r above on. Here you would use

```
r = r | 0x0c;
```

The number 0x0c is a hexadecimal number that has 2 and 3 bits turned on and other bits turned off. This OR operation will leave bits 2 and 3 on all other bits will remain unchanged.

Suppose that you want to complement a bit in a variable. For example, bit 0 the memory location PORTA must be toggled each time a certain routine is entered. The expression

```
PORTA = PORTA ^ 1;
```

will perform this operation. Because the exclusive OR with a 0 will not change the bit value so the all bits will remain unchanged except for bit 1 of PORTA. However, if bit 1 in PORTA the exclusive OR will force this bit to 0. If this bit is 0, the exclusive Or will force this bit to a 1. Therefore, the above expression will complements bit 0 of PORTA each time it is executed.

The bitwise operators &, 1, and ^ are of lower precedence than the equality operators, and higher precedence that the logical AND operator. The bit shift operators are of the same precedence, of lower precedence than the arithmetic operators + and-, and of higher precedence than the relational operators.

**Increment and Decrement Operators**

To write a language that is concise and yet unambiguous the C language was written every effort. For shorten the program several powerful shorthand operators were included in the language. The increment and decrement operators are examples of such short-hand operators. In the examples earlier there were instances of expressions such as

```
i = i + 1;
```

Here the i value stored in memory is replaced by one more than the value found there at the beginning of execution of the expression. The C expression

```
++i;
```

will do exactly the same thing. In the memory location is the increment operator ++ causes 1 to be added. Either prefix or postfix operators the increment and decrement operators can be used. If, like above, the ++ operator precedes the variable, it is called a prefix operator. If the variable is used in an expression, it will be incremented prior to its use. For example, suppose i = 5. Then the expression

```
j = 2 * ++i;
```

will leave a 12 for the value j and 6 for i. On the other hand, if i again is 5, the expression

```
j = 2 * i--;
```

will leave a value of 10 for j and 4 for i

*Assignment Operators*

Assignment operator are another shorthand that was included in C. You will find that expressions when you are programming such as-

```
i = + = 2;
```

or

```
x = x << 1;
```

are used often. On the right side of the expression any binary operator can be found. To simplyfy these expressions a special set of operators were credited in C. The first expression can be written

```
i +=2;
```

and the second

```
x <<= 1;
```

What is defined as an assignment operator used these expression. The operators that can be used in assignment operators are

- \+ • >>
- \- • <<
- * • &
- / • ^
- % • |

If you have two expressions el and e2, and let the operand $ represent any binary C operator, then

```
el $ = e2;
```

is equivalent to

```
el = (el) $ (e2);
```

The precedence of all of the operator assignments are the same and less than the precedence of the conditional operator discussed in the next section. These operators assignments and the = operator are associated from right to left.

*The Conditional Expression*

Another code sequence found frequently is

```
if (expl)
exp2;
else
exp3;
```

The logical expression expl is evaluated. exp2 executed if that expression is TRUE. Otherwise, exp 3 is executed. The above code sequence can be written in the compact notation of C.

```
exp 1 ? exp 2: exp 3;
```

This expression is read if ex;1 is TRUE, execute exp 2. Otherwise, execute exp 3. This expression accomplishes exactly the same as the above if sequence.

In macro definitions the conditional expression often found. which we discuss later.

**Precedence and Associativity**

Here is a summary of the rules of both precedence and association of all operators. The higher an operator falls in the table, the higher its precedence. Operators are all of the same precedence which fall on the same line. All symbols used in are operators. Therefore, the operator ( ) refers to the parenthesis enclosing arguments to a function call. To the brackets enclosing the argument of an array referred by the operator [ ]. The period operator, and the comma operator, will both be discussed when introduced. Later, the-> and the size of operators 679 will be introduced.

<table>
<tr><th>Operator</th><th>Associativity</th></tr>
<tr><td>( ) [ ]-> .</td><td>left to right</td></tr>
<tr><td>! ~ ++-+-* & (type) sizeof</td><td>right to left</td></tr>
<tr><td>* / %</td><td>left to right</td></tr>
<tr><td>+-</td><td>left to right</td></tr>
<tr><td><< >></td><td>left to right</td></tr>
<tr><td>< < + > = ></td><td>left to right</td></tr>
<tr><td>== !=</td><td>left to right</td></tr>
<tr><td>&</td><td>left to right</td></tr>
<tr><td>^</td><td>left to right</td></tr>
<tr><td>|</td><td>left to right</td></tr>
<tr><td>&&</td><td>left to right</td></tr>
<tr><td>| |</td><td>left to right</td></tr>
<tr><td>? :</td><td>right to left</td></tr>
<tr><td>= + =-= * = % = & = ^ = | = << = >> =</td><td>right to left</td></tr>
<tr><td></td><td>left to right</td></tr>
</table>

Note the very high precedence of the parenthesis and the square brackets. To force operations that are not in line with the normal precedence of the language it is the high precedence of these operators that allows the prgrammer. The second highest precendence is the list of unary operators. These operators are all associated from right to left.

**Program Flow and Control**

To control the execution of a program, program flow and control comprise several different means. Looping constructs, for example, control the repeated execution of a program segment while adjusting parameters used in the execution at either the beginning or the end of the loops. The choice of one of many operations can be accompanied with the else if or switch/case statements and two way branches are created by if / else statements. The following paragraphs will provide a quick look at each of these program flow and control methods.

*The While Statement*

For the C programmer there are three looping constructs available, the while ( ) statement, the for ( ; ; ) statement and the do/while ( ) statement. The use of the while looping construct along with some other concepts demonstrated by the following program. We have seen the while statement earlier, but the following program will provide a new look at its use.

```
# include <stdio.h>
void main (void)
(
int guess, i;
i = 1;
guess = 5;
while (guess ! = i )
{
i = guess;
guess = ( i + ( 10000/i ) ) /2;
}
print f ( "The square root of 10000 is %d\n", guess);
}
```

As in the first example. To bring standard input/output features into the program the # include statement is used and with the function definition main ( ) the program starts.

Inside of the main program, the first statement is

```
int guess, i;
```

The variables guess and i identifies by this statement as integers. No value is assigned to i at this time, but a space in memory is allocated to guess and i and the space is sufficient to store an integers. The first executable statement in the program is.

```
i = 1;
```

this is an assignment statement. Here equal sign is a misnomer. The statement is read "replace the contents of the memory location assigned to i with a 1." The next statement

```
guess = 5;
```

assigns a value 5 to the variable guess.

The statement

```
while (guess !=i)
```

invokes a looping operation. To execute the statement while operation is used. At the beginning of each loop execution, the while argument guess ! = i is checked. This argument is read "guess is not equal to i." So long as this argument is TRUE, the statement following the while will be executed. The statement following the while will be skipped when guess becomes equal to i.

The while is followed by a compound statement that contains two statements:

```
{
i=guess;
guess = ( i + ( 10000/i ) ) /2;
}
```

This calculation is known as a Newton loop. It states that if i is a guess at the square root of 10000, then ( i + ( 10000 /i ) ) /2 is a better guess. Until i is equal to guess the loop will continue to execute. At this time the compound statement will be skipped.

The program control is passed to the statement when the statement following the while is skipped.

```
print £ ( "The square root of 10000 is %d\n*, guess );
```

this statement prints out the last guess which will be the square root of 10000.

*The For Loop*

Many times, a sequence of code like

```
statement 1;
while (statement 2 )
{
.
.
.
statement 3;
}
```

will be found. In the above example this exact sequence was seen. There is a short-hand version of this sequence that can be used. It is as follows:

```
for ( statement 1; statement 2; statement 3 )
```

Three arguments taken by for construct which separated by semicolons. The for construct is compiled exactly the same as the above sequence in operation. In other words, statement 1 is executed followed by a standard while with statement 2 as its argument. The compound statement that follows will have statement 3 placed at its end, so that statement 3 is executed just prior to completion of the statement following the while construct.

To write the above program the for construct is used in the following manner.

```
# include <stdio.h>
void main (void)
{
int guess, i;
for ( i=1, guess=5; i ! = guess; )
{
i = guess;
guess = ( i + (10000/i )) /2;
}
print £ ( "The square root of 10000 = %d\n*, guess );
}
```

As for allows three arguments but all arguments are not, necessary for proper execution of the for. Only two arguments are included in this case. The first argument is really two initialization arguments separated by a comma operator. When the comma operator is used, the statements separated by commas are each evaluated until the semicolon is found. At this time, the initialization is terminated. By the way, the comman operator can be used in normal code sequences so that you can string several statements in a row without separating them with semicolons. The second argument of the for construct is i ! = guess. As long as this expression is TRUE the for loop will execute. In the for invacation there is no third statement.

This argument is where you would normally place the change in i that is to take place at the end of each loop. In this case, the operation on i is i = guess. At the end of the first loop the second argument would be FALSE if this expression were used for the third argument and execution of the calculation would be prematurely terminated.

***The Do/While Construct***

Do/While is the another loop structure & prior to executing the statement following the argument of a while statement is tested. If the argument of the while is FALSE to begin with, the statement following will never be executed. Sometimes, it is desired to execute the statement at least once whether the argument is TRUE or not. The argument should be tested at the end of the loop in such case rather than at the beginning. This operation accomplished by the do/while construct. The construction of a do-while loop is as follows

```
.
.
do
{
.
.
.
} while ( expression );
.
```

The program will enter the do construct and execute the code that follows up to the while statement. At that time, the expression is evaluated. If it is TRUE, program control is returned to the statement following the do. Otherwise, if the expression evaluates to FALSE, control will pass to the statement following the while. Following the while (expression) there is a semicolon. For correct operation of the do-while loop this semicolon is necessary.

**The integer number n converted into the corresponding ASCII string by the following function. The function has two parts: the first part converts the number into an ASCII string, but the result is backward in the array; the second part reverses the data in the array to that the result is correct.**

```
/* convert an integer to an ASCII string; valid for
positive numbers only */
void itoa (int n, char s [ ] )
{
int i=0, j=0, temp;
/* convert the number to ASCII */
do
{
```

```
s [ i++ ] = '0' + n % 10;
n / = 10;
} while ( n ! = 0 );
s [ i ] = 0;
/* but it is backwards in the array-reverse t * /
i-; /* don't swap the NULL */
while ( i > j )
{
temp = s [ j ];
s [ j++ ] = s [ i ];
s [ i-] = temp;
}
}
```

Three integer variables are used in this function. The variable temp does not need to be initialized and the variables i and j are both initialized to zero. The first portion of the program contains a do-while loop, the number is converted into string. The statement

```
s [ i++ ] = '0' + n % 10;
```

first calculates the value of the integer modulo 10. In the number this value is the number of 1s. The character corresponds to the number of 1s will created by adding that value to the character '0'. This value is stored in the location s [ i ] with i = 0 and then i is incremented.

n is replaced by n divided by 10 in the second statement in the loop. this code removes any 1s that were in the number originally, and now the original 10s are in the 1s position. If the result is between 0 and 1 it will be rounded to 0, since this division is an integer division. Therefore, the test in the while argument allows the above two statements to repeat unitl the original number n is exhausted by repeated divisions by 10.

S [ i ] will be the character in mediately following the string of characters when the do-while loop is completed. A string is created by placing a 0 or a NULL in this location of the array.

The program starts by decrementing i so that s [ i ] is the last entry in the array to reverse the data. This entry is the most significant character in the number, and it must be placed in the first array location s [ 0 ]:. Likewise, the character in s [ 0 ] must be placed in s [ i ]: and so forth. the while loop that follows accomplishes this requirement.

***The If/Else Statement***

The if/else statement has the general form

```
if (expression)
statement 1;
else
statement 2;
```

Statement 1 will be executed if the logical evaluation of the expression that is the argument of the if is TRUE. Program control will pass to the statement following statement 2 and will not be executed after statement 1 is executed.

The use of the if/else flow control method is demonstrated by the following program.

```
/* count number of numbers and other characters in input
*/
# include <stdio.h>
void main (void)
{
int c, nn, no;
no=0;
nn=0;
while ( ( c=getchar ( ) ) ! = EOF )
if ( c> = '0' &&c< = '9' )
nn++;
print f ( "Numbers = %d and other characters = %d\n", nn,
no );
)
```

The statement

```
int c, nn, no;
```

declares the three variables c, nn, and no to be integers. With a single declaration statement you may declare as many variables as you wish. The next statements

```
no = 0;
nn = 0;
```

initializes the values of no and nn to 0. Automatic variables are the variables declared with the above sequence of instructions. These variables are not initialized by the compiler, and the programmer must initialize them to a required value. Otherwise the variables will contain garbage.

The expression sequence

```
while ( ( c = getchar ( ) ) ! = EOF )
if ( c>+ '0' && c<= 'g' )
nn++;
else
no++;
```

comprise the while and its following statement. The value of c tested and determined by the if portion of the statement. A character is identified as a specific value by placing the character value in single quotes. Therefore, the expression c>='0' dermines if the character in the location c is greater than or equal to the character. The result of this expression is TRUE if it is. Otherwise, the result is FALSE. If the input character is less than or equal to the character g determined by the expression c<='g'. If both of these logical expressions are TRUE, and the statement nn++ will be executed to count the numbers found in the input stream. Program control will then skip to the end of the if statement and continue to execute the while loop. If, on the other hand, either of these expressions are FALSE, then the AND of the two results will be FALSE, and the statement no++ will be executed. The number of characters that are not found in the input stream keep count by this statement.

The get char ( ) will return an EOF character and the program will fall out of the while loop at the conclusion of the program. It will than execute the following statement:

```
print £ ( "Numbers = %d and other characters = %d\n", nn,
no );
```

A combination of text plus calculated values of variables to printed out caused by the string contained within the double quotes in this argument. Suppose that the program would have found 51 numbers and 488 other characters. The printout fom the program would then be:

```
Numbers = 51 and other characters = 488
```

Before it is sent to the screen each %d is associated with its corresponding argument and converted to a numerical value.

### *The If-Else If Statement*

To select among several alternatives it is necessary sometimes. One of the methods that C offers is the if-else is sequence. Examine the following program that counts the number of occurrence of each vowel in an input. The program also counts all other characters found in the input.

```
/* Count the number of occurrences of each vowel found
in an input and also count all other characters. */
# include <stdio.h>
void main (void)
{
int na=0, ne=0, ni=0, no=0, nu=0;
int nother=0, c;
while ( ( c=getchar ( ) ) !=EOF)
if ( c=='A' || c=='a' )
na = na + 1;
else if ( c =='E' || c=='e' )
ne = ne + 1;
else if ( c =='I' || c=='i' )
ni = ni + 1;
else if ( c =='O' || c=='o' )
no = no + 1;
else if ( c =='U' || c=='u' )
nu = nu + 1;
else
nother=nother + 1;
print f ( "As = %d, Es = %d, Is = %d, Os = %d, Us = %d
and" )
"Others = %d/n, na, ne, ni, no, nu, nother" );
}
```

Several new features of c shown by this program. The first is found in the program lines.

```
int na=0, ne=0, ni=0, no=0, nu=0;
int nother=0, c;
```

They are assigned initial values of 0 when the variables na and so forth are declared where variables are declared then such an initialization is always possible. The next statement of the program is

```
while ( (c=getchar ( ) ) ! = EOF )
if ( c == 'A' || c == 'a' )
na = na + 1;
else if ( c == 'E' || c == 'e' )
ne = ne + 1;
else if ( c == 'I' || c == 'i' )
ni = ni + 1;
```

```
else if ( c == 'O' || c == 'o' )
no = no + 1;
else if ( c == 'U' || c == 'u' )
nu = nu + 1;
else
nother = nother + 1;
```

There are some new concepts and this single statement has a quite a few lines of code associated with it. First, the arguments of the if s are combination of two logical expressions. The expression

```
c = = 'A' || c == 'a'
```

Says that the argument is TRUE if c is equal to uppercase a or if c is equal to lowercase a. The vertical bars || are the logical operator OR.

The first if statement is evaluated. If its argument is TRUE, the statement following the if is executed and program control moves to the end of the if statements. Otherwise, the first else if statement argument is evaluated. The following statement is executed and program control moves to the end of the if statements if this argument is TRUE. Until one of the arguments is found to be true this process is repeated or all of the else if statements are evaluated. At that time, the final statement following the else entry is evaluated. The final else is not required.

The print £ function call

```
print £ ( "As=%d, Es=%d, Is=%d, Os=%d, Us=%d and"
"Others=%d\n, na, ne, ni, no, nu, nother );
```

has the normal print £ arguments. Note however that the string is not confined to one line. In a program c compilers will not allow a string to be split among several lines. However, ANSI C causes two adjacent strings to be concatenated into a single string so the above code will compile without error.

***Break, continue, and goto***

To alter its program flow these commands will cause a c program. The program will exit the loop in which it is executing if a break statement is encountered. Break can be used in exit for, while, do-while, and switch statements. An example of the use of the break statement is shown in the next section.

The next iteration of a for, while or a do-while loop to be started caused by the continue statement. In the case of the fore statement, the last argument is executed, and control is passed to the beginning of the for loop. For both the while and the do-while, the argument of the while statement is tested immediately, and the program proceeds according to result of the test.

The continue statement is rarely used and the break statement is seen frequently. Goto is the another rarely used statement. In C, the programmer can create a lable at any location by typing the label name followed by a semicolon. If it is necessary, the goto-<lable> can be used to transfer control of the program from one location to another. In general, C provides enough structured language constructs that the use of the goto <lable> sequence will rarely be needed. One place where the goto can be used effectively is when the program is nested deeply and an error is detected. From a deep loop to an outer loop to process the error the goto statement is an effective means of unwinding the program in such a case.

*The Switch Statement*

The switch statement is a second approach for selection between several alternates. This approach is sometimes called the switch/case statement. As the above program following is a program that accomplishes exactly the same. In this case the switch statement is used.

```
/* Count the number of occurrences of each vowel found
in an input and also count all other characters. */
# include <stdio.h>
void main (void)
{
int na=0, ne=o, ni=0, no=0, nu=0;
int nother=0, c;
while ( ( c=getchar ( ) ) !=EOF)
switch ( c )
{
case 'A' ;
case 'a' ; na=na+1;
break;
case 'E' ;
case 'e' ; ne=ne+1;
break;
```

```
case 'I';
case 'i'; ni=ni+1;
break;
case 'O';
case 'o'; no=no+1;
break;
case 'U';
case 'u'; nu=nu+1;
break;
default;
nother=nother+1;
}
print £ ( "As=%d, Es=%d, Is=%d, Os=%d, Us=%d and"
"Others=%d\n, na, ne, ni, no, nu, nother );
}
```

As the earlier one this program performs exactly the same function. The data are read in a character at a time as before. Here, however, the switch statement is used. The comparison of the argument of the switch with the constants following each of the case statements caused by the statement switch (c). When a match occurs, the next set of statements to follow a colon will be executed. Once the program starts to execute statements, all of the following statements will be executed unless the programmer does something to cause the program to be redirected. The break instruction does exactly this operation for us. When a C program encounters a break, it jumps to the end of the current block. The program to jump out of the executing sequence and return to get the next character from the input stream caused by the breaks following the executable statements above.

When all options have been exhausted without a match, the statements following the default line will be executed. It is not necessary to have a default line.

## Functions

The heart of a c program is the function. In fact, any C program is merely a function named main To provide a mechanism to allow a single entry of a code sequence that is to be repeated many times its the purpose of a function. In c language a function is the most reusable element. Properly written and debugged functions can be collected into a program when needed. Therefore, the use of functions will allow the programmer to write smaller programs and it is not necessary to rewrite common functions that are used often.

Many arguments may present in a function or may not following the function name function arguments are contained in parenthesis. The values of the arguments are the parameters needed to execute the function. A function can return a value, or perhaps it will not have a return value. An example of a function the returns a value is getchar ( ) which will return a character from the input stream. A function will retrun no value is put char (c) which puts the character c onto the output stream.

Inside another function a function may not be nested. Out side of the boundaries of any other function or program structure any function must be created. Functions have only one entry point, and they return only one return item. The return can be of any type that C supports. Functions can have several arguments. The arguments can be of any valid C type.

The type to be returned from the function is the first type preceding the function. A function prototype is a statement of the following form:

```
type function_name (type, type, type, . . .);
```

The type to be returned from the function is the first type preceding the function. The several types found in the argument are the types of the corresponding arguments that are sent to the function. Variable naes may or may not be used for the arguments of a function prototype. The type list is the important item and in the argument list the types are separated by commas.

Thus far, it might seem that we have beeen blindly using functions like print £ ( ), getchar ( ), and putchar ( ) without the benefit of function prototypes. Not so! It is not necessary for you to put a function prototype in your code for these functions because the headerfile studio.h contains the function prototype of all input/output related functions.

Compilers will differ. If a programmer attempts to send the wrong type of data to a function through its argument, the compiler might consider it an error or it might well convert the argument to the correct type prior to calling the function. To use the wrong type of data as an argument to a function the compiler will not let a program in either case.

Before it is passed to the program data returned from a function will always be converted to the correct type. If you wish to have a different type returned, the cast operator can be used to change the return data type to any desired.

ANSI C defined the type void. This type is used in several different ways. The prototype must identify the function as type void if there is no function return. Also when there are no function arguments, the argument list must contain the type void. This use of the keyword void will prevent problems is function calls.

Note that the function prototype above is terminated with a semicolon. The semicolon is needed in the function prototype, but it is not to be used after the name of the function in the code where the function is defined.

To use functions with little provocation is the philosophy in c and produces code that is easy to read and follow by using many functions. Often it is easier to debug many small functions rather than a larger program. One must temper these ideas somewhat when writing code for small microcontrollers. Calling a function requires some overheawd that is repeated each time the function is accessed. If the total overhed is more than the length of the function, it is better to use in-line code. In-line code implies that the function code is repeated in-line every time that it is needed. If the function code is much greater than the calling overhead, the function should be used. It is difficult to determine a hard-and-fast rule in between these limits. To use function calls to a single function if there is a net savings of memory as a result it is probably best in microcontroller applications. This savings is calculated by first determining the code needed prior to calling the function, the code needed to clean up the process after the function call, the number of times the function is called and the length of the function. The in-line code will be smaller than the corresponding function code. Therefore, if the total code for the number of function calls listed first exceeds the total in-line code required to accomplish the same operations, then use the in-line code. Otherwise, use function calls.

For microcontroller applications code the above argument is valid. It does not necessarily follow the code written for large computers. There are usually few memory constraints when writing for a large computer. In those cases, it is probably best to use more function calls and not be worried about the memory space taken up by function calls unless there is serious speed constraint. When speed is a problem, the programmer must go through an analysis similar to that above wiht the dependent parameter being time rather than memory space. Single instructions can require many clock cycles in small computers where several registers can be saved and restored when a function is entered and exited. When deciding whether to use a function or in-line code, the programmer must assess the total time lost to entering and exiting a function each time it is entered, and weight that time lost as a fraction of the total time the program resides in the function. If this time is large, and the program requires too much execution time, consider the use of in-line functions.

To exercise the small functions it is always good to write small functions and create simple calling programs. These programs are used to debug the functions, and they are discarded after the functions are debugged. If later, the program constraints dictate that in-line code should be used, the essential code of the function can be written into the program wherever it is needed. Another approach that will be discussed in the next chapter is to use a macro definition to specify a small function. Whenever the function is invoked the function code is written in-line to the program with a macro definition.

Let us revisit an example used ealier. Write a program to calculate and display the square root of each integer less than 11"

```
/* Calculate and display the square roots of numbers
1 <=x <=10 */
# include <stdio.h.>
#define abs (t)  ( ( t) >=0 ) ? (t) :-(t) )
#define square (t)  (t) * (t)
double sqr ( double );
void main (void)
{
int i;
double c;
for ( i=1 ; i<1 ; i++ )
{
```

```
c=sqr (i);
print £ ( "\t%d\t%£\t%£\n", i, c, square (c) );
}
}
double sqr ( double x )
{
double x1=1, x2=1, c;
do {
x1=x2;
x2=(x1 + x/x1)/2;
c=x1-x2;
}
while (abs (c) >= . 00000001);
return x2;
}
```

The calculation's result is as follows:

1. 1.000000 1.000000
2. 1.414214 2.000000
3. 1.732051 3.000000
4. 2.000000 4.000000
5. 2.236068 5.000000
6. 2.449490 6.000000
7. 2.645751 7.000000
8. 2.828427 8.000000
9. 3.000000 9.000000
10. 3.162278 10.000000

The second line of code

```
#define abs (t) ( (t) >=0 ) ? (t) :-(t) )
```

is called a macro definition. The macro definition has the appearance of a simple functin in this case the absolute value of the argument will calculated by this function. The absolute value of the argument is a positive value. If the argument is positive, it is returned unchanged. If it is negative, it is multiplied by-1 before it is returned. A macro definition is a type of character expansion. Whenever the function abs (x) is found in the code, the character string ( ( (x)>=0) ? (x) :-(x) is put in its place. The argument x can be any valid C expression. The absolute value of its argument returned by this function. The macro definition

```
#define square (t) (t) * (t)
```

returns the square of t It is neccessary to be coutious when writing the macro definitions since these arguments can be valid in any c operation. Suppose that the parenthesis were left out of the above expression, and the macro were written

```
#define square (t) t * t
```

Also suppose that the code using this function were as follows:

```
x=square (y+3);
```

* The character expansion of this expression would be

```
x=y+3*y+3;
```

The result of this calculation is 4*y+3 and not ( y+3 ) * ( y+3 ) as expected. Surround all arguments and functions created by the macro with parenthesis when uniting macro definitions so that arguments are evaluated prior to use in the macro definition function.

At the end of the macro definition there is no semicolon. There should not be. If a semicolon were placed at the end of a macro definition, and a semicolon placed at the end of an expression using the macro definition, extra semicolon would be entered into the expression with unpredictable results.

The function prototype

```
double sqr ( double );
```

notifies the compiler that the function returns a double and takes a double argument. Inside of the main function, the for loop

```
for ( i=1; i<11; i++ )
{
c=sqr (i);
print £ ( "\t%d\t%£\t%£\n", i, c, square (c) );
```

is used to calculate the several results. The variable c is of the type double, and an int. The expression c=sqr (i) will be accepted by the compiler. A double which can be stored in c returned by this function, the compiler recognizes that sqr requires a double argument but the argument is an int and before it is sent to the function sqr ( ) converts it to a double.

The code in the function sqr ( ) is a statement of a square root operation we saw earlier. Three double variables are used in this case and rather than using integers function processes floating point numbers. The variables x1,x2 are the current and last values found in the Newton iteration. As the reconverges to the correct value for the square root, several things happen. Variable x1 and x2 become equal. The square of x2, and x1 for that matter, becomes equal to x. The product of x1 and x2 become equal to x. To determine if the estimate has been through enough iterations to be accurate any of these tests can be used.

To test for the end of the loop the macro definition abs (x) is used. You will see that the argument is evaluated three times for the expansion of the macro. If we plan a lot of calculation within the argument of a macro definition, the expansion of the macro may cause the code to calculate the argument to be repeated several times, this reason, the expression.

```
c = x1-x2;
```

is placed inside of the while loop, and the test to determine loop termination arg (c).

The value of the expression following the word return to be evaluated and returned to the calling function a return statement will cause that at the end of a function. This expression is not of the type specified by the function prototype and the found definition, it will be converted to the correct type prior to being returned to the call function. The expression following the return statement can be enclosed in parenthesis or not.

Another example will show the use of static external variables.

```
/* Read in a string from the keyboard and print it
out in reverse order. */
# include <stdio.h>
/*some function prototypes */
void push (int);
int pull (void);
void main (void);
{
int c;
push (NULL);
while ( ( c=getchar ( ) !='\n' )
```

```
push (c);
print £ ( "\n" );
while ( ( c=pull ( ) ) !=NULL )
putchar (c);
print £ (\n );
}
```

The following code is to be compiled in a separate file from the code above:

```
# define MAX 100
staticf int buffer [MAX];
static int sp;
void push ( int x )
{
if ( sp < MAX )
buffer [ sp++ ] =x;
else {
print £ ( "stack overflow\n" );
exit (1);
}
}
int pull (void)
{
if ( sp > 0 )
return buffer [-sp ];
else
{
print £ ( "stack underflow\n" );
exit (1);
}
}
```

A stack is a last in, first out (LIFO) structure. To reverse the order of data sent to it a stack can be used. A stack operation used in the above program. The functions push and pull identified in the function prototypes perform the stacking operations for the main program. To identify the end of the data as it is pulled off of the stack a character at a time a NULL is pushed in the main program. Data are read in a character at a time, and as each character is read in, it is pushed onto a stack. The input phase is stopped and the data written to the stack is pulled off and printed when a new line character is detected.

When the NULL is detected, the data have all been pulled off the stack, and the program is ended.

The function exit ( ) is used in the function above which is simmilar to return function. Whenever a call to the function exit is called, the argument is evaluated, any files open for write are flushed and closed, and the control of the computer is returned to the operating system. The evaluation of the argument is returned to the operating system. Whenever a return is encountered, the expression following the return call is evaluated and returned to the calling function. The evaluation of the expression is returned to the operating system is control is in main ( ) and whenthe return is encountered. Also, from main ( ) all files open for write are flushed and closed.

The stack functions are compiled in a separate compilation the macro definition MAX is defined as 100 in that function. Macro definitions can be used to define any character string that is needed in a program. They are not limited to defining pseudo functions. An array of MAX integer named buffer and an int called sp are the two global variables defined in this file. These variables are declared to be static. As such, these variables can be accessed by any function in the file, but they are not available to any function outside of the file. The variable sp is used as an undex into the array buffer. When a push is executed, a test to determine if sp is less than MAX is completed. If sp is less than MAX, the data are stored at the sp location in buffer and sp is then incremented. Otherwise, an error message that indicates that a stack overflow has occurred and the program is exited.

The pull ( ) function is the reverse of the push ( ) operation. To see if there are some data on the stack to be pulled off a check is made first. The stack pointer is decremented if there are data and the content of the buffer at that location in returned to the calling program. In the event that sp is when the pull operation is executed, a stack underflow message is sent to the screen prior to exiting the program.

The advantage to our making the buffer and the stack pointer in the stack functions static can be easily see. Suppose that these variables could be accessed from anywhere in the program. To call the functions push or pull to stack and unstack data it would not be necessary for the programmer in this case.

If several different programmers were using the same stack for different tasks in one large program, it would be possible for different programmers to access the stack as expected, or from their own tasks. Suppose a programmer would make the mistake of pre-decrementing the stack pointer on stacking and post-incrementing the stack pointer on unstacking. The whole program would suddenly be in chaos. Serious debugging problems can reduced by masking these variables from rest of the program.

# Chapter 9

# Arrays, Pointer and Functions

In consecutive memory locations a collection of like types of data that are stored is called an array. By appending a pair of square brackets to the array name an array is designated at declaration time. If the size of the array is to be determined at the declaration, the square brackets can contain the number of elements in the array. Following are proper array declaration.

```
extern int a [ ];
long rd [100];
float temperatures [1000];
char st [ ] = { "Make a character array"};
float pressure [ ] = { 1.1, 2.3, 3.9, 3.7, 2.5, 1.5, 0.4
};
```

Before you can use empty square brackets in the designation the size of an array must be designated. In the first case above, the array a [ ] is defined in global memory, so all that is necessary for the compile to know is that a [ ] is an array. The argument of an array is sometimes called its index. It is a number that selects a specific entry into an array. Array arguments start with zero always. By using the arguments 0 to 99 these elements are accessed when an array of 100 elements is created. The element corresponding to 100 will not be a part of the array, and its use will cause unpredictable results.

Arrays can be initialized at declaration. these values must be seperated by commas, if there are several individual numerical values and must be enclosed in braces. In the case of a string intialization, it is necessary to include the string in quotes and also enclose the string along with its quotation marks within the braces. In both of these cases, the size of the array is calculated at compile time, and it is unnecessary for the programmer to figure the size of the array.

A special case of an array is a string and an array of characters is created a string is generated in C. The length of the array is one greater than the length of the string. The individual characters from the string are placed in the array entries. To be a proper C string, the array's last character must be a zero or a NULL. All strings in C are NULL terminated. If you as a programmer create a string in your program, you must append a NULL on the end of the character array to be guaranteed that C will treat the array as a string.

C provides you with no array boundary checking. The array arguments do not violate the boundaries of the array to guarantee that it is programmers responsibility.

**Pointers**

From most of other high level languages the use of pointers sets the C language apart under the name of indirect addressing pointers are commonly used in a assembly language. Most high level languages ignore completely this powerful programming technique. In C, pointers are simply variables that are the addresses of other variables. These variables can be assigned, be used as perands, and treated much the same as regular variables. Their use, however, can simplify greatly many of the truly difficult problems that arise in day-to-day programming. Let's discuss pointers with the view that to make our programming job easier they offer us a powerful new tool.

***How to use Pointers***

The address of a variable is a pointer to a variable depending on the type of the standard variable types were found to occupy 8-16-or 32-bits. Pointers are not types in the sense of variables. Pointers might occupy 16-or 32-bits, and their size is implementation dependent. In fact, there are cases of pointers to like types having different sizes in the same program depending on context.

If the variable px is a pointer to the type int and x is an int, px can be assigned the address of x by

```
px = *px;
```

To use the address of x rather than the value of x in the above assignment the ampers and (&) modifies the compiler. The reverse operation to that above is

```
x = * px;
```

To use the address of x rather than the value of x in the assignment the arterisk (*) is a unary operator that applies to a pointer. The unary * is referred to as the deference operator. With these two operators, it is possible to move from variable to pointer and back again with ease.

If the lexical value of a one word is smaller, equal or larger to that of another word then a comaprison is needed first. Above such a compare routine was outlined. Second, a swap routine that will swap the words that are in the wrong order. Here is a case where an array of pointers can be quite useful. Assume that the program that reads in the data will put each word into a separate memory location and keep an array of pointers to the beginning of each word rather than just the array of the words themselves. Rather than swapping the words swap the pointers in the array when a swap is required in the shell sort swap pointers in the array are very easy to implement. On the other hand, swap routines to swap two strings in memory are difficult and slow. Therefore, we can create a sort routine that is much more efficient if we use an array of pointers rather than an array of strings.

```
/* shell_sort ( ) : sort the contents of the array char*
v [ ] into ascending order */
void shell_sort ( char* v[ ], int n )
(
int gap, i,, j;
char* temp;
for ( gap = n/2; gap / = 2 )
for ( i = gap; i < n; i++ )
for ( j = i-gap; j>=0 &&
strcmp (v [j], v[j+gap]); j-= gap)
(
temp = v[j];
```

```
v [j] = v [j+gap];
v [j+gap] = v[j];
)
```

To determine if a swap is needed the strcmp ( ) routine is used. In header file string n strcmp ( ) is identified. When needed, the contents of the array of pointers to the beginning of the words is swapped rather than swapping the words themselves.

**Multidimensional Arrays**

Multidimensional arrays supported by C. For multidimensional arrays will go away with the availability of pointers the programmers after find that much of the need. Multidimensional arrays in C are thought of as arrays of arrays. This idea can be extended to more than tw3o dimensions, but most compilers will limit the dimensionality of an array to five or less. A two dimensional array is identified as array [x] [y]; /* [row] [column] */

As the row dimension the first argument to the right can be thought and the second the column dimension. Elements specified by the rightmost argument are stored in adjacent memory locations.

At declaration time an array can be identified. For example:

```
int array [3] [4] = ( (10, 11, 12, 13 ),
( 14, 15, 16, 17 ),
(18, 19, 20, 21 ) );
```

It is equally valid to initialize the array as follows:

```
int array [3] [4] = ( 10, 11, 12, 13, 14, 15, 16, 17, 18,
19, 20, 21 );
```

In the proper location in the memory either form of intialization will place the proper numbers and in either case the two dimensional indices will work properly.

Frequently, it is needed to know the size of a variable in C. This variable can be a basic type, an array, a multiple dimensional array, or even a structure that will be introduced later. C provides an operator that has much the appearance of a function called size of ( ). The size of ( ) operator is use to determine the size of any variable as follows :

```
a = size of (array);
```

which will return the number of bytes contained in array [ ] [ ] above.

To determine the Julian data is an example program that is frequently found with two dimensionally arrays. The Julian date is simply the day of the year. The following function is one that allows counting the number of days that have passed in a year.

```
int month_days [2] [13] = {
{ 0, 31, 28, 31, 30, 31, 30, 31, 31, 30, 31, 30, 31 },
{ 0, 31, 29, 31, 30, 31, 30, 31, 31, 30, 31, 30, 31 }
};
int Julian data ( int month, int date, int year )
{
int i, leap;
leap = year%4==0 && year%100!=0 ||year%400==0;
for ( i=1; i<month; i++)
day += month_days [leap] [i];
return day;
int month_days [2] [13] = {
{ 0,, 31, 28, 31, 30, 31, 30, 31, 31, 30, 31, 30, 31 },
{ 0, 31, 29, 31, 30, 31, 30, 31, 31, 30, 31, 30, 31 }
};
```

types month_days as an array of 26 integers. This array is a two-dimentional array of two rows of 13 columns each. The values assigned are shown. To allow the conventional month designations 1 through 12 to be used as indices and the extra 0 entry at the beginning of each array and not have to worry about the fact that arrays in C start with a 0 index.

The introduction of the program is normal. The function expects to receive three int arguments, one for month, one for the day of the month, and one for year and the function returns an int. Note that the year must be the full year, like 2013, rather than merely 13. Logical statement is the first executable statement.

```
leap = year%4==0 && year%100!=0 || year%400==0;
```

Leap years are usually ever four years. However with the "once each four years" correction a small discrepancy still exists. The calender makers have decided that years divisible by 100 will not be leap year unless the year is divisible by 100 to further correct the error. The above statement is a logical statement that it is then checked to determine if it is divisible by 100. The result of this much of the analysis will be TRUE for any year divisible by 4, and not divisible by 100. If this portion of the calculation is TRUE, leap will be assigned a value TRUE, or 1, and the evaluation will terminate. It will be neccessary to evaluate the last term to determine if the whole statement is TRUE or FALSE if the result of the first portion of the calculation is FALSE. The variable leap will be assigned the result of

```
year%400==0
```

in this case.

According to the result of the logic evaluation leap is assigned a value of 1 or 0. This value can be used as an index into the two dimensional array to determine if the number of month days in a leap year or a nonleap year will be used in the calculation of the Julian date.

**Pointers and Multidimensional Arrays**

Multidimensional arrays are one of the most widely misunderstood and mysterious aspects of pointers and C. These problems are really not difficult. A multidimensional array must always be understood as being arrays of arrays of arrays and so forth. For example, the declaration

```
int ar [3] [5];
```

defines three arrays of five elements each. We have already seen that data stored this array is column major. ar [n] [0] and ar [n] [1] are stored in adjacent memory locations and the second arguments points to a column in two dimensional array. Following the logic of arrays names and pointers, the array name ar is pointer to the first element in the array. The value obtained when using ar as an rvalue is &ar [0] [0]. The order of evaluation of the square brackets if from left to right so that * (ar + 1) is a pointer to the element ar [1] [0] in the array. Think of the two-dimensional array as being * (ar + n) [i] where n has a range from 0 to 2 and i has a range from 0 to 4. The absolute value of the pointer incremented by 5* size of (int) by increment in n.

To the next level these ideas can be carried. To the first element of a 5 element array the element *( ar + n ) is a pointer. Therefore, the evaluation of * (*(ar+n) +i is the value found in the location ar [n] [i]. The important item is that the right most argument in multiple dimensional arrays point to adjacent memory locations and the increment of the left arguments step the corresponding pointer value from array to array to array.

To arrays of more than two dimensions these ideas can be extended. Had the array been

```
double br [3] [4] [5];
```

then * (* (* (br+1) +2) +3) would be the element br [1] [2] [3] from the above array, and * (* (br+1) +2) +3 is a pointer to this element.

## C's Dynamic Allocation Functions

For C's powerful dynamic allocation system pointers provide necessary support. A program can obtain memory while it is running by means of dynamic allocation. As you know, global variables are allocated storage at compile time. Local variables use the stack. However, neither global nor local variables can be added during program execution. Yet, there will be times when the storage needs of a program cannot be known ahead of time. By using C's dynamic allocation system these programs most allocate memory.

From the heap the region of free memory that lies between your program and its permenent storage area the memory allocated by C's dynamic allocation functions. Although the size of the heap is unknown, it generally contains a fairly large amount of free memory.

## malloc ( ) and free ( )

The core of C's allocation system consists of the functions malloc ( ) and free ( ) Several other dynamic allocation functions are supplied by most C compilers but these two are most important. To establish and maintain list of available storage these functions work together using the free memory region. The malloc ( ) function allocates memory and the free ( ) function releases it. That is, each time a malloc ( ) memory request is made, a portion of the remaining free memory is allocated. Each time a free ( ) memory release call is made, memory is returned to the sysem. Any program that uses these functions should include the header file stdlib.h.

The malloc ( ) function has this prototype:

```
void *malloc(size_t number_of_bytes);
```

The malloc( ) function returns a pointer of type void, which means that you can assign it to any type of pointer. After a successful call, malloc( ) returns a pointer to the first byte of region of memory allocated from the heap. An allocation failure occurs and malloc( ) returns to a null if there is not enough available memory to satisfy the malloc( ) request.

The code fragment shown here allocates 1000 bytes of contiguous memory.

```
char *p;
p = malloc(1000); /* get 1000 bytes */
```

After the assignment, p points to the first of 1000 bytes of free memory.

The next example allocates space for 50 integers. Notice the use of size of to ensure portability.

```
int *p;
p = malloc(50*sizeof(int));
```

Since the heap is not infinite. You must check the value returned by malloc( ) to make sure that it not null before using the pointer whenever you allocate memory.

Using a null pointer will almost certainly crash your program. The proper way to allocate memory and test for a valid pointer is illustrated in this code fragment:

```
if(1P=MALLOC(100))
{
PRINTF("Out of memory,\n");
exit(1);
}
```

In place of the call to exit ( ) you can substitute some other sort of error handler. Just make sure that you do not use the pointer p if it is NULL.

The free function returns previously allocated memory to the system hence it is opposite of malloc( ). Once the memory has been freed, it may be reused by a subsequent call to malloc(). The function free ( ) has this prototype:

```
void free(void *p);
```

Here, p is a pointer to memory that was previously allocated using malloc( ). It is critical that you never call free( ) with an invalid argument; this will destroy the free list. A couple of points to be noted regarding free( ) has this operation are:

- Because malloc( ) stores this information at the time of allocation along with the space allocated to you so you do not have to tell free( ) how many bytes it has to free.
- You cannot use the sizeof operator to find out the size of the space pointed to by the pointer that was assigned space by the malloc( ). In such a case, all that the sizeof can tell you is the size of the pointer itself and not the space that the pointer points to.

For keeping track of the free and occupied memory while using the dynamic allocation it is unfortunately very easy to corrupt the internal data structures. The resulting problems can be very tricky to find and debug. The most common source of problems is that you may write more to a malloc region than it was allocated to hold. Consequently, some other items in memory may be overwritten inadvertently. The impact of this may show up long after the actual mistake and in unrelated sections of code, making the diagnosis of the problem because they store crucial pieces of information directly adjacent to the blocks of memory they return, making it very easy to overwrite them with pointers gone astray.

To support a variety of important programming constructs such as linked lists and binary trees C's dynamic allocation subsytem is used in conjunction with pointer. You will see several examples of these in a course on Data Structures.

## Pointers to Functions and Complicated Declarations

To functions C has pointers. In creating vector tables for microcontrollers pointers to functions are commonly used. Most microcontroller applications will involve the use of interrupts. When an interrupt occurs, the machine status is saved, and program control is transferred to an interrupt service routine. At the close of the interrupt service routine, the machine status is returned to the earlier condition, and control is returned to the interrupted program. An address table in memory called the vector table contains the addresses of each interrupt service routine. It is the programmers responsibility to fill the vector table with the proper addresses for the various interrupt service routine. To access the addresses of the interrupt service routines pointers to functions allow the programmer. To create the vector tables on the individual microcontrollers we will see several different methods in the chapters.

A pointer to a function is idendified by

```
int ( *funtion_ptr) ( );
```

The above declaration says that function_ptr is pointer to a function that returns a type int. The arguments are not declared here. The parenthesis surrounding * funtion_ptr are required. The declaration would declare function_ptr as a function that returns a pointer to the type if they were not included. If function_ptr is a valid pointer to a function, the function can be accessed by

```
( *function_ptr) (args);
```

the above declaration form can be used for arrays as well as functions. The declaration

```
char (* array_ptr) [ ];
```

states that array_ptr is a poiter to an array of char. The declaration

```
char* array [ ];
```

states that array is an array of pointers to the type char. These declarations can be combined to create very complicated declarations although you will find them rarely used.

One construct from the general area of complicated declarations is so important to microcontroller code that it must be covered. l values are the type variable supported by 'C' that can be destination for an assignment. Most variables in C are 1 values. Notable exceptions are function names and array names. If a program deals with a number that can be a memory address, it can be made accessible to the language by casting the address to an appropriate type. For example, suppose that a special table is located at the address 0x1000 in memory. Further, suppose that the type to be stored at that address is an integer. Here, the code sequence

```
( int * ) 0x1000
```

forces the number 0x1000 to be a pointer to a type int. If the programmer wants to put a value into a specific address then after this idea must be carried further. the above representation is a pointer to the type int. Therefore, a value can be assigned to that int by

```
*( int * ) 0x1000 = integer_value;
```

will place integer_value into the location 0x1000 in the computer memory.

At specific locations in memory control registers, data registers and input/output port registers are frequently placed. These register locations can be converted to tractable C names by use of the #define macro capability of C. Suppose that an I/O port is located at the address.

```
#define PORTA ( * ( char * ) 0x1000 )
```

allow the use of the variable PORTA in the computer program. this variable is of the type char, and its address is 0x1000. In programming microcontrollers this capability is very useful.

Why it is necessary to be able to manipulate direct address in memory when programming microcontrollers there are two reasons for it. To specific memory locations most high level languages will not allow the programmer direct access. As seen above, C does allow the programmer to bend these rules enough to be able to store data into a specific memory address. Another feature that is highly desirable is to be able to place the address of a function at a specific address. The capability is necessary when implementing an interrupt service routine. When an interrupt occurs the computer will stop its current operation, save at least the values contained in the status register and the program counter, and begin execution at an address contained in a vector location. Each interrupt will require its own interrupt service routines and will have a unique vector address. Program initialization when interrupts are involved will require that the program place the addresses of any interrupt service routines into the specific vector addresses for each interrupt.

In this case a continuation of the above approach can be used to receive the interrupt service routine address there is a direct address in memory. Let's think for a moment about what this address is. The address is goint to contain the address of a function. The address itself is a pointer to a memory location. The contents of this location is a pointer that points to a function that is the interrupt service routine. All interrupt service routines are the type void. Therefore, the vector address is a pointer to a pointer to a type void. We must assert one addition of level of indirection to access the content of the specific memory location to be able to place the value of the pointer to a type void into this location. Therefore, the following line of code

```
* (void **) 0xfffc = isr;
```

will place the beginning address of the function isr into the memory location 0xfffc. To create a macro is a convenient method of excuting this operation. The following macro definition works:

```
#define vector ( isr, address ) ( * ( void ** ) (address
) = ( isr ) )
```

Now the function call

```
vector ( timer, 0xffd0 );
```

will place the address of the function named timer into the location 0xffd0 in the computer memory map. It is important that timer defined as a function that returns a type void.

## Functions

The one of the most important features of 'C' are functions they are building blocks of programmed where all program activity occurs. A function encapsulates one or more statements, variables and parameters into a unified package that you can call into action whenever needed.

Dozens of functions from which each designed to perform a particular task present in 'C' to write programs. A program's functions are small but independent pieces of code that each performs relatively simple but well-defined tasks, when combined, perform the task required of the program.

At least one function called main ( ) present in all C programs which contains initial statements of the program. This is the function to which the control is first passed when the program is executed. All the other functions are called directly or indirectly from the main function. These other functions are at the same level as the main function. C does not permit functions to be declared within a function, although other languages like PASCAL do so. The implecations shall be highlighted later.

To create a larger program the concept of small but independent functions being combined together is very popular with the C programmers because of several reasons. Here it suuices to say that any programmer wanting to learn C has to necessarily master the technique of visualizing and implementing functions. Hence, you are advised to spend considerable time in mastering the basic ideas presented in this chapter.

## Writing and Calling Functions

A simple design that is easy to learn used by functions. A simple functiion that consists of a single statement in the body looks like this:

```
int square (int v)
{
return v*v;
}
```

You are advised to note the following points in this example:

(i) First comes the functions data type-the type of the value computed in the function.

(ii) Then, the name of the function being defined is written. This can be any valid identifier name.

(iii) Follows the functin name a pair of parenthesis enclosing the arguments passed to the function. The pair of parenthesis has to be present even if there are no arguments in the function. This is to enable the compiler to distinguish between the definition of an identifier and the function name. You shall learn more about these arguments later.

(iv) Then comes the body of the i.e. the statements that shall be executed when the function is called. With in a pair of curly braces these statements are enclosed. The above example consists of just one statement in the body-in general there could be several of these statements constituting the body of the function.

(v) A function must have at least one return statement that is executed when the function is called if it is to return some value that is to be used at the place at which the function is called. A return statement passes a value of the appropriate type as the function result. In this example, the parameter v is squared and the resulting value is returned by the function. The return statement has two important uses. First, it couses an immediate exit from the function that it is in. That is, it causes program execution to return to the calling code. Second, it may be used to return a value.

This function can be used anywhere in the program as shown below:

```
int k = 45;
k = square(k) ;
```

The second statement calls the function square with the value of k i.e. 45 as an argument. The value 45 *45 is dutifully computed by the function the value that is returned as the result of the function i.e. the right hadn side of the second statement. This result is assigned to the variable k that is on the left hand side of the assignment. Thus, k has the value 2025 now. After this, the program continues where it left off with the next statement in line.

## SOME IMPORTANT TERMS AND CONCEPTS REGARDING FUNCTIONS

**In the context of functions these are several terms that are used very frequently. By any aspiring C programmer these terms embody concepts that need to be well understood. You shall now look at some these terms and concepts in this section.**

### Function Type

The type of data that the function returns specified by the type-specifier in the function definition also called the type of the function. Functions that declare a return data type other than void must return a value of that type for all possible exit paths from the function. This means that every time such a function is executed a return statement must be executed as the last statement in the execution of the function. The compiler issue

**the error "function should return a value" if it fail to execute a return statement.**

**What type of values may be returned by a function? Any type of data except array may return by a function. Most functions return simple data types like int, float, double and so on. Function may also return pointers, structures and a pointer to an array.**

**If no type is specified, the compiler assumes that the function returns an integer result. You must speciality dealer it to be of void type if your function does not return any value as shown below:**

```
void myfunc(int k)
{
....
}
```

**When you write programs, your functions generally will be of three types.**

**(i) The first type is simply computational. To perform operations on their arguments and return a value based on that operation these functions are specifically designed. A computational function is a "pure" function. Examples are the standard library functions sqrt() and sin() etc.**

**(ii) The second type of functions manipulate information and return values that simply indicate the success or failure of that manipulation. close() is an exchange of the library function used to close a file. If the close operation is successful, the function returns 0; if the operation is unsuccessful, it returns an error code.**

**(iii) The last type of function has no explicit return value. In essence, the function is strictly procedural and produces no value. As returning type void all functions should be declared that do not return values. By declaring a function as void, you keep it from being used in an expression, thus preventing accidental misuse.**

**Although all functions, except those of type void, return values, you don't have to use the return value for anything. A**

common question concerning function return values is, "Don't I have to assign this value to some variable since a value is being returned?" The answer is no. The return value is simply discarded if these is no assignment specific. For example, even scanf and printf functions return values but you hardly ever use them!

Some additional points about the function names and types may be looked at here. A declared function variable is made up of the function definition and a variable parameter. The function definition or code is required to computer a value and the variable parameter is required to hold the returning value until it is effectively used in the calling expression. Hence there are two associated storage spaces involved for each function definition.

(i) For storing the function definition.

(ii) For storing the computed value.

Thus if myfunct is the name of a function, then

(i) The address of that function definition represented by myfunct which is a constant pointer that cannot be altered.

(ii) Myfunct () represents the function's value parameter indicating the current value.

(iii) & (Myfunct() represents the address of that function variable in the memory. To the constant type this address also belongs and this address may change from one function call to the other depending on the implementing.

## Specification of arguments type

In two ways the parameters that a function takes may be declared. In the first method, the parameter list and their type is specified immediately after the function name inside the brackets as follows:

```
Void myfunc (int a, float b, char c)
{
...
}
```

Alternatively, you can specify them as follows:

```
Void myfunc (a, b,c,)
int a, float b, char c;
```

```
{
...
}
```

C programmers use both the methods. In this book, you would follow the first method.

Thus, the parameter list is a comma-separated list of variable names and their associated types that receive the values of the arguments when the function is called. In case when the parameter list is empty a function may be with out parameters. However the parentheses are still required even if there are no parameters.

By using a comma-separated list of variable names you can declare many variables to be of a common type in variable declarations.

```
f(type variable1, type variable2,....type variableN)
```

**Recursion**

*A recursive* routine is one that calls itself. The C language is supposed to produce recursive code. Recursion is often one of the first casualties on small microcontrollers but compilers usually support recursion for large machines. Automatic variables are created when a function is entered, and they are stored on the stack. Such a function is called *reentrant,* and reentrants functions are also recursive. An example of a simple recursive function is the factorial:

```
n! = n* (n-1)* (n-2)*....*2*1
```

An interesting observation that can be made of factorial is that

```
n! = n* (n-1)!
```

or n factorial equals n times n-1 factorial. Also, the factorial of 0 is defined as 1. To calculate the factorial of a number it is possible to write the following recursive function with there definitions.

```
long factorial (in n)
{
if (n == 0)
return 1;
else
return n*factorial (n-1);
}
```

This surprisingly simple function calculates the factorial. It is important to have means of getting out of the routine whenever you write a recursive routine. The function returns a result rather than calling itself again when the argument reaches zero in above case. At that time the routine will work itself back a level at a time until it reaches the initial factorial call, and the calculation will be done.

Recursion can create some elegant code in that the code is very simple. Often too simple. There is a cost in the use of recursive code, and that is stack space. The argument is placed on the stack and a subroutine call is executed each time a function call is made. As a minimum, the return address is two bytes, and the value of the argument is also two bytes. Thus at least four bytes of stack space are needed for each function call. That is no problem when the factorial of a small number is calculated (The factorial of 13 is larger than can be held in a long, so only small numbers can be considered for a factorial). It is possible to get into stack overflow problems if a recursive function is written that calls itself many times.

Another interesting recursive routine is the function to calculate a Fibonacci number. A Fibonacci number sequence is described by the following function:

```
long fib (int n)
{
if (n == 1)
return 1;
else if (n ==0)
return 1;
else
return fib (n-1) + fib (n-2);
}
```

This sneaky function calls itself twice. Some interesting characteristic of this function included in the following exercise.

## Input and Output

### *Printf and Scanf Statement*

With in the 'C' in language there is hot provision for either input or output. Any such operations must be programmed as functions that are called from the programs complier. However, in many instances, compilers for very small microcontrollers will have no built-in input/output capability.

In complete E compiler there are several 40 functions are included.

File accesses are through a set of functions and a special structure. All parameters needed to access a file contained by a structure the struck File. The pointer to file is usually called a file handle in MS-DOS or PC-DOS vernacular. The file handle is given a value by

```
FILE *FP;
FILE *fopen (char* name, char* mode);
```

The name of file contained by name here which is a pointer to a character arrary. This name can be simply the file name if the file resides in the default directory, or it can be the complete path name-file name combination for files elsewhere in the file system. A one or two character string is the string pointed to by mode. The various modes are

```
"r"     read only
"w'     write only
"a"     append
        and sometimes
"b"     binary
"rw"    read/write
```

To open a file, the program must contain a statement

```
fp=fopen (name, mode);
```

where fp is declared as a pointer to the type FILE. All file accesses will use fp as an argument in some way, once the file is opened. There are two single character file access functions:

```
int getc (FILE* fp);
int putc (int c, FILE* fp);
```

The first function returns a character from an open file fp and the second puts a character c onto an open file fp. When program is loaded then there are three special file handles that are created by the operating system. These three file handles and stdin, stdout, and stderr. stdin is the standard input, and defaults to the keyboard. Stdout in the standard output and defaults to the terminal screen, and stderr is the standard error output which defaults to the terminal screen. When the program is executed then through the case of redirection operators and pipe operators these defaults can be redirected by the operating system.

The functions get char () and putchar () are macro definitions:

```
#define getchar () getc(stdin)
#define putchar (c) putc (c,stdout)
```

Therefore a put char() will put a single character to the terminal screen and get char() will read a single character from the keyboard.

There are string I/O with the file functions. A string can be put to a file by

```
int fputs (char* string, FILE* fp);
```

If an error access this function returns an EOF otherwise there is no error then it returns to zero.

A string can be read from a file by

```
int fgets (char* string, int maxline, FILE* fp);
```

From the file fp fgets return the next input line. This data are written into string, and can at most maxline-1 characters. The string is NULL terminated. fgets will return a zero when an error occurs. If there is no error, fgets returns the pointer string.

Another important file access function is

```
int fclose (FILE* fp);
```

This function release the file handle fp and it causes any data written to the file, but not written to the final destination, to be written. For example, To storeup a significant amount of data before it is written to the disk most disk file systems use a buffer. If data are buffered when the fclose() routine is executed any buffered data is written to the disk and the program connection to the file system is dissolved.

Several file handling routines are present in different compilers. To obtain the maximum advantage of these routines, you should consult the manual that comes with your specific compiler.

We have seen several instances of input/output functions. The most common is the prinɪf () function Under the category formatted input/output function printf () function can be grouped. The formatted output functions include

```
int printf (char* format, arg1, arg2,...0;
int sprint (char* string, char* format, arg1, arg2,...);
int fprintf (FILE* fp, char* format, arg1, arg2,...);
```

The function printf() has been used throughout the text so far, and there should be little question as to its use. This function prints data to the terminal screen. The pointer format points to a character string that contains the information to print out. Within the format, there can be conversion commands identified by a percent sign%. These commands will be discussed in detail later. With in the format string the number of arguments arg1, arg2 etc depend on the number of commands.

The second function above, sprint f(), performs exactly the same conversion as print f(). Rather than printing the result to the screen, it is written into the character array string in memory.

With the third function fprintf () data can be printed to a file. Here fp is the file handle of an open file, and the remainder of the arguments are exactly the same as with the printf () function.

All the conversion commands and their meanings are given here in this list. If the character following the % in a format string is not found in the table, function behaviors will be undefined.

| *Character* | *Printed as* |
|---|---|
| d,i | int : decimal number |
| o | int : unsigned octal number |
| x,X | int : unsigned hexadecimal number |
| u | int : unsigned decimal number |
| c | int : single character |
| s | char* : print characters from string until NULL is detect. |
| f | double : floating point[-]m.dddd where the number of ds is given by precision. Default precision is 6. |
| e, E | double : floating point [-]m.ddddExx where the number of ds is given by the precision, and the power of 10 exponent can be plus or minus. Default precisions is 6. |

*Contd.*

| *Character* | *Printed as* |
|---|---|
| g, G | Uses e or f format which ever requires least space. |
| % | N argument is converted. Print as a %. |

Additional formatting capability exists. Between the % sign and the conversion command a decimal number can be placed. Suppose this number is f.p. Here the field width provided for the conversion is f, and the precision--the number of decimal places--is p. The program takes the space needed if the conversion requires a field width greater than. Therefore, if the programmer is careless and tries to squeeze more information into a field than can fit, the program automatically provides a correct result with the format disrupted. The data output will started at the life side of the field if this number is preceded by a negative sign. Otherwise, the output will be justified to the right edge of the field.

This formatting approach works with strings as well as numerical outputs. A string output works much the same as an numerical output if it contains a field width or a precision. If the field width specified is not long enough to hold the output string, the specified field with is ignored. The complete string is printed out. With a string, precision specifies the number of output characters. If the precision is smaller than the field width, the width of the output field will be the precision specification. A minus sign applied to field width will cause the data to printed to the left edge of the field. Otherwise, the data will print to the extreme right edge of the field.

Formatted input is also provided in C. The three formatted input functions are

```
int scanf (char* format, arg1, arg2,...);
int scant (char* string, char* format, arg1, arg2,...);
int fscanf (FILE* fp, char* format, arg1, arg2,...);
```

The formatted data from the standard input read by the first function, formatted data from a string in memory read by should and formatted data from an open file fp is read by third function. There is a significant difference between the formatted inputs and outputs. Recall that the arguments in the formatted outputs are data values. In the formatted inputs, all arguments must be pointers to locations in memory that can hold the data types specified in the data string. If the program should contain

```
int ;
•
•
•
scanf ("%d", i); /* BAD */
```

the program will probably compile, most compilers will not note an error, and the program will not run correctly because the scanf () argument is not a pointer.

## What is a Function

A self-contained block of statements that perform a coherent task of some field is called a function. As collection of these functions every C program can be thought. As we noted earlier, using a function is something like hiring a person to do a specific job for you. Sometimes the interaction with this person is very simple, sometimes it's complex.

Suppose you have a task which is always performed exactly in he same way... say a bimonthly servicing of your motorbike. When you want it to be done, you go to the service station and say, "it's time, do it now". You don't need to give instructions, because the mechanic knows his job. You don't need to be told when the job is done. You assume the bike would be serviced in the usual way, the mechanic does it and that's that.

Let us now look at a simple C function which operates in much the same way as the mechanic. Actually, we will be looking at two things: The function and the program that calls or activates the function.

```
main ()
{
```

## Why Use Functions

Why write separate functions at all? Why not squeeze the entire logic into one function, **main()**? Two reasons:

(a) Rewriting the same code over and over writing functions avoids. Suppose you have a section of code in your program that calculates area of a triangle. If, later in the program, you want to calculate the area of a different triangle, you won't like it if you are required to write the same instructions all over again. Instead, you would prefer to jump to a 'section of code' that calculates area and then jump back to the place from where you left off. This section of code is nothing but a function.

(b) To write programs and keep track of what they are doing becomes easier by using functions. If the operation of a program can.

## Passing Values between Functions

The functions howen't been very flexible that we have used. The do what they are designed to do when we call them. Like our mechanic who always services the motor-bike in exactly the same way, we haven't been able to influence the functions in the way they carry out their tasks. It would be nice to have a little more control over what functions do, in the same way it would be nice to be able to tell the mechanic," Also change the engine oil, I am going for a outing".

Between the 'calling' and the 'called' functions we want to communicate now. You have unknowingly used the arguments in the print() and scanf() functions; the format the format string and the lis of variables used inside the parentheses in these functions are arguments. The arguments are sometimes also called' parameter'.

Consider the following program. To convey information to the function the mechanism used is the 'argument'. However, the calculation of sum is done in a different function called **calsum ()**. If sum is to be calculate in **calsum ()** and values of **a, b** and **c** are received in **main**.

## Advanced Features of Functions

Let us now get into their intricacies with a sound basis of the preliminaries of c functions. Following advanced topics would be considered here.

(a) Function Declaration and Prototypes

(b) Calling functions by value or by reference

(c) Recursion

One by one let us understand there features.

## Functions Declaration and Prototypes

By default any c function returns an int value. If we desire that a function should return a value other than an int, then it is necessary to explicitly mention so in the calling function as well as in the called function. The compiler assumes that this function would return a value of the type int whenever a call is made.

## Call by Value and Call by Reference

Now we clearly familiar how to call function. We have always passed the 'values' of variables to the called function whenever we called a function and passed something to it. Such function calls are called 'calls by value'. By this what we mean is, we are passing values of variables to it on calling a function. The examples of call by value are shown below:

```
Sum = calsum (a,b,c);
f = factr (a);
```

We have also learnt that variables are stored somewhere in memory. So instead of passing the value of a variable, can we not pass the location number (also called address) of the variable to a function? It would become a call by reference f we are able to do so. We would find out a little later that what purpose a 'call by reference' serves. First we must equip ourselves with knowledge of how to make a 'call by reference'. This feature of C functions needs atleast an elementary knowledge of 'pointers' So let us first acquire the basics of pointers after which we would take up this topic once again. Which is discussed in another segment.

# Chapter 10

# Structures and Files

Till now you have looked at data structures that are relatively independent i.e. By declaring an integer you stored a number that has a meaning of its own and Because the data make sense so you need to club together some data. For example, if you were storing information about the students in your class i.e. their serial numbers, names, addresses, age, height, weight etc. A particular address makes sense only if you know whose address it is. Of course, you can declare an array for each of the above and use he index into the arrays as the connecting link between the arrays. Data don't have anything which show that arrays are related the relation is only in the code that accesses the data structures. That will make it very difficult even for you to remember what is related and what is not (imagine you look at the code after six months!). And, if that is so, think of the difficulty if someone else has to maintain your program. C provides structures to get over this problem.

In earlier chapters you studied about arrays. Two basic problems are related with the arrays:-

- At the time of declaration the array the dimension of the array is to be declared at run time it cannot be decided. What is the implication? You must decide once and for all times what would be the maximum size that the array would be needed to accommodate and use it as the dimension. Now, this is difficult to predict. Imagine you are writing a text editor program. How can you decide the maximum size of the data that you would type in apriori? You may feel that this is no big problem. All that you have to do is to fix the size so big that you never run short of space. There are two problems with this approach. One, for that kind of sizes your system and or may not be having that support. Two, even if memory is available, it may not be available in one continuous piece. Remember that in an array you need space in contiguous locations. So, you need to trade - off. The size of your file you can change as per your need.

- The second problem is in processing large chunks of data. As mentioned earlier to store very large pieces of data you may not have the enough space in internal memory. What you can do is store them in external storage and get them into internal storage as and when necessary for their processing. Further, arrays stored in internal memory are washed out when you power down. If you most to store the data in external storage and require it later then files are useful for it.

In this chapter, you shall look at these two important constructs in C – structures and files. This chapter would sort of put together all that you have picked up in the earlier chapters and lead you to the development of meaningful applications.

## STRUCTURES

For grouping data elements together suitable data type is structure. For storing the data crate a suitable data structure. Use the basic data types that you have learnt about earlier. As with the other variables, a definition for the structure is first required. This allows the compiler to determine the storage allocation needed, and also identifies the various subfields of the structure.

```
struct date {
int month;
int day;
int year;
};
```

A new data type called date declared by this which consists three basic data elements of type integer. This is a definition to the compiler. It does not create any storage space and cannot be used as a variable. In essence, it is the specification of new data type, like int and char, and you can now use it to create other variables of his type. For example,

```
struct date data1;
```

defines a variable called date 1 to be of the same data type as that of the newly defined data type struct date.

**Assigning values to structure elements**

To access the individual elements the (dot) operator can be used. For example, to assign a particular date to the individual elements of he structure data 1, statements that you would need to write are:

```
date1. date = 17;
data 1. month =03;
date 1. year = 1966;
```

will place the beginning address of the function isr into the memory location oxffic.

To create a macro is a convenient method of executing this operation. The following macro definition works:

```
#define vector (isr, address) (*(void**) (address) =
(isr)
```

Now the function call

```
vector (timer, oxffdo);
```

will place the address of the function named timer into the location oxffdo in the computer memory map. It is important to define a function as timer that returns a type void.

**Structures**

Structure is the another feature of e not found in many high level long usage. Generally a structure is similar to an array. A structure is a collection of one or more variables identified by a single name. The variables can be of different types. Structures are types in the sense that an int is a type. Therefore, if you have properly declared a structure, you may declare another structure of the same type. Examine the following structure:

```
struct person
{
char name [20];
char address [20];
```

```
char city [20];
char state [2];
char zip [10];
int height;
int weight;
float salary;
```

Some of the features that describe a person contained in this structure. Character strings are given to the person's name and address. The person's height and weight are integers, and the salary is a floating point number. The structure declaration must be followed by a semicolon. This combination of variables is created every time a structure of the type person is declared. The name person following the struct declaration is called the structure tag or merely the tag. Tags are optional Once a tag is used, it may be used to declare other structures of the same type by

```
struct person ap, bp, cp;
```

Here ap, and cp are structures of the type person. A single instance of a structure can be declared by

```
struct {...} a;
```

In this case a is a structure with the elements defined the braces.

Members are the elements that make up a structure. Members of a structure can be accessed by appending a period followed by the member name to the structure name. For example the name of the person represented by ap is accessed by

```
ap.name [ ]
```

and that person's salary is

```
ap. salary
```

A pointer to a structure can be used. The pointer pperson is created by

```
struct person *pperson;
```

Members of the structure can be accessed by the use of a special operator – if a pointer to a structure is used. This operator is created by use of the minus sign (-) followed by the right circumflex character (>). The height of a person identified by the pointer person is accessed by

```
pperson->height
```

To increment the pointer arrays of structures are used when dealing with pointers to arrays of structures and the pointer move to the next structure. If a program has

```
struct person people [20], *pp;
```

and pp is made to point at people [10] by

```
pp = people
```

then

```
people [1] . name
```

is the same as

```
++pp->name
```

As a member element a structure can have another structure. Consider

```
Struct point
{
int x;
int y;
};
```

where point contains two integer elements, x and y. A circle can now be defined by

```
struct circle
{
struct pointer center;
int radius;
};
```

To the members center the access in this case is by

```
circle.center.x
```

or

```
circle.center.y
```

Of course the radius is accessed by

circle.radius

Structures can take as arguments by functions and they can letter structure. For example the function make point () that follows returns a structure.

```
struct point make point (int x, int y)
{
struct point hold;
hold.x=x;
```

```
hold.y=y;
return hold;
```

In this function the struct point is traded as a type with no difficulty. The return type is struct point, and within the body of the function hold is also a type struct point. The x argument passed to the function is placed in the x member of hold as is the y argument placed in the y member. Then the struct hold is return to the calling function. All of these operations are legal.

Structures can have structures members since structures create types. For example, suppose that the struct rect for a rectangle is defined as

```
struct rect
{struct point p1;
struct point p2,
};
```

Let's outline a program hat will inscribe a circle within a rectangle. The circle is to be centered in he rectangle, and to be tangent to the sides that make up the narrowest dimension of the rectangle.

```
/* Inscribe a circle in a rectangle */
struct point
{
        int x;
        int y;
};
struct circle
{
        struct point center;
        int radius;
};
struct rect
{
        struct point p1;
        struct point p2;
};
struct circle make_circle (struct point ct, int rad)
{
        struct circle temp;
        temp . center .x = ct . x;
        temp . center . y = ct . y;
```

```
        temp . radius = rad;
        return temp;
}
# define min (a,b) (((a)<(b)) ? (a) : (b))
# define abs (a) ((a)<0 ? - (a) : (a))
void draw_rectangle (struct rect);
void draw_circle (struct circle);
void main (void)
{
        struct circle cir;
        struct point center;
        struct rect window = { {80, 80}, {600, 400} };
        int radius, xc,yc;
center .x = (window .p1 x+window .p2.x) /2;
center .y = (window .p2 .y+window .p2.y) /2;
xc = abs (window .p1.x-window.p2 .x) /2;
yc = abs (window .p1.y-window.p2 .y) /2;
radius =min (xc,yc);
cir = make_circle (center,radius);
draw_rectangle (window);
draw_circle (cir);
```

Several important struct types are defined at the beginning of the program. These include a point, a rectangle, a circle, and a function to make circle given its center and its radius. Two macro definitions are needed. The first is the calculation for the minimum value of a and b and the second returns the absolute value of the argument. Two function prototypes are included. A Rectangle and a circle is drawn by these functions on the screen.

Inside the main program cir is declared to be of the type struct circle, center is struct point, and window is of the type struct rect. It is initialized to the values shown when window is defined to the structures as well as arrays this type of initialization is acceptable. The rectangle is defined by two points. The point {80, 80} is the lower left hand corner of the rectangle, and the point {600,400} is the upper right corner. These locations are implementation dependent, and in some cases might represent the upper left corner {80,80} and the lower right corner {600,400}.

By determining the average value of the X members of each point along with the average value of y members the centre of window is calculated. These values are the exact center of the rectangle. The center of the inscribed circle will lie at this point.

The radius of the inscribed circle will be one-half the length of the shortest dimension of the rectangle. The two potential value are calculated as xc and yc. Here the absolute value is used, because in general, it is impossible to know that the rectangle will be specified by the lower left hand corner in p1 and the upper right hand corner in p2.

Negative values would be calculated if these points were interchanged. This problem avoided by the selection of the positive result through the abs () macro. The final choice for radius is the minimum value of xc or yc.

The above calculations provide enough information to specify the circle, so cir is calculated as the return value from make_circle (). Finally, two complier specific functions, draw_rectangle () and draw_circle, are used to draw the calculated figures to the screen.

It is obvious that the structure formulation of the program makes a much earlier and simpler program so it is not difficult to execute these calculation with out the use of structure. The variables and program elements are objects here rather than mere numbers.

For the convince of program typedef command can removal a specified type. It does not create a new type, it merely renames an existing type. For example.

```
typedef int MILES;
typedef char BYTE;
typedef int word;
typedef long DWORD;
```

are all valid typedef statements. After he above invocations, a declaration

```
MILES m;
BYTE a [20];
WORD word;
DWORD big;
```

would make m an int, a an of 20 characters, word the type int, and big long. All that has happened is that these types are a redefinition of the existing types. Typedefs defined new types which are usually written in upper case letters. This is the requirement of the c language not a tradition.

Structure used earlier could be modified by use of the typedef. Consider

```
typedef.struct
{
int x;
int y;
} POINT;
```

This typedef redefines the earlier struct point as POINT. The judicious use of typedefs can make a program even easier to read than the simple use a structs. The program that follows is the same as that above where all of the structures are typedef new names.

```
/* Inscribe a circle in a rectangle */
typdef sruct
{
int x;
int y;
} POINT;
typedef struct
{
POINT center;
int radius;
} CIRCLE;
typedef struct
{
POINT p1;
POINT p2;
} RECT;
CIRCLE make_circle (POINT ct, int rad)
{
CIRCLE temp;
temp .center .x = ct .x;
temp .center .y = ct .y;
temp .radius = rad;
return temp;
#define min (a,b) ((a)<(b)) ? (a) : (a))
#define abs (a) ((a)<0 ?-(a) : (a))
void draw_rectangle(RECT);
void draw_circle(CIRCLE);
void main (void)
{
```

```
CIRCLE cir;
POINT center;
RECT window = { {80,80}, {600,400} };
int radius, xc,yc;
center .x = (window .p1 .x+window .p2 .x) /2;
center .y = (window .p1 .y+window.p2 .y) /2;
xc = abs (window .p1 .x-window .p2 .x) /2;
yc = abs (window) .p1 .y-window .p2 .y) /2;
radius = min (xc,yc);
cir=make_circle (center, radius);
draw_rectangle (window);
draw_circle (cir);
```

A type CIRCLE returned by the function make circle () and argument POINT and int required by it. CIRCLE is used to declare the variable temp in make_circle () Within the main program CIRCLE, POINT, and RECT are used as types in the declaration of the several structure type variables used in the program.

Draw_rectangle () and draw_circle () are not standard c functions. These functions are programmed and the listing of the final program is shown in Appendix B.

### Self Referential Structures

A structure cannot contain itself as a member. Structure definitions are not recursive. A pointer to a structure of the same type contained by structure. In dealing with completed restore listing problems this capability has proven quite useful. One sort problem that can be easily treated is the *binary tree* sort. A tree sort receives data, such as a word. Within the tree there is a *root node* that contains a word. The node also contains a count of the number of times the word has been seen and two pointers to additional nodes. These nodes are called *child* or *descendent* nodes. Traditionally, the node to he left contains a word that is less than the root word, and the node to the right contains a word that is greater than the root node. The new word is compared with the root word. If it is equal to the root word, the count in the node is incremented, and a new word is received. If the word is not the same and is less than the root word, the node to the left is accessed and the comparison is repeated. This process is repeated until a match is found or a node with no descendants is found. If a match is found, the count of that node is incremented. If no match is found a new node is created and placed at the bottom location, and the word is inserted into the new node. With the smaller words always going to the left and the larger words always going to left hence this process is repeated.

Eventually a tree that contains all of the different words entered into the program will have been created. The tree has several properties. The tree builds in a binary manner because each node has two nodes. The root level has exactly one entry, the second level has two entries, the third level has four entries, and so forth. If the tree is balanced, each level will have a power of two entries. It is possible that some tree branches will terminate early and other will extend to a depth or level that exceeds some of word data are taken in land only.

It is possible to sort it or to arrange the words in alphabetical order once the data are placed into the tree. If we traverse the tree from the root node to the extreme left, we will find the word that is smallest. Immediately above that word will be the next larger word. To the right of the second word will be words larger than itself but smaller than the word in the next node above. Therefore, the right path must be traversed to the left to find the next larger words. All of this--right and left, larger and smaller--sounds complicated. It is not.

Here is a case where a little thought and recursive code will help things along easily. To alphabetize and count the number of times that each word is used in a document the code is a complete function. Several new concepts will be shown in this program, so it will be broken into short blocks and described in these small pieces of code rather than trying to bite into the whole program at one time.

The structure tnode is listed below.

```
typedef struct tnode
{ /* the tree node */
char *word; /* points to text */
int count; /* occurrences */
struct tnode *left; /* pointer to left child */
struct tnode *right; /* pointer to right child */
} TNODE;
```

The first two elements to this structure are a pointer to the word contained in the node, and the number of times that the word has been seen. The last two elements are pointers to structures of the type tnode. The structure tag was used in the typedef of the struct node. Because self preferential pointers inside of the structures needs the tag to find the correct type it is necessary to use the tag in this case. For the remainder of the programm, he typedef TNODE is used.

In the include files some new files are included and in a following section there will be discussed. The first is ctype .h. This program uses several character tests that are identified in ctype .h. There are string operations found in string .h, and there are standard functions defined in stdlib .h.

```
#include <stdio .h>
#include <ctype .h>
#include <string .h>
#include <stdlib .h>
```

The list of function prototypes for the functions written in this program follow:

```
TNODE *addtree (TNODE *, char *);
TNODE *talloc (void);
void treeprint (TNODE *);
int getword (char *, int);
char *strsave (char *);
```

To add a tree to the program the first function is used. *talloc () is a function that allocates memory for a TNODE. The function treeprint () prints out the tree, and getword () reads in a word from the input stream. There are two function prototypes defined within the program getword (). These functions are used by getword () only. The final function above saves the string pointed to by the argument in a safe place and returns a pointer to the word location in memory.

The main program is relatively simple. The maximum number of characters that can be allowed in a word is the constant MAX WORD. With main () a pointer to structure TNODE name root is declared along with a character array named word and an integer i.

```
/* word frequency count */
#define MAXWORD 100
int main (void)
{
```

```
TNODE *root;
char word [MAXWORD];
int i;
root = NULL;
while (getword (word, MAXWORD) ! = EOF)
if (isalpha (word [01])
root = addtree (root, word);
treeprint (root);
return 0;
```

A NULL value is assigned to root, and the program enters a loop that read words from the input stream. The word has been read in if the first character if the word is letter. If the argument is letter then the function is alpha () returns a TRUE other wise FALSE. If the input is a letter, the routine addtree is executed with the arguments root and word. The first time that the function is executed, root is a NULL. This loop is repeatedly executed until getword () receives an EOF character from the input stream. At that time the input loop terminates, and the function treeprint () is executed. When treeprint () is completed, main () returns a 0 to the calling program or the operating system. To notify the operating system that the program has execute correctly this signal can be used.

The most complicated function in this program is addtree (). A pointer to a TNODE and a pointer to a character string as arguments received by this function. It returns a pointer to a TNODE. If the TNODE pointer argument is a NULL of entry to the function, the first if loop is executed. Within that loop, talloc () return a pointer to a new TNODE. The function strsave () copies the string into a safe place and returns a pointer to this location. This pointer is put into the word pointer location in the new TNODE. A value of 1 is put into the count location, and the pointers to the left and right child TNODES are set to NULL. At this time, the word has been put in the TNODE, and the pointer to this TNODE is returned to the calling program.

```
/* addtree: add a node with w, at or below p */
TNODE *addtree (TNODE *p, char *w)
{
int cond;
if (p = = NULL) /* new word has arrived */
p=talloc (); /* make a new node */
```

```
p->word = strsave (w);
p->count = 1
p-> left = p->right=NULL;
}
else if ((cond = stremp (w,p->word)) = = 0)
p->count ++; /* repeated word */
else if (cond <0) /* less than into left subtree*/
p->left = addtree (p-> left,w);
else /* greater than into right subtree */
p->right = addtree (p->right,w);
return p;
```

Suppose now that at a later time addtree () is called and this time p is no longer a NULL. In this case to determine if the word that has been passed is equal to that in the TNODE pointed to by p, a string compare test will be executed. If it is equal, it is a repeated word for that node, so the word count is incremented and control is returned to the calling program. If it is not equal (say, it is lexically less than the word of the node), it is necessary to either traverse to the node on the left or add a new node on the left if there is none there. The code

```
p->left = addtree (p->left,w);
```

does exactly what is needed in this case. If one exists then this recursive call to addtree () will descend to the left TNODE and the pointer to the left TNODE will be NULL if one does not exist.

The addtree () call would work on the pointer to the right childnode if the lexical value of the word been greater than that of the word stored in the node. Therefore, the function addtree () will start at the root node and traverse down the tree to the right or left child nodes depending on the size of the word relative to the sizes of the words in the tree. Its count is incremented if the word is found in the tree. If control proceeds down the tree, and the word is not found, eventually, a TNODE with a NULL pointer to the direction that the path must move. A new TNODE is created and the word is assigned to that TNODE at that time.

The control is passed to the function tree print () when all of the date to be input into the tree are read in. The argument of treeprint () is a pointer to the root node and treeprint () returns nothing to the calling program. Efficient printing out of the data requires recursive routine. The function treeprint () shown below shows this routine. Treeprint () is called with the root pointer as a argument. The Code following the if statement will be executed because the root pointer will not be a NULL. The first

```
/* treeprint : in-order print of tree p */
void treeprint (TNODE *p)
{
if (p !=NULL)
{
treeprint (p->left);
printf ("%4%15s\n", p->count, p->word);
treeprint (p->right);
}
```

statement of this code is a recursive call to treeprint () with the pointer to the left child pointer as an argument. To propagate to the lowest and left most level of the tree this recursive call will cause control. At this time treeprint () will return normally, and the word pointed to in the TNODE will be printed out by the printf () call. The program will then start a recursive treeprint () to the right of this node. Control will immediately go to the left side of the right branch and will descend the lowest level and print out the word found. Until the whole tree control has been printed this routine wil repeat up and down.

The function strasave () copies the word passed to it as an argument into a save place and returns a pointer to this memory location to the calling program. C provide for dynamic allocation of memory. Up to this point, all memory access

```
char *strsave (char *s) /* make a duplicate of s*/
{
char *p;
p = (char *)malloc (strlen (s)+1);
if (p ! = NULL)
strcpy (p,s);
return p;
```

was to memory allocated by declaration statements. The program can go to the operating system and request memory at any time with dynamic allocation. This memory is from a memory area called the *program heap*. The first call to allocate memory is malloc () shown above. The function prototype for this function is found in stdlib .h, and the function requires an argument that is the length of the memory space needed. The program returns a pointer to the base type of the system, probably bytes, to the required block of memory. The function returns a null pointer if there is not enough memory available.

The function talloc () also makes use of the malloc () function. In this case, the argument of the malloc () call is the sizeof () function. sizeof () is a C operator that returns the size of the argument. This function is a keyword in C and requires no prototype.

```
/* talloc : make a tnode */
TNODE *talloc (void)
{
return (TNODE *) malloc (sizeof (TNODE));
```

To the basic memory size of the system the memory allocation function malloc() returns to a pointer. It is always necessary to cast the return from malloc () onto the type of variable that the return must point to. In this case, the cast is to the type pointer to TNODE. In strsave (), the cast was to the type pointer to char. Therefore, the statement

```
return (TNODE *) malloc (sizeof (TNODE);
```

will return to the calling function a pointer of the type TNODE to a free memory space the size of a TNODE. Function addtree () called is this function. Good programming practice would dictate that the return from talloc () should be tested to make certain that malloc () did not return a NULL pointer.

Getword () is the next function that must be incorporated into the program. getword () returns the first character of the word or an EOF in the case hat an EOF is detected. It requires two arguments. The first is a pointer to a character array into which the input data is to be stored. The second argument is the length of the array and hence the maximum length of any word that can be read into the program by getword (). Two functions are accessed by getword (). The first is geton () which returns a character from the input stream. Ungetch () is the second one which restores a character back onto the input stream.

It must pull one more character that the length of the word in some cases to work correctly. When that happens, the extra character must be put back onto the input stream so that it will be available for the next getch () call.

```
/* getword: get next word or character from input */
int getword (char *word, int lim)
{
int c, getch (void);
void ungetch (int);
char *w=word;
while (isspace (c=tolower (getch ())));
if (c! = EOF)
*w++=c;
if (!isalpha (c))
{
*w=NULL;
return c;
}
for ( ; -lim >0 ; w++)
if (!isalnum (*w=tolower (getch ())))
{
ungetch (*w);
break;
}
*w=NULL;
return word [0];
}
```

The first executable statement

```
while (isspace (c=tolower (getch ())));
```

includes two standard C functions. + In the header file ctype .h the function is space () has its prototype. If its argument is a space then this function returns a TRUE otherwise FALSE. The second function, tolower (), is also protctyped in ctype. h. It tests he argument and returns a lower case letter if the argument is upper case and a lower case letter if the argument is an upper case letter. Until it receives a nonspace input this operation will loop, and the lower case version of the letter input will be stored in c.

It is put into the next open location of the word array and the pointer into this arrays is incremented if c is not an EOF. If the return is an EOF, the second if statement will execute. The if statement

```
if (!isalpha (c))
{
```

```
*w=NULL;
return c;
}
```

tests to determine it the character from the input stream is a letter. It its argument is letter then isalpha () returns a TRUE otherwise FALSE. If the character taken from the input stream is an EOF, isalpha () will return a FALSE and the statement following the if will be executed.

In this case to the word a NULL is written and to the calling function the EOF is returned.

If the return is a letter, the following sequence will be executed:

```
for (; -lim >0 ; w++)
if (!isalnum (*w=tolower (getch ())))
{
ungetch (*w);
break;
}
```

The central loop here is the if statement. To read in characters from the input stream its argument executes getch (). These inputs are converted to lower case and stored into the array location pointed to by w. The result is then checked to determine if it is a letter or a number. If it is not, it is put back onto the input stream and the loop is exited by the break instruction. If it is a letter-or a number, the pointer to the output array w is incremented and the maximum length of the array is decremented.

The next character is read in if this last result is greater than zero. Otherwise, the if statement is skipped.

The last wo statements in the function are

```
*w=NULL;
return word [0];
```

The last entry of the character array is made a NULL to satisfy the C requirement that a string must terminate with a 0, and the first character of the word is returned to the calling program. To just guarantee that an EOF is not returned this value is returned.

There are two final function required for this program. These functions work together to form the getch () /ungetch () pair. A global integer bufp is declared and a global buffer with an argument BUFSIZE is created. Since these variables are global, they are initialized at the beginning of the program, and they will not be changed when control is returned to a calling function.

The value of bufp is tested in getch () the character returned is taken from buffer and the buf is decremented if it is greater than 0. Otherwise, a new character is read from the input stream by getchar ().

```
#define BUFSIZE 100
char buf [BUFSIZE]; /* buffer for ungetch */
int bufp=0; /* next free position in buffer */
int getch (void) /* get the next character from the
buffer */
{
return (bufp>0) ? buf [-bufp] : getchar ();
}
void ungetch (int c) /* put character back onto input */
{
if (bufp>=BUFSIZE)
printf ("ungetch: too many characters \n");
else
buf[bufp++]=c;
}
```

A test is made to determine this store would exceed the buffer length when ungetch () is executed. If bufp will be greater that BUFSIZE after it is incremented, an error return is executed. Otherwise, the return character is put in the buffer and it is there to be read the next time getch () is executed.

Several c functions are introduced by this program. In fact, C has a ungetchar () that does the same function as ungetch () above. It has given examples of structures containing pointers to like structures, recursive functions to process data, and dynamic memory management.

**More Structures**

There are two more important considerations that should be placed under structures. The first of these is the *union*, and the second is *bit manipulations* and *bit fields*.

### *Unions*

A union is defined same as a struct although there is a significant difference. A union can have several different arguments, each of which is a different type. The compiler, when it sees a union declared, provides enough memory to hold the largest argument of the union.

The different types occupy the same memory location when different arguments are used. Consider the following sequence:

```
struct bothints
{
int hi, lo;
};
union both
{
long l;
struct bothints b;
} compound;
```

To generate a structure that contains two into this sequence will cause the compiler. The union both will provide space for whichever is larger, a long or a struct bothints. Of course, a long is the size of struct bothints, so enough memory will be provided to store a long. In use, a sequence like

```
compound .h .hi = a;
compound .b. lo = b;
```

will place the int a into the upper location of compound, and b will go into the lower location of compound. Compound .1 will contain in is upper word and be in its lower word after there operations. If compound .1 were used as a variable, it would be this combination.

As a method of saving memory unions are most often thought of. If several variables are completely independent and never used at the same time, a union that contains these several variables will allow the programmer to store each in the same memory location.

### *Bitfields*

The concepts of *bitfields* fall loosely under structures. The first built in operation involves an enum that allows bit manipulations from C. Consider the following enum:

```
enum {PB1=1, PB2=2,OUT1=4, OUT2=8};
int PORTA;
```

Notice that the different elements of the enum are each powers of 2. We can then use an expression like

```
PORTA I= PB1 I PB2;
```

to turn on bits corresponding PB1 and PB2 in the integer PORTA. Or in PORTA these corresponding bits might be turned off by

```
PORTA & = ~ (PB1 I PB2);
```

Tests can be executed like

```
if (PORTA & (PB1 I PB2) = = 0)
```

Here the argument of the if call will be TRUE if both bits corresponding to PB1 and PB2 are turned off in PORTA.

These manipulations are not really special bit manipulations It is a merely creation of bit like operations using normal C. C does support bit fields. Bit fields are created in the form of a struct. The following struct defines several bit fields:

```
struct
{
unsigned int PB1 : 1;
unsigned int PB2 : 1;
unsigned int OUT1 : 1;
unsigned int OUT2 : 1;
unsigned int ALL : 4;
} FLAGS;
```

Several bit fields consists this struct. The colon that follows the field name designates the size of the bit field. The first four fields are each 1 bit wide, and the final field ALL is 4-bits wide. These bits can be turned on by

```
FLAGS.OUT1 = FLAGS.OUT2 = 1;
```

or off

```
FLAGS.OUT1 = FLAGS.OUT2 = 0;
```

and they can be tested

```
if (FLAGS.PB1 == 0 && FLAGS.PB2 ==1)
```

Some special bit constructs the compilers. These constructs are usually structs that have either 8-or 16-bits within the field. As Boolean variables these structs are useful.

The programmer will frequently want to have bit fields at specific locations in memory when setting up a microcontroller program. These bit fields can be used is I/O ports, control registers and even arrays of bits to be used internally as flags. An approach to this problem is found in the bit array.

```
typedef struct
{
bit_0 :1;
bit_1 :1;
bit_2 :1;
bit_3 :1;
bit_4 :1;
bit_5 :1;
bit_6 :1;
bit_7 :1;
} BITS:
```

A macro definition is used to create a variable:

```
#define PORTA ( * ( BITS *) 0x1000)
```

With these definitions, instruction statements like

```
PORTA.bit_7 = 0;
if (PORTA.bit_3 == 1 && PORTA.bit_2==0)
```

etc. can be used in dealing with the bits within this memory location.

## Files

Because it is difficult to handle the large volume of data by programs so it is necessary to keep data in the permanent storage and after execution of program is over all the entered data will be lost because the data stored in the variables are temporary.

There is a concept of file in C through which the data can be stored in the disk or secondary storage device. So the data can be read when required. A file is a collection of data or text, placed on the disk.

Sequential file and random access file are the two types of files. Data are kept in sequence in sequential file. As example if we want to access the forty fourth record then first forty three records should be read sequentially to reach the forty fourth record. In the random access file, The data can be accessed and processed randomly i.e. in this case the forty fourth record can be accessed directly. It takes less time than the sequential file.

The steps for file operation in C. Programming are as follows-

1. Open a file
2. Read the file

   or-write data in the file
3. Close the file

## Opening of A File

First we need a temporary area in memory where we store the data/records then we transfer it to it when we store a record in the file. For storing these records in the memory, The starting address where this data/record is stored use pointer to point. We write this as-

```
FILE *p;
```

Here p is a pointer of file type. It is necessary to write FILE in capital and then pointer variable name for declaring any variable to file type pointer.

We use the library function fopen () to open a file. First we declare pointer variable and fopen () as file type pointer. We write this as-

```
FILE *p, *fopen ();
then p=fopen ("filename", "mode");
```

Here filename is the name of datafile where data/record is stored. With data file which operation (read, writ or append) is to be performed decided by Mode.

## Modes

### *1. w (write)*

This mode open a new file for writing a record, if the filename already exists then using this mode, the previous data/records are erased and the new data/record entered is written to the file.

Ex-

```
p=fopen ( "rec.dat", "w");
```

Here rec.dat is the filename and w is the mode.

**2. a (append)**

For appending a data/record this mode open a file. If the file doesn't exist then the work of this mode is same as "w" mode.

Ex-

```
p=fopen ( "rec.dat", "a");
```

Here rec.dat file can be already exist or new file.

***3. r (read)***

For opening a file for reading purpose only this mode is used.

```
p=fopen ( "rec.dat", "r");
```

If the file rec.dat doesn't exist then compiler return NULL to the file pointer. This is written as-

```
p=fopen ( "rec.dat", "r" );
if ( p= =NULL)
print ( "File does not exist");
```

We can also write this as-

```
if ( ( p=fopen ( "rec.dat", "r"))==NULL)
printf ( " This file doesn't exist" );
```

***4. w+ (write+read)***

For both reading and writing purpose this mode is used. This is same as the "w" mode but we can also read the record which is stored in the file.

Ex-

```
p=fopen ( "rec.dat", "w+" );
```

***5. a+ ( append+read)***

For both reading and appending the record this mode is used. This mode is same as the "a" mode but we can also read the record which is stored in the file.

```
p=fopen ("rec.dat", "a+" );
```

***6. r+ (read+write)***

For both reading and writing purpose this mode is used. We can read the record and also write the record in the file. From this mode the previous record of file is not deleted.

```
p=fopen ( "rec.dat", "r+" );
```

The compiler, return the NULL to the pointer if the file does't exist. This is written as-

```
p=fopen ( "rec.dat", "r+" );
if (p = =NULL)
print ( "This file doesn't exist" );
```

We can also write this as-

```
if ( ( p=fopen ( "rec.dat", r+" )) = NULL)
printf ( "This file doesn't exist" );
```

## Closing a File

At the end of the program the files which are opened from the fopen () function must be closed. This is written as-

```
fclose(p);
If the opening file is more than one then we close all
the file.
fclose ( p1);
fclose ( p2);
---------

---------
```

Structure of The File Program

```
main ()
{
FILE *p, *fopen ();
p=fopen. ( "filename", "mode" );
-------------------
-------------------

-------------------
fclose ( P );
} /* End of main */
```

## Input / Output Function

C support three tupe of input / output functions.

```
-character I/O
-string I/O
-file I/O
```

### *Character I/O*

*1. getchar ( )*

From standard input this function read character type data as one character at a time.

```
/*program to understand the use of getchar ( ) */
#include<stdio.h>
main ( )
```

```
{
char arr [100];
int i=0;
while ( ( arr [i] = getchar ( ) ) ! = '\n' )
i++;
arr [i] = '/0';
printf ( " %s", arr );
}
```

**2. *Putchar ( )***

This function print one character at a time which is taken by the standard input.

```
/*program to understand the use of putchar ( ) */
#include<stdio.h>
main ( )
{
char arr [100];
int i=0;
printf ( " Enter the string :" );
sanf ( "% s", arr );
printf ( " The accepted string is:" );
while ( arr [i] != '\0' )
{
putchar ( arr[i] );
i++;
}
```

**3. *getch( )***

From the standard input this function read any alphanumeric character. The difference between getchar( ) and getch( ) is that getchar( ) continue access the key-board until the carriage return key is pressed.

**4. *putch ( )***

As soon as key is pressed it stops accessing the keboard.

```
/*Program to understand the use of getch ( ) and putch (
) */
#include<stdio.h>
main ( )
{
int ch;
printf ( "Enter a character:" );
```

```
ch=getch ( );
printf ( "The character is:" );
putch ( ch );
}
```

### *String I/O*

#### *5. sscanf ( )*

This function is same as the scanf ( ) function except that data is read from memory pointed by array rather than the standard input.

Syntax-

```
sscanf ( array-name, "control characters", variable-
names);
#include<stdio.h>
main ( )
{
char arr[20];
int i;
float x;
gets (arr );
sscanf ( arr, "%d %f \n", i,x );
print ( "%\n ", arr );
}
```

#### *6. sprintf ( )*

This function is same as printf ( ) function except. This write the output to an array instead of sending the output on to the screen.

Syntax-

```
sprintf ( array-name, "control characters", variable-
names );
/*program to understand the use of sprintf ( ) function
*/
#include<stdio.h>
main ( )
{
char arr [20];
int i;
float x;
sprintf ( arr, " %d %f ", i, x );
}
```

*7. gets ( )*

From the standard input this function reads the character and store then in character type array.

Syntax-

```
gets ( array-name);
/*program to understand the use of gets ( ) /
#include<stdio.h>
main ( )
{
char arr [100];
printf ( " Enter the string :" );
gets ( arr );
printf ( "The accept string is : %s", arr );
}
```

*8. puts ( )*

The string which is already accepted in the character type array printed by this function.

Syntax-

```
puts(array-name);
/*program to understand the use of puts ( ) */
#include<stdio.h>
main ( )
{
char arr[100];
printf ( "Enter the string :" );
gets ( arr );
printf ( "The accepted string is :" );
puts ( arr ) ;
}
```

***File I/O***

*9. fprintf ()*

This function is same as he printf ( ) function but it has one more parameter the file pointer because it writes the data into the file.

Syntax-

```
fprintf ( fptr, "control character ", variable-names);
/* program to understand the use of fprintf ( ) */
```

```
#include<stdio.h>
main ( )
{
FILE *fopen ( ), *p;
char name[10];
p=fopen ( "rec.dat", "r" );
printf ( "Enter your name :" );
scanf ( "%s", name );
fprintf ( p, "My name is %s", name );
fclose ( p );
}
```

## *10. fscanf ( )*

This function is same as the scanf ( ) function but it has one more parameter the file pointer because it reads the data from the file.

Syntax-

```
fscanf ( fptr, "control character ",&variable-names);
/*program to understand the use of fscanf ( ) */
#include<stdio.h>
main ( )
{
FILE *fopen ( ), *p;
char name[10];
int sal;
p=fopen ( "rec.dat", "r" );
fscanf ( p, "% %d", name &sal );
printf ( "NAME\t SALARY\n" );
while ( !feof (p) )
{
printf ( " %s\t% %d\n", name, sal );
fscanf ( p, "%s %d",name, & sal );
}
fclose ( p );
```

## *11. getc( )*

To read a single character from a given file and increment the file pointer a macro the getc( ) is used. It returns EOF, if the end of file is reached or it encounters an error.

Syntax-

```
getc( fptr );
```

```
ch=getc( fptr );
where fptr is a file pointer.
/*program to understand the use of getc( ) function */
#include<stdio.h>
main ( )
{
FILE *fptr;
char name[15];
int ch;
printf ( "Enter the file name:" );
scanf ( "% s", name );
if ( ( fptr=fopen ( name, "r" ) ) = = NULL)
{
printf ( "File doesn't exist  \n");
exit ( );
}
else
{
while ( ( ch=getc( fptr ) != EOF )
printf ( "%c", ch );
}
fclose ( fptr );
}
```

**12. *putc ( )***

To write a single character into a file a macro putc( ) is used. value EOF if an error occur.

Syntax-

```
putc( ch, fptr );
```

where fptr is a file pointer and ch is a variable written to the file which is pointed by file pointer.

```
/*program to understand the use of putc( ) function */
#include<stdio.h>
main ( )
{
FILE *fptr;
char name[15];
int ch;
printf ( "Enter the file name:" );
scanf ( "% s", name );
if ( ( fptr=fopen ( name, "w" )) = =NULL)
```

```
{
printf ( "File can't be open \n");
exit ( );
}
else
while ( ( ch = getchar ( ) ) != '$' )
putch( ch, fptr );
fclose( fptr );
}
```

### 13. *fgetc ( )*

To read a single character from a given file and increment the file pointer position This function is used which is same a getc( ) function. It returns EOF if end of file is reached or it encounters an error.

Syntax-

```
fgetc( fptr );
ch=fetc(fptr);
```

where fptr is a file pointer and ch is a variable which receive the character returned by the function.

```
/* program to understand the use of fgetc ( ) */
#include<stdio.h>
main ( )
{
FILE *fopen ( ), *p
char ch;
if ( ( p=fopen ( "rec.dat", "r" )) = =NULL )
printf ( " This file doesn't exist\n' );
else
{
while ( ( ch = fgetc ( p ) ) !=EOF )
printf ( "%c", ch );
}
fclose ( p );
```

### 14. *fputc ( )*

To the specified stream at the current file position this function writes the character and then increments the file position indicator.

Syntax-

```
fputc( ch, fptr );
```

where fptr is a file pointer and ch is a variable written to the file which is pointed by file pointer.

```
/*program to understand the use of fputc ( ) */
#include<stdio.h>
main ( )
{
FILE *fptr;
char name[15], ch;
printf ( "Enter the file name:" );
scanf ("%s", name)
if( (fptr=fopen (name, "r" ) = =NULL)
{
printf ( "File doesn't exist\n");
exit (1);
}
else
{
fptr1=fopen ( "rec.txt", "w" );
while ( ch=fgetc (fptr) !=EOF)
fputc (ch, fptr1);
}
fclose (ftpr);
fclose (fptr1);
```

### 15. *fgets( )*

To read a string copies the string a given file and location this function is used which is referenced by an array.

Syntax-

```
fgets( sptr, max, fptr );
```

Where sptr is a string pointer, which points to an array, max is the length of the array and fptr is a file pointer which points to a given file.

This function is used to read max-1 characters which is pointed by sptr and places them into the array. This function read character until either a newline or an end of file or size of the array occurs.

At the end of the string it appends a null character ( '\0' ).

```
/*program to understand the use of fgets( ) */
#include<stdio.h>
man( )
```

```
{
FILE *fptr;
char name [20], arr [50];
int i=0;
printf ( " Enter the file name:' );
scanf ( "% s", name );
if ( ( fptr = fopen ( name, "r" ) )= =NULL)
{
printf ( "File doesn't exist \ n" );
exit ( );
}
else
if ( fgets ( arr, 50, fptr ) != NULL)
while ( arr[i] != '\0' )
{
putchar ( arr[i] );
i++;
}
```

### 16. *fputs( )*

To write a sring to a given file this function is used.

Syntax-

```
fputs( sptr, fptr);
```

where sptr is a pointer which points to an array and fptr is a file pointer which is pointed to a given file.

```
/*program to understand the use of fputs( ) */
#include<stdio.h>
main ( )
{
FILE *fptr;
char name[20], arr[50];
printf ( "Enter the file name:" );
scanf ( "% s", name );
if ( ( fptr = fopen ( name, "w" ) ) = = NULL)
{
printf ( "File can't be open \n" ) ;
exit (1);
}
else
{
printf ( "The string is:" ) ;
```

```
gets ( arr );
fputs( arr, fptr ) ;
}
fclose( fptr ) ;
```

*17. getw( )*

The integer value from a given file returned by this function and increment the file pointer position to the next integer.

Syntax-

```
getw( fptr );
```

where fptr is a file pointer which takes the integer value from file.

```
/*program to understand the use of getw( ) function */
#include<stdio.h>
main ( )
{
FILE *fptr;
char name[20];
int value;
printf ( "Enter the file name:" );
scanf ( "% s", name );
if ( ( fptr = fopen ( name, "r" ) )= =NULL)
{
print ( "File doesn't exist \n" ) ;
exit ( ) ;
}
else
while ( ( value=getw ( fptr ) !=EOF )
printf ( " %d \t", value ) ;
fclose ( fptr );
```

*18. putw( )*

For writing an integer value to a given file this function is used.

Syntax-

```
putw (value, fptr ) ;
```

where fptr is a file pointer and value is an integer value which is written to a given file.

```
\*program to understand the use of putw ( ) function */
#include<stdio.h>
```

```
main ( )
{
FILE *fptr;
char name[20];
int value=0;
printf ( "Enter the file name:" ) ;
scanf ( "% s", name ) ;
if ( ( fptr = fopen ( name, "w" ) ) = = NULL)
{
printf ( "File can't be open \n" ) ;
exit (1) ;
}
else
while ( value < 10)
{
putw ( value, fptr) ;
value++;
}
fclose (fptr) ;
}
```

*Block read / write*

To store the block of data into the file rather than individual elements it is useful. Each block has some fixed size, it may be of structure or of an array. It is possible that a data file has one or more structures or arrays. So it is easy to read the entire block from file or write the entire block to the file. There are two useful functions for this purpose:-

*19. Fread ( )*

To read an entire block from a given file this function is used.

Syntax-

```
fread (ptr, size, nst, fptr);
```

where ptr is a pointer which points to the array which receives the structure, size is the size of the structure, nst is the number of the structure and fptr is a file pointer.

```
/*program to understand the use of fread( )*/
#include<stdio.h>
main ( )
{
```

```
struct rec {
int code ;
char name[20] ;
} person [10] ;
FILE *fptr ;
int i=0; j ;
char str [15];
printf ( "Enter the file name :" ) ;
scanf ( "%s", str ) ;
if ( fptr=fopen ( str, "r" )) = =NULL) ;
{
printf ( "File doesn't exist \n" ) ;
exit (1) ;
}
else
while (! feof (fptr) )
{
fread (&person, size of (person) ,1, fptr) ;
i++;
}
for ( j=0 ; j<i ; j++)
{
printf ( "Code: %d\t", person [j] .code) ;
printf ( "Name: %s\n", person [j] .name) ;
}
fclose (fptr) ;
}
```

**20. *fwrite ( )***

For writing an entire block to a given file this function is used.

Syntax-

```
fwrite(ptr, size, nst, fptr) ;
```

where fptr is a pointer which points to the array of structure in which data is written, size is the size of the structure. Nst is the number of structure and fptr is the file pointer.

```
/*Program to understand the use of fwrite ( ) */
#include <stdio.h>
main ( )
{
struct rec {
```

```
int code ;
char name [20];
} person [10] ;
FILE *fptr ;
int i, j=0 ; n;
char str [15];
printf ( "Enter the file name:" ) ;
scanf ( "%s", str ) ;
if ( ( fptr=fopen ( str, "w" ) ) = = NULL)
{
printf ( "File doesn't exist \n" ) ;
exit (1) ;
}
else
{
printf ( "How many records:" ) ;
scanf (%d", &n) ;
for (i=0) i < n; i++)
{
printf ( "code:" ) ;
scanf ( "%d", & person [i] .code ) ;
printf ( "Name:" ) ;
scanf ( "%s", & person [i] .name ) ;
}
while (j<n)
{
fwrite ( & person, sizeof (person), 1, fptr) ;
j++;
}
}

fclose (fptr) ;
}
```